"[Twight] is brutally honest, and nobody, inclun

his high standards and criticism. Many of thes d

new light on his earlier work.... This is literat a

blow-by-blow account of climbing drudgery f.
   —*Rock & Ice*

"The character who emerges [in *Kiss or Kill*] is a walking cautionary tale, one who has given in to his climbing obsession—to be the hardest man on the hill—and is willing to pay dearly."
   —*Outside*

"Deeply personal, arrogant, grandiose, thrilling and unapologetic, this record of [Twight's] career will gratify and repel extreme athletes, their admirers, and their detractors."
   —*Publishers Weekly*

"With chapter titles such as 'House of Pain' and 'I Hurt, Therefore I Am,' no one would mistake Twight for a member of the Von Trapp family.... A bracing tonic for us desk-bound wussies."
   —*Pittsburgh Tribune-Review*

"Twight's writing may be as risky as the routes he's climbed. I enjoyed reading what I would not dare write myself. [It's] an accurate, painfully honest, and sometimes uncomfortable account of the price he paid for climbing at the highest level."
   —John Bouchard, Ice Climbing Prophet, Paragliding Pioneer,
      and Alpine Climbing Iconoclast

"Most mountaineering literature reads like a cross between forensic pathology and the Hardy Boys. Just as punk music ripped a hole in the dead world of eighties rock, Twight's punk-fueled writing put the soul back into climbing literature. One copy of *Kiss or Kill* is worth hundreds of times more than all the Everest dreck put together."
   —Will Gadd, Mixed Climbing Visionary, 2000 Ice World Cup Champion,
      Paragliding Distance Record Holder 1999 (180 miles)

"Climbing can be as addictive as heroin, and sometimes just as dangerous. Twight pulls you into his world of fear, death, and brief, impossible highs—then won't let you go. A fascinating and often disturbing glimpse into obsession."
   —Kyle Mills, author of *Free Fall* and *Burn Factor*

KISS or KILL

MARK TWIGHT

CONFESSIONS OF A
SERIAL CLIMBER

THE
MOUNTAINEERS
BOOKS

Published by
The Mountaineers Books
1001 SW Klickitat Way, Suite 201
Seattle, WA 98134

Cloth: First printing 2001
Paper: First printing 2001, second printing 2002, third printing 2004, fourth printing 2005, fifth printing 2007

Published simultaneously in Great Britain by Cordee, 3a DeMontfort Street, Leicester, England, LE1 7HD

Manufactured in the United States of America

Project Editor: Kathleen Cubley
Editor: Paula Thurman
Cover and book design: Ani Rucki
Layout: Alice C. Merrill

All photos by the author unless otherwise noted

Front and back cover photographs by Brooks Freehill
Frontispiece: *The Rupal Face of Nanga Parbat, Pakistan*

Library of Congress Cataloging-in-Publication Data
    Kiss or kill : confessions of a serial climber / Mark Twight.— 1st ed.
      p. cm.
    ISBN 0-89886-763-0 (cloth)
    ISBN 0-89886-887-4 (paper)
    1. Twight, Mark, 1961– 2. Mountaineers—United States—Biography. I. Title: Confessions of a serial climber. II. Title.
    GV199.92.T87 A3 2001
    796.52'2'092—dc21   00-012356
                                                      CIP

 Printed on recycled paper
ISBN 10: 0-89886-887-4 (paper)
ISBN 13: 978-0-89886-887-6 (paper)

To
LISA,
my wife,
AND ZUMA,
who reigned.

CONTENTS

FOREWORD

I first met Mark on a pistol range in Colorado. Even as a novice his movements were fluid and smooth. I saw the same effortless manner while rock climbing with him and some friends a few years later, as if he were part of the mountain. As I watched him train with the pistol, I could see he had *it:* the ability to listen, assimilate, and execute. Although our paths of expression differ, I realized our driving force is the same—to master our personal environments, whatever the conditions at the moment.

Curious, I asked what attracted a professional climber to pistol training. He said his best climbs were accompanied by a feeling of becoming one with the environment. At his best, he was the environment. I understood his answer. "I" disappear during an impeccable performance. He said this feeling, if it arrived at all, typically followed six months of training, two months in a foreign country, and acclimatizing at altitude for two weeks. He found he could challenge himself in a similar way while training and competing with a pistol without leaving the state. This comment surprised me. I figured climbers would believe nothing challenged you like the fear of death. At that point I knew Mark had realized that fear takes different forms depending on the individual. Life is fear: fear of alpine climbing, fear of competition, fear of failure, fear of death. Mark found a way to grapple with his personal fears without being "Mark the Climber."

We were talking after a pistol competition and one of the top shooters was joking and clowning around. Later I asked Mark, "You probably have those kind of guys in climbing, right?" His quick reply: "Not that are still alive." There is a saying I learned while road racing motorcycles, "When the green flag drops, the bullshit stops." While this holds true in all forms of human endeavor, I can't think of a better analogy than extreme alpinism. However, in Mark's case there is no bullshit to drop—he is pure action.

A friend and I were looking through Mark's book *Extreme Alpinism: Climbing, Light, Fast, & High.* She commented that Mark doesn't seem like the type of guy who would do the extreme climbing depicted in the book. Just looking at the pictures is overwhelming. The average person can't even imagine what it would take to attempt those situations, let alone survive them. That *is* Mark—he doesn't display his climbing ego in order to justify his self-worth.

Shortly after meeting Mark, I learned through his friends that his nickname was Dr. Doom. I had a good laugh over this because the Mark I knew appeared as nothing of the sort. I knew Mark Twight the shooter: confident, deliberate, and emphatic. Even when climbing with Mark, I had never seen a dark side, someone who longed to be on the precipice of death. However, after reading his earlier writings, I unearthed Dr. Doom. In "House of Pain" he writes, "I really don't give a shit what anyone thinks. I do what I do. I succeed. I fail. Sometimes I'm so lazy I do neither. I live and breathe along with my problems and my work and my self-inflicted pain." When we undeniably *see* that we create our own misery, we stop. The force generated by this insight changes anyone. Even Mark. His internal struggle for personal freedom, outwardly manifested through his climbing, eventually transformed Dr. Doom into Dr. Om.

I was struck when he wrote, "The future progression of alpine climbing resides in the mind. Improvements in physical fitness and equipment offer relatively limited advances to be made, while great strides may result from perfecting the minds of a few gifted climbers." An impressive statement from a man in a sport dominated by egos. I was surprised to find references to Krishnamurti and Carlos Castenada in the bibliography, another departure from the usual climbing book fare.

Without any effort on his part, Mark inspired me to improve in areas where, despite lifelong interest, I have a tendency to be lazy. The tangible effects of his knowledge of diet, exercise, and dedication to training have benefited me immeasurably. His "They all died" mantra has helped me through many a hot Arizona summer's run.

Everything in life is a challenge. You can accept the challenge to improve, or you can bask and distract yourself with success. Mark has accepted and survived the challenge, emerging as a true human being. The reward is personal freedom—not the illusion of the freedom to choose, but the freedom to confidently follow the heart.

Sport is about personal growth, whether in competition or on the mountains. You have the opportunity to challenge yourself beyond any means available in daily life. You choose what you get. You can waste it on your identity, or you can give back some of what you take. It's up to you.

POSTSCRIPT

Three days after writing this, I witnessed one gang beating that day's rival gang member nearly to death. I commented, to no one in particular, "What a waste of life, their whole culture is one big ego." Someone nearby responded, "That's true, but they're happy." "But at what price?" was my reply. Just as I said this, Mark's words formed in my mind, their meaning penetrating the temporary confusion, "It doesn't have to be fun to be fun."

Brian Enos
Apache Junction, Arizona
July 2000

INTRODUCTION

I began working on this collection in France in 1993. That original version included a fair amount of poetry. Jean-Marc Porte from *Montagnes Magazine* and Cathy Beloeil worked on the French translations. Nothing came of the book because it lacked depth. The singular point of view showed little personal evolution. The past seven years caused a lot of change and I think the work written in that time shows it. *Kiss or Kill* would not have come together had it not been for Jim Martin. His critical eye and editing skills were invaluable to the rewriting process.

The book is a one-time deal. I don't anticipate writing enough of these types of pieces in the future to put another collection together. That's why this one carries some weight. It's a knockout punch because there's no combination of weaker blows to follow.

Kiss or Kill features a collection of writing produced between 1985 and 2000. All of the work was previously published. However, these are Author's Cuts, not the homogenized fluff offered up by specialty climbing magazine editors who are often unwilling to offend subscribers and advertisers. Some material was only released in France, Italy, or England. One older piece titled "The Reality Bath" appeared in a forgotten Canadian review called *Alpinism*, printed once in 1989.

Each essay has been rewritten and annotated with a year 2000 perspective wherein I describe some of the writing's inspiration or events following publication. I think this collection offers a frightfully lucid look into my personal life as both man and hardcore alpine climber. The dissection scares me sometimes, but I'm oblivious to the lessons learned at others. I realize my emotional surgery in print has gone too far for some but deeply affected others in a positive manner. I care only for the latter. My climbing career mirrors that of many other professions: there were successes, failures, and a learning curve paralleled by a process of becoming. Sometimes this evolution demanded that I solo hard routes, taking extreme risks in order to see clearly. Sometimes all I had to do was wipe the glass with a clean cloth. This book is a memoir documenting my journey toward maturity as a climber and, consequently, as a human being.

After commenting that the book's power might cause people to put it down, my editor was surprised to hear me say I hoped so. Each piece was originally written for a magazine format. They are printed here in approximate chronological order of publication and not intended to flow smoothly from one to the next. I don't want it to be an easy read. I want you to put it down, to think about it. I want this book to help you recognize your own anger, which will help you understand mine.

My language and attitude come from a specific period in musical and social history: I'm a Punk, and Punk rock fueled my rebellious nature and its expression for years. Some folks will laugh, claiming Punk died 20 years ago along with Sid, but its anger and energy blaze on for many. If you read these articles before, or read them now without sharing the language of Punk, you'll likely consider them posturing or arrogant. So be it, but somewhere out there somebody understands these words and knows they matter. They were written in blood, learned by heart.

Despite my age, I'm still raving, kicking against mediocrity. I'm not as angry as I was in the old days, but I am still intolerant of empty words and arrogant about taking action. Put up or shut up.

Mark F. Twight
Boulder, Colorado
September 2000

SOLO ON THE

The north
face of
Grands
Charmoz,
November 2,
1984
Chamonix,
France

CHARMOZ

Your letter asked where I've been. The usual Chamonix hangs, I suppose. The waiting is frustrating, but the locals don't even notice. They can afford to watch good conditions pass. I'm on a time limit, so things aren't the same for me. Before, I thought I was going to stay the winter. I don't know what changed my mind, but something stretched too tightly and snapped. A voice I'd been ignoring finally started screaming, "Get out Mark, it's time to go home."

Things were tough but going well. The franc is weak so my money buys a lot, and I knew I could get by until I found work. When I came here from Grindelwald, I hit three weeks of good weather and even better ice conditions. By the time normal fall weather returned, I was happy. My hands were so swollen from whacking my knuckles against the ice that I needed a break. I spent a few days reluctantly looking for work, and went to Geneva to pick up a wire transfer from my dad. Then the weather turned good again.

It was my birthday, so I decided to treat myself to the north face of the Grands Charmoz. My friends had gone home in October so I went alone, but I felt comfortable with the process.

The Charmoz is a difficult climb—what we did on the Eiger was offensively easy by comparison—and a storm caught me near the top. It wasn't supposed to blow in for another 12 hours. Hard luck, I guess, and it scared me badly remembering that Welzenbach sat through four days of foul weather. I began rushing a bit, climbing carelessly. I expected to cruise the Heckmair finish because the crux is purportedly in the rock bands down low. I was wrong. The ice was extremely thin over steep rock; it was rotten or hollow in places.

At one point when I eased my frontpoints into the ice and weighted them, the whole plate cut loose, and my crampons scraped down the rock underneath. I transferred the force onto my tools instinctively, but one of them ripped out, too. I thrashed around swinging at patches that weren't even ice. Sparks showered down as the pick hit rock in rat-a-tat-tat repetition.

My head spun with fear—I had the sensation of falling over backwards and tumbling end over end. I imagined my head breaking open like a carelessly dropped cantaloupe, my precious life making an ugly mess of the ice field below me. No witnesses or shock, just a lonely, soloist's end.

The music in my headphones shouted:

> *I was going to drown, but then I started swimming.*
> *I was going down, but then I started winning.*

Living the words, I stemmed out onto good ice and pulled for all I was worth, climbing to a relatively secure rest. I shook, barely holding it together, but I held it because I had to, because I needed to keep climbing. And the hardest part—finding a way down—still loomed ahead of me. It was snowing harder. I took an extra wrap in my ice tool leash and turned up the volume.

I crested the ridge in a whiteout and didn't bother with the summit, which was 200 feet away. I jumped into the nearest couloir I saw figuring that as long as it didn't cliff out, I'd be able to get down. Descent, descend, sanctuary, survival. I did not philosophize beyond recognizing that luck runs out all at once, never by degrees. I performed only primary survival functions, feeling neither hunger nor thirst.

I downclimbed until it became too steep and then rappelled, leaving gear behind without caring because money meant nothing at the time. I went off single-piece anchors as I had so few, playing for all the marbles at every throw. Then the avalanches began, small at first, but growing larger as more snow fell and I put more above me by losing altitude. The slides roared down without warning. I'd hear one, sink my tools, tuck my chin to my chest, and hope it wasn't too big, that there were no rocks in it. I descended faster than ever before, overcoming my best efforts as I was overcome by events.

Eventually, I reached relatively level ground. I breathed easier in the temporary sanctuary. I didn't know where I was, but I'd come through worse and believed I could handle the rest of the journey. Intuitively, I found my way back to the Mer de Glace and down to town. Being lost was trivial compared to the rest of the descent.

There was nothing for me in the valley, no comfort or understanding or friends. I was a soloist who almost died, which is nothing special in Chamonix. I wandered the streets alone, but it was the last thing I wanted. True, I came here by myself in the first place, but that was a month ago, before the Super Couloir, before the Charmoz, not today. I didn't want to be alone. I didn't want to stay here any longer. The voice said, "Go home," and I didn't have the energy to argue with it anymore.

As the bus headed toward Geneva, I gave Chamonix a warm smile and fond "Adieu." I didn't say "Good-bye" because I knew I would be back.

2000 AUTHOR'S NOTE

I rewrote this article extensively. I thought it sad to have described such an important event with lame writing. It was one of my first efforts (November 1984) and I hadn't yet found my voice. I penned it on the Swiss Air flight home, making few modifications before submitting it to *Climbing*.

The climb on the Charmoz ended my first trip to Europe. I'd gone over with Jon Krakauer to attempt the north face of the Eiger. We sat out three weeks of the wettest September since 1864 hoping the weather would improve. During a two-day high pressure, which we deemed too brief to tackle the Nordwand, I soloed the north face of the Monch. It opened my eyes to my own potential and an ambition I did not know existed. Eventually, Jon and I got on the Eiger, but snow conditions convinced us to descend from the base of the Second Icefield. Beaten, Jon flew home while I took a train to Chamonix.

As I rolled toward France that autumn, the haze of burning vineyards clung to the bottom of the Rhone Valley and the Alps shot into clear blue sky. The Rhone was more open than the valley below the Eiger, and the mountains less oppressive. The rhythm of wheel to track hypnotized me. I knew I traveled toward my destiny. As the train exited the tunnel at Montroc and I glimpsed the Chamonix valley my gut told me I was home, that this would be my home.

During the next two weeks I soloed the Triangle du Tacul, the Gabarrou-Albinone, and the Super Couloir on Mont Blanc du Tacul and the Swiss Route on the north face of Les Courtes. Bad weather closed me out of the mountains for a few days, so I went to Geneva to pick up some money my father kindly wired to me. I bought a tape by The Stranglers and played the song "The European Female" over and over all the way back to Chamonix. I hatched a plot to remain in France. I thought I was ready for it. The near fatal climb on the Charmoz interrupted my plans and sent me scurrying for the States, which was for the best because most 22-year-olds don't survive their alpine learning curves if they play the game full-time. I went back for four months the following year, a month in 1986, six weeks in 1987, and finally moved for good in November 1988. I stayed five years, learned to speak French, was married and divorced, and climbed a lot of hard, beautiful mountains.

The power of the Mont Blanc Massif changed me forever, and I consider Chamonix my spiritual home. It was pure chance to have turned up there during the best ice conditions I have ever seen in the range. Had I arrived during a dry year, my whole life might have taken a different course.

KISS OR KILL

I've always dreamed that I would die being eaten by rats. Maybe I've read Orwell's *1984* once too often. Indeed, 1984 was the beginning of my descent into the black depths of extreme alpinism. This obsession destroyed my relationships, drove me into depression, and changed me from a happy, future-hopeful young man into an embittered cynic.

In 1984 I went to the Eiger because it was the most radical, dangerous climb I could imagine myself doing. To prepare, I backed away from everything except the mountain and my ambition. They were all that mattered. Relationships that were incomplete or inconsequential were cut away. I consolidated my power by not sharing it. Sure, I'm a self-centered asshole, but being obsessed is something not easily shared, nor is it often appreciated.

I suppose it came from the music. Joy Division taught me that cynicism is okay. Ian Curtis, the band's vocalist, was so consumed by it that he hung himself as a solution. Johnny Rotten stated that "the future is a pointed stick," so why bother? The young punks and the music generated in me such a vehement intolerance of stupidity and mediocrity that extremism became *my* solution.

Kiss or Kill.

The Eiger wasn't enough. Alaska wasn't enough. The wild soloing didn't do it either. No matter what I did, the suffering I experienced did not satisfy me. I had to have more. Then I met Jeff Lowe.

Jeff is 10 years my senior. He's not into my scene. In fact, he used to be a hippie. Being so young, I don't know exactly what that means, but I suspect that the hippies were basically punks that weren't angry. Mind you, Jeff is intense, although without my kind of dark intensity. He wouldn't have a birthday party where all the guests wear black.

I don't care about the cash.

I don't care about life's "necessary accessories."

I only care when provoked.

I care about climbing, period.

Jeff invited me to Kangtega and Nuptse: "New routes, Mark, hard, high, unknown ground . . ." I'd met Jeff once before. I knew he was good. I accepted. With only 10 days' notice I cut off everything that might have held me back. I am very good with the knife now.

Twelve days after Jeff's call I arrived in Katmandu, which is a Third World cesspool no matter what the travel books allege. I hated it and couldn't wait to get out, but I had to wait because there are no schedules. There are no exceptions made for climbers, and the bureaucrats do not understand ambition which one does not profit from—which *they* do not profit from.

I hated Katmandu, but I understood it: the crying souls, the poverty, the futurelesssness. This condition disgusts some, enlightens all, and inspires others to join the Peace Corps to "help." As I trudged through the filth, I understood it.

Entire chapters of expedition tomes dwell on the approach toward the Khumbu. That horse is well flogged, but it's no longer necessary because the approach has been modernized. Now, we fly to Lukla, above the leeches, above the wasted landscapes, above the porter hassles.

Both Jeff and I came down with amoebic dysentery in Lukla and spent three days weakly laughing at each other as we alternately vomited and shat without control. Feverish, shivering, always hoping it would end. Two high-altitude athletes driven to their knees by something microscopic—too poetic. Now *that* was suffering. I flip on the Skinny Puppy tape: "The world's a hell, what does it matter what happens in it?" Yeah, what's it matter?

"Base camp was languorously pitched at 14,000 feet among blossoms and boulders, with waterfalls that lulled us to sleep at night and birds to wake us at dawn." Waxing eloquent? Lying. Base camp was at 14,000 feet, but we'd come too high too fast and headaches shrieked like jackhammers. Our stomachs hadn't adjusted to the food, and the only birds to be seen were crows the size of baseball mitts. We gave *them* anything they wanted.

We wasted no time at Kangtega Base Camp, moving immediately up to Lobuche village beneath the mighty Lobuche Peak. We intended to acclimate. The collection of stone shelters awakened new states of disgust in me. A trekking group had pitched their toilet tent over the water supply, raw sewage polka-dotted the few campsites, and Western garbage, American garbage, was piled high everywhere. Yeah, I felt like a gringo. Yeah, I felt sick.

After climbing the peak, I left the others behind and ran away. I ran 10 miles back to Kangtega Base Camp. I couldn't embrace what our presence had done to that awesome place. I had to escape. I had to forget. So I drank. I drank all that I could. I crawled semiconscious from my tent on hands and knees, and I vomited long and hard. Morning found me half-in and half-out of my sleeping bag. I was hung over, but I felt cleansed. That same morning we started up Kangtega, an epic that lasted through 10 long and hungry nights. I knew I'd get up the mountain, but a voice inside sadly assured me that it would not be enough.

I returned to base camp lean and wasted, the warm-up climb had worn me out. I needed rest but never got it. On May 7 we began trekking toward the apocalypse.

At anxious last I saw it: the southeast spur of Nuptse was terrifyingly beautiful. It had the elegance of a Halston dress and the aggressiveness of a metal-studded dog collar. There was a hollow feeling in my stomach. It became an ache, the ache became a stabbing pain. I fell to the rocks clutching my frightened head in my hands . . . I wanted like I had never wanted before.

Oh, precious ambition that feeds me, I worship your power with emotional violence. I am struck down by watching angels and paralyzed by haunting fear in the final hour. I must go to the wall, driven by anger, by anguish, by anxiety. Oh, precious ambition, I just want to die with a smile on my face.

> *No conscience, just confidence*
> *Your glue-on smile, your social style*
> *You're tired, you're ruled, you're such a fool.*
>
> **Skinny Puppy**

"You never run out of batteries for that thing do you?" Jeff pointed at my Walkman. It'd be poor style to run out of batteries. Besides, it's my survival mechanism. When the going gets tough, the tough turn up the volume.

The avalanches had a tremorous effect on my bowels. The sustained primal groan excited my fight-or-flee reaction even when nothing could be achieved by either. We were quite safe out on the spur. We continued upward day after day. It was enjoyable. It was horrifying. Always it was painful. I was a drowning man climbing desperately: pushing, demanding, trying to lose my mind in my body. I may be possessed, I may be obsessed, but I can feel, I can love just like the rest of you. I didn't have a Walkman with me so I sang, and I suffered when Jeff did.

> *This is the crisis I knew had to come, destroying the balance I kept. Doubting,*
> *unsettling and turning around, wondering what will come next . . .*
>
> **Joy Division**

The storm hissed against my bivy tent, we were burned. It couldn't kill us, but it was fierce enough to stop us. We'd climbed 4000 feet toward clear skies until the seventh day when it began to snow. I pushed one more pitch into the spindrift and wind on the morning of the eighth day. At the top, I set a rappel anchor and dropped back to the belay for a decision. At 1 P.M. we began descending. At 6 P.M. the next day we walked into base camp with no hardware left, no food or fuel, no bivouac gear, and nothing material to show for our desperate act of volatile ambition. All we had was a resolve to return in November.

There is a damp smell in my tent. I stare at the waxy yellow ceiling and turn myself inward, introspection that eventually ends in pain.

Back in the city the darkness stalks me with cold skill. I dash down bombed-out streets through a hard and dirty rain. Pavement scatters as my feet pound beneath the cliffs of buildings, soaring into the filthy mist. I see faces that carry the marks of strain, faces that wear weariness like lumps of clay—tired, danceless faces. I see people who are stained and damp, with ashtray breath like the smell of decay. Everywhere I look I see hope that's been smothered by deadly routine. And I see the rats hunting.

I remember the mountain from a distance and I try to convince myself that the rats will not catch up to me. At long horrible last, I am truly suffering.

And long hearses without drums or music drag
in slow file through my soul; hope vanquished
weeps, and atrocious, despotic anguish
plants on my bowed head her black flag.

Unknown French poet, 1800s

2000 AUTHOR'S NOTE

Of all my experiences and the articles I've written about them, this one affected me the most. I left it basically untouched while I rewrote every other piece in the collection. Despite being heavily laden with adjectives, the pace is fast and the story lean. I cringe at some of the descriptive phrases after 14 years' worth of perspective. I could write them better now. But like a 1980s hairstyle, while the fashion may be questionable today, it seemed appropriate at the time. I used what tools I had to express myself. The experience and the way I told it shaped my life for years to come.

"Kiss or Kill" was the fourth article I'd had published. It messed with more heads than any piece I've written before or since. I hand-wrote it on a yellow legal pad in a single sitting. *Climbing* ran it almost verbatim, adding only the word *Orwell's*, before setting the type. For a while I thought they'd done so because I wrote so well. I later concluded that being such a personal and painful account rather than a boring "we went there, we did that" narrative, they dared not mess with it too much. Perhaps they weren't sure how to edit it. Clearly, they did not leave it alone because of its brilliant construction.

I was heavily influenced by punk music both on the trip and while writing "Kiss or Kill." The title, in fact, was stripped from a song by Los Angeles favorites X. Punk songs were all short, spare, and packed a wallop. The confrontational attitude broadcast by the punk movement was mantra and method for me. Punk music's message of personal reinvention and its Do-It-Yourself ethic remain with me today.

The article reached out to a few men who have become very important in my life. Barry Blanchard admitted to reading it more than 40 times before we met. Scott Backes was so familiar with the piece and its "feeling" he quoted Skinny Puppy to me the first day we met. Both have told me how comforting and inspiring it was to learn there was another climber out there who held similar attitudes. They were not alone. They honor me with their words, and their friendship.

But Jeff Lowe had some trouble with the article. He could not believe what had been going on in my head during that expedition. It was my third trip ever outside the USA; my first to a Third World country. I was with people I did not know, and one was a climbing legend. The routes we planned to attempt were harder and higher than anything I could imagine doing. I was scared out of my mind and trying to cover it up. That fear, present 24 hours a day until we began the trek out, filtered each experience. Even the ones I was equal to.

The expedition was an epiphany. I learned that I had talent. I also learned I was not as good a climber as I thought I was. At the time, climbing the new route on Kangtega was little consolation for the failure on Nuptse. Years afterward, I appreciate Kangtega for the transformation it caused. I stepped out of the bush league up there. After Alison Hargreaves, my partner on the summit of Kangtega, died, the mountain meant even more. That and Lobuche were the only two peaks we ever climbed together. Others found her too ambitious, but this was a trait I knew well and encouraged. She was incredibly strong, and delightful to be around in the mountains.

GLITTER AND DESPAIR

I hear the pitter patter of tiny claws on my stairway and shiver with the fever. I stare across vacant rooftops into the fluorescent high-rise windows; television screens that look down upon the ooze of the city. The waste is atrocious. Garbage piled in the alleyways gags the stoutest throats. I watch the migration of homeless people as the winter forces them south. I pretend to empathize.

The rats are everywhere. I used to fight them; I used to care a bit. Today, I retreat. In the streets I watch the battles both inevitable and lost. I sleep wrapped in the cynical strength of my arms, peace interrupted by thoughts of my discarded past. Bones show through my smooth hard skin, they are not broken yet. I am starved of emotional nourishment, denied respite, refused satisfaction. I accept this punishment for over-stepping my limitations. I failed as miserably as is possible. Every poisoned breath I share with this city is atonement for being unable to overcome.

The nights are filled with lips that don't move and cynicism that kills my pen. I wake wearing a necklace of unfulfilled dreams. Last summer I overflowed with the wild hope of youth. I was a young man and faithful to my goals. I was concentrated, fierce, and alert; a mercenary fighting an epidemic of the lame and the weak. Today as I reach for my death-stick cigarettes I laugh at my deficiencies. I'm not disappointed with myself anymore. I used to hide my tears because tomorrow is another day. Now I let them flow for much the same reason.

I was strong. I could have done anything. I seethed with desire. Believing in my self-importance, I stroked and blessed my ego. Ambition was so precious. I worshipped it and stole for it. I rationalized every evil thing I ever did by weigh-ing it against my ambition. I wanted to be a god without enduring the boredom of sainthood.

I trained. I punished myself. I thought making myself suffer on a day-to-day basis would prepare me for climbing hard at high altitude. I slept on the floor. I carried ice in my bare hands. I beat them against the concrete just to see if I could handle it. I never missed an opportunity to train. I ran stairs until I vomited, then ran more.

I ruined relationships to get used to the feeling of failure and sacrifice (it was much easier than holding on). I trained in the gym on an empty diet to learn how far I could push myself without food or water. I imitated and plagiarized the heroes who lived and died before me. I spoke only strong words and ignored weakness at every turn. I subdued my fears. I was opinionated and direct. I became a man either well loved or truly hated. I was ready for anything.

I returned to the South Pillar of Nuptse despite the warnings, and my bad dreams. I knew I could handle it. I knew I'd summit in winter, even in carnivorous winds and crippling temperatures. But our technology was impotent against the winter storms. We watched in silence as piece by piece, tent by tent our base camp was destroyed. The murderer was benevolent with us by comparison to the two lives it claimed a scant 10 miles away. We faced the wall awed by the storm's power. I thought I knew the meaning of the word *wind* until I went to Nepal in winter. I finally understood after hearing the howl for days and nights strung on end. It shook my organs, conjuring atavistic feelings, "I should be in a cave, underground." The pit in my stomach came from the wind. I wanted a bunker, not a nylon bag. Three days later we packed our gear. The two of us were incredibly small in the vastness of Himalayan winter. We approached the pillar knowing we were doomed. But also knowing we were beautiful to hope our ideals would triumph over the heaviness of fear.

On Christmas day I searched for perfection, for God under an ultraviolet sky rather than beneath a crucifix. Exhaled haloes wreathed our heads, distressed and furious. I watched nightfall without moonrise. The sun went down on our efforts to find a bivouac cave. Blood, hope, and sweat froze all at once in the dusk.

New Year's Eve I lost all feeling in my feet and hands. I belayed Jeff for hours as he did what he does best on radical mixed terrain. The pitch would have been ED+ in the Alps. We were at nearly 23,000 feet.

When he climbed, I loved to watch his hands. His tools caressed the ice, without it shattering. Jeff applied perfection earned through years of practice. But doubt beat its way into my head with more determination each hour. I wondered whether our efforts would be sufficient. By questioning at all, I began to fail.

The storm arrived while we slept. It whipped this way and that, freezing eyelids, nostrils, and eventually words in our throats. I screamed at Jeff to hurry up. I was more worried about losing my fingers than my life. He never heard me. I dropped a jumar. I dropped my belay plate. I carelessly lost some of the keys to success. Tears froze on my cheeks before they could disappear into the snow.

That night I shivered. I couldn't force my body to obey me. The smell of 10 days' effort fouled the air in our one-man bivy tent; the rank ammonia odor of

Jeff Lowe at
20,000 feet
on Nuptse's
South Pillar
during the
winter
attempt,
January
1987

the body burning muscle tissue in order to survive. The sickening and sweet taste of defeat overcame me. It promised respite from struggle bolstered by the relief of knowing that there was absolutely no hope for success. By morning I'd succumbed to an attack of amoebic dysentery. I shat in my altitude suit, unable to get it off fast enough. After the first time I cut my underwear out, but after the third time all I could do was leave the shit where it was. Without conversation Jeff and I agreed to go down.

Wind surged across the frozen wastes. Our bodies moved restlessly, we could not feed them enough. Dusk upon us, we crept across the ghetto of boulders, our headlamps sometimes eerie, then like rockets in the fog. Total darkness ambushed us short of our destination. The hours wore on. The moraine wore us down. My eyes were riveted to the rising scythe of a moon. In that instant I figured out what was killing me. It wasn't the quick blow of an ax, but the slow torment of the rack: each day I was weaker, each hour a little more sick. With every night that passed I shuffled a bit nearer to death. I made life-and-death decisions like I was choosing between two brands of beer. In the end, I knew it was time to give up and consider escape the only success. I gave way to fear, trading my dreams for the bland taste of survival. I turned my back and crawled away.

I sold all of my gear in Katmandu. After I got I home I threw away all of the elitist books in my apartment. Eventually, I tore down the pictures of summits and dream climbs from around the world. I promised that I would never ever go back to the mountains. I vowed that I would not climb again.

The bed embraces me warmly. I accept the solace it offers. I went to the edge, I thought it was important. I thought the view would be crystal clear. Now I don't care. I give in. I give up. I just want to be ordinary, to have meager needs and mediocre ambitions. I want each day to be enough on its own, without risk or fear or the pressure to succeed. I wish I was like everybody else. I squeeze the narrow face in my hands. Its eyes ask me for encouragement, its frail voice distracts me, hoping to find consolation in my company. But my shoulder's not for comfort, my hand not for support. I cannot give anymore. Time bleeds away with every heartbeat and I carefully inspect my lean bitterness of purpose. The weight of it forces me to the bed. I sprawl face down and sleep through nightmares now because I've seen how bad it can really get. I'm not afraid of dreams anymore.

But the threat still lingers like a steel sprung trap. Though obsession rests, I know it will attack without warning. Possession will come back to disrupt the quiet. I know that sharp and dripping teeth wait calmly behind seductive lips; wait to crush, wait to tear with vicious, hungry breath. I know that sensitive eyes rest quietly behind fiercely made-up lashes, behind a calculated mask. Capable of opening without consent, they are neither placid nor menacing. I bow my head once more, and while ambition sleeps inside of me I content myself with memories of glitter and despair.

2000 AUTHOR'S NOTE

I fought one of the biggest fights I've ever had with a woman over this article when she asked if it was fiction. Jeff read it and said the same thing he said about "Kiss or Kill": "It's like we weren't even on the same route." The experience I had in my head was totally different than what happened in his despite sharing the same physical reality. The same theme came up several times later in life. It took years to become comfortable with it, longer still for others to do so.

A lot of bad things evolved from this trip. The failure caused such self-loathing that I broke up with my girlfriend. I didn't love myself, so how could I love her? Besides, she wanted much more than I could give at that point in my life. I soloed some good routes in the Alps on my way back to the States, though, and enjoyed the time I spent in France. Once home, my mother and stepfather, who had both read "Kiss or Kill," tried to check me into a drug and alcohol rehabilitation clinic. They were convinced I was addicted to alcohol and Valium. Had I actually been dabbling in depressants to the degree they suspected, I think I'd have found it difficult to get out of bed in the morning, much less climb hard in the Alps and Himalayas. My stepfather wondered why I "dreamed I'd die being eaten by rats." Then his employer's daughter told him of her rehab session and how during the worst of the DTs she'd hallucinated that she was being chewed on by giant rodents. Bingo! Paul and Jan did not interview Jeff, other climbing partners, or my former-girlfriend, Anne. Nor did they document events resulting from my being fucked up all the time, like losing a job or beating up my woman. Lacking evidence, they still attempted Intervention. I laughed, I denied, I became sarcastic; all expected reactions, apparently. Finally, I read the AA manual they'd been studying. I told them to stuff themselves until such time as they compiled evidence supporting their theory. They never produced any, they never apologized, and I never forgave them.

My stepfather died, and Mom still clings to what he believed. The photo (in my book *Extreme Alpinism*) she prefers to show her friends is one where I am feigning unconsciousness on a lawn chair at Kahiltna Base Camp. The liquor bottle in my hand is partially hidden by a joke label. I know she loves me and is quite proud of my achievements. She simply can't reconcile her own feelings versus what Paul believed. She treats me like the adolescent I was when all that happened. Although I love her, I can't change her or teach her who I am. So I watch and am disappointed by how ordinary our dysfunctional family really is.

the REALITY BATH

RANDY RACKLIFF APPROACHES THE REALITY BATH ON WHITE PYRAMID: GRADE 6+, VII. 600 METERS. BECAUSE OF A FIFTY-FIFTY CHANCE OF BEING KILLED ON THIS UNREPEATED ROUTE, SPEED IS SAFETY.

(A FRAGMENT)

I shook the broken tool off my wrist and with wooden fingers unholstered a spare. I sank the pick into more rotten ice just as the serac wall five pitches above calved off for the second time. Hyperventilating in the spindrift, I watched the bulk of the ice blocks rush past less than a hundred feet away.

Fifteen feet higher the ice looked thick enough to take a Snarg. I hammered until it hit rock. After tying the 7-millimeter haul line to my lead rope, I rappelled back to the cave where Randy Rackliff was belaying. We were freaked out, out of control. He agreed the route might actually be too dangerous—even for sick men like us, men willing to play for more than we could afford to lose.

We rapped five pitches to the ground and did not return to the northeast face of the White Pyramid for three weeks. Warm and unstable weather created serious avalanche danger. Our heads and the weather settled toward the end of February. After soloing Slipstream in two hours and filming Randy soloing Polar Circus, I felt fast and strong. Above all I felt ready to stick my neck out. I didn't care much about coming back because the rest of my life wasn't going too well.

We skied to the face via Epaulet Lake. The snow, melted by Chinook winds, had refrozen hard as asphalt. The serac barrier threatening the waterfall still appeared 150 to 200 feet high, although portions of it had fallen away. The debris and craters at the bottom of the face told us tons of ice had avalanched. We put on our crampons, threaded hands through the wrist leashes of our tools, and began climbing without the rope.

I wanted to vomit all day long. I was sick with the fear of being unequal to the climb, afraid of getting splattered by falling ice. My muscles cramped as subconscious battled conscious. Dark music looped through my head and a black, suicidal mood pooled around me. I broke my ice tools on the frozen crucible. Instinct forced me to live through it.

RANDY

RACKLIFF

APPROACHES

THE SERACS

AT THE TOP

OF THE

REALITY

BATH, WHITE

PYRAMID,

CANADA.

Every time Randy's tool bounced off the old, dense serac ice I thought of the two tools we'd already broken and how bad it would be if he snapped another pick. The ice wall cracked and shuddered, settling on the topography underneath. Our first rational choice of the day was to avoid the direct finish, to get out from under the threat because if you lose control, you lose. Period.

Afterwards, Barry Blanchard tried to convince me that V+ is the hardest technical grade that exists on ice. I don't contest it—we all attach the number grade for different reasons. I graded The Reality Bath 7 because of its length, sustained difficulty, and insane objective hazard. Maybe it'll be repeated, gang-soloed, down-rated, dismissed. So what? I respect action and competence. Words and numbers are meaningless to the artist. The number VII+ simplifies conversation. It offers a notion of what to expect.

Looking back I wonder why we bothered with the route at all. Waterfall climbing is tedious and uncomfortable. The same motions and noises and impressions over and over again. The only way to make it more meaningful is to use it as a thermostat. How "bad" can I be? How hard can I solo? How many waterfalls can I climb in one day? How much objective danger am I willing to accept? I don't care about what I climb, only how it affects me. Success merely punctuates the experience.

2000 AUTHOR'S NOTE

The Reality Bath was a pivotal moment in my climbing career. I learned that safety is relative to one's consciousness and the exigencies of a particular route. One must be adaptable to internal and external conditions. On our second attempt, Randy and I realized that true safety resided in not being there at all, and if compelled to be there by whatever desires and demons we faced, it was better to be on the climb for as little time as possible.

We simul-soloed the first five pitches because it was faster than belaying. Then we tied into one 9-millimeter rope. Randy clipped the two screws I'd left on the sixth pitch, but we never placed another point of protection on the route. We didn't use the rope to stop a leader fall but to make it safe for the second to follow as fast as possible, without needing to place each tool securely. We were under the seracs for more than eight hours, on the route for nine. Conditions were perfect: three weeks of warm weather followed by a week of hard freezing. Such ideal conditions may never occur again. Nonetheless, the route was still incredibly dangerous.

The Reality Bath hasn't seen a second ascent as of this writing. In the recent guidebook *Waterfall Ice*, a new grading system, divided into two categories respectively addressing technical difficulty and commitment, has replaced the old single numeral system. Our original grade of VII covered all aspects of the climb, from technical difficulty to engagement.

Under the new system The Reality Bath received a technical grade of 6+ and an engagement Grade VII, which according to the new guidebook's author, Joe Josephson, means "you have a 50-50 chance of getting the chop."

Albi Sole, author of the previous two Canadian Rockies ice guides, stated that "'Reality Bath' seems so dangerous as to be of little value except to those suicidally inclined." This is the assessment of a nonparticipant. What remains to be seen is the judgment of whoever has the balls to make the second ascent of this remarkable route. We climbed it, we lived, we remember it well.

THE RISE AND FALL

ATTEMPTING A
NEW ROUTE
ON THE
NORTH FACE
OF EVEREST'S
NORTHEAST
RIDGE

(Photo by Barry

Blanchard)

OF THE AMERICAN ALPINIST

The bell announces the third round. There's blood everywhere. Every tendon is blown and crying eyes are swollen shut. Biceps poisoned, once proud American faces are aimed at the floor. We went down to Le Menestral, Raboutou, and Tribout in Round One. We begged for mercy during Round Two as Beghin, Boivin, Chamoux, and Profit cramponed our Alpine and Himalayan "successes" to death. I think it's time to start kicking ass.

Although Dale Goddard and Scott Franklin are resuscitating the rock scene, Americans still fail miserably in the mountains. Our "significant achievements" pale in comparison to the European efforts. Christophe Profit soloed the Three Great North Faces of the Alps in 24 hours. He repeated this apocalyptic trilogy in winter. Jean-Marc Boivin combined extreme skiing, paragliding, and hang gliding with alpinism to enchain the north faces of the Aiguille Verte, Les Droites, Les Courtes, and the Grands Jorasses into one marathon day. He flew his hang glider 15 kilometers down the Vallée Blanche at one o'clock in the morning.

Until 1987 the closest Americans had come to doing an 8000-meter peak in Alpine Style was the Unsoeld-Hornbein traverse of Everest in 1963. Last September Steve Untch (USA) partnered Alan Hinkes (GB) for a new route, Alpine Style on Shishapangma. Score one for Old Glory. In contrast, Jean Troillet and Erhard Loretan demeaned Everest by climbing up and sliding down its 10,000-vertical-foot north face in 43 hours. No oxygen, no Ten Essentials, and no drugs. Voytek Kurtyka and Robert Schauer snuck up the west face of Gasherbrum IV (a route often tried by Americans) shortly after Nil Bohigas and Enric Lucas flashed a new route on the south face of Annapurna.

American teams grovel in the Himalayas despite technological, financial, and manpower advantages. They suck down thousands of dollars worth of oxygen, hire Sherpas to carry loads that the climbers can't handle, then fix ropes, camps, and

33

gear to within easy reach of the summit. Occasionally, someone stands on top.

What's the problem? European climbers are not superhuman. But their Himalayan successes directly reflect immense skill, training, sponsorship, and a sort of social Darwinism in choice of team members. Rarely is an American expedition composed of the nation's best climbers. But Europeans are fairly nationalistic about Himalayan summits; they want the flag on top, so send the country's finest to place it there. Neither are they averse to heroes or leaders. They understand that all climbers are not created equal. Not all deserve the chance. The heartless, dedicated assholes are the ones that succeed. American expeditions get nowhere because democracy is useless in the harsh environment of the Himalayas. Besides that, Americans consider themselves "entitled" to a chance even when they're a liability to the organization. What is needed for success is a leader and a few crack troops, not a group of inexperienced friends arguing and voting over how much gas to cache at Camp 3 or whether the line is too dangerous. These petty conflagrations erupt from the fact that the climbing itself is not the most important thing to the team players. Trivial social conflicts prevent or soil successful expeditions all too often. The French do so well because they are willing to give up everything for the CLIMBING. But in American camps, leaders fear the tread of assistant leaders, and both worry over whether their thunder will be usurped by the louder clap of the climber who stands on the summit with a video camera.

Face it, Americans have an inferiority complex when it comes to Himalayan mountaineering. We content ourselves with lower summits and justify them by claiming they are more technically difficult. Or we climb expedition style on known routes to well-trod summits. Standards have not been pushed by an American team since the Lowes, Kennedy, and Donini attempted Latok in 1978. Although Jeff Lowe's unfinished route on the south face of Nuptse offers a glimpse into the future, for the most part we are wasting money, effort, and time.

Closer to home, the only significant advances in American alpine climbing were made by "North Americans," i.e. Canadians. In the last three years new routes have been put up on the north faces of North Twin and Temple. Both the east face of Mount Chephren and the northeast face of Howse Peak were climbed by new routes in the winter. Either Barry Blanchard or Ward Robinson has been a player on every one of these climbs.

The Canadian Rockies are the only arena on this continent where we can train to compete on an international level, but every time I'm there I rarely see fellow countrymen. Even in winter when the stones are frozen silent and the waterfalls are thick, few climbers come north. When they arrive, all they do is make bigger craters in the trade routes. This is sad because waterfalls are one discipline where we lead the European competition. The hardest waterfalls on the planet are in North America. We have a 20-year history of curved picks, frontpoints, and vertical ice.

Each winter the envelope is stretched. A few Americans push the extreme while the Europeans fly paragliders, ride monoskis, or enchain routes of moderate difficulty. The deficiencies of European waterfall climbers are glaring.

For example: in the Cirque de Gavarnie—France's premier waterfall site—only two of the 15 routes would merit a Canadian Grade VI; Thanatos and Overdose, the latter only because of its length. Fluid Glaciale and Adrenaline are given ED and ED+ grades—the top of the French system. I soloed both of them and would apply Grades IV and V- if they were in Canada. Adrenaline is similar in length and ambience to Bourgeau-Left. During the Premieres Journées de Glace meet at Gavarnie in February 1987, fewer than 10 of the 70 competitors could competently lead Grade VI ice. At this same time in Canada, however, Jeff Marshall created Riptide, 200 meters VI+, a five-pitch bolt-protected heinousity. Kevin Doyle and Tim Friesen's Gimme Shelter, 350 meters VI+, went unformed and unrepeated. The Terminator was heralded as the world's first Grade VII (after four ascents the consensus dropped to VI+) and the classic VIs were being gang-soloed into submission. Guy Lacelle did Polar Circus, 600 meters VI, in two and a half hours. Jeff Marshall soloed Polar Circus and Weeping Pillar, 280 meters VI, in one day. I brought the Euro-flavor home by soloing Slipstream, 925 meters VI, in two hours and four minutes. February 1988 saw another advance in standards when Randy Rackliff and I established The Reality Bath, 600 meters, 11 pitches Grade VII. It is certainly the most sustained and dangerous waterfall route in the Rockies. Time marches on.

When I speak of competing with others in the mountains, I'm sure it disgusts some of you. You say it is contrary to mountaineering spirit. I can't agree, nor will I argue. Whether it's right or wrong, it happens. This unspoken, unorganized competition is the only way to force alpine climbing standards higher.

The traditionalists also blather about risk in the wake of K2 1986 and numerous tragedies during 1987. The safety margins of today can't compare to those of 20 years ago, or even 10. To succeed on the modern desperates, food and fuel must be pared to a minimum. Carrying insufficient gear is normal practice these days. The new climbs of the age are yesterday's death routes. People die. Alpine climbers die. It is part of the game. However, we don't shoot with the same dice our predecessors used. The equation is simple: as technological and psychological advances increase, the danger and difficulty of the routes must be raised as well to maintain an equivalent human experience. We are not satisfied by repeating what others have done. The risks young alpine climbers take today are justifiable in order to make the artistic statements of the age. Don't try to hold us back.

In conclusion, American standards are rising in both rock and ice venues, but the young climbers lack opportunities to perform in the Himalayas. The alpine climbers of the 1960s and 1970s abandoned their duty to help perpetuate the group. By failing to outgrow traditional practices while opposing new methods and style, they've made Himalayan climbing a gross endeavor. It is unappetizing to the few aspiring alpinists in this country. It looks like a dead end in terms of sponsorship and modern artistic expression. Sport Climbing and windsurfing are more attractive to the young men of the day.

Although I have been most fortunate to have the support of the American Alpine Club, Brenco Enterprises, John Bouchard, and Jeff Lowe, I am an unrepresentative example. Until young alpinists are supported through grants or sponsorship, America's success rate on modern Himalayan routes will remain at zero.

The unfortunate result of these circumstances is that I must look outside the United States for partners. This year I'm going to the Rupal Face of Nanga Parbat with Barry Blanchard, Kevin Doyle, and Ward Robinson—three of Canada's best. We will attempt the 4000-meter-high face in Alpine Style. No fixed ropes, camps, or attitudes. I hope to God this example will be contagious because I'm sick of being classified with the other American alpinists who are the laughingstock of world mountaineering.

2000 AUTHOR'S NOTE

Little has changed despite appearances. It seems all the sponsorship dollars waved at today's climbers are spent on Himalayan or Baffin Island Big Wall climbs, where film crews join the climbers, Internet companies pose like vultures on their shoulders, and media exposure is guaranteed to the sponsors. The public, the vicarious adventure-parasite consumer, can trudge slowly up the wall with the slow-moving climbers and imagine themselves doing the same thing. None of those viewers could possibly place themselves in the boots of the small team climbing with no bivy gear or ropes on a Himalayan face in the winter; therefore, ascents of this nature are not attractive to potential sponsors.

Granted, new routes in "new" Single-Push Style are being done in Alaska and the Yukon by Americans, but no Americans have participated in Alpine Style or Single-Push ascents in the greater ranges like the Karakoram or Himalayas. No evolution in the American alpine climbing consciousness blossomed from increased corporate sponsorship. The obvious conclusion is that throwing money at a problem does not solve the problem, especially if it derives from the nature of man. So I guess I was wrong: climbers can't buy balls with their grants. And until balls hang naturally from tomorrow's pioneering alpinists, we'll be at the back of the line, happily repeating routes climbed more than two decades ago in a style I was slagging in the 1980s.

The "race" to be first to solve the current last, great problems appears to revolve around being first rather than attending to any particular style. If someone does climb the South Pillar of Nuptse in Siege Style, when it has received seven Alpine

Style (and one Siege Style) attempts, their success should be ignored. IGNORED. If Siege-Style transgressions are unreported or, better yet, ridiculed, glory seekers will stop climbing in that style. The conscience of the climbing community can be brought to bear on the attitudes of whoever is active, inspiring or coercing them to climb in better style. Look at the evolution in "clean" climbing during the Yosemite years. Once it was agreed that pitons were irreparably damaging the resource, new ways were invented to protect climbers on those routes—methods that preserved the environment and purified the style of climbing. This needs to happen in the Himalayas. Until the scrutiny of the whole community becomes unbearable, until climbers who go against a consensus (which does not yet exist) are publicly castigated in the press, sieging and littering and the like will continue unobstructed. Alpine Style will remain the province of the mystic and the truly talented.

We may still look to Europe for the highest standards in alpine climbing, waterfall climbing (yeah, and it didn't take 'em long to catch up), mixed climbing, rock climbing, and Himalayan climbing, although the Himalayan talent pool has shifted eastward from France in the last decade.

Cash is not the answer.

As a comic aside, after the initial article appeared in *Climbing,* Yvon Chouinard penned a note to the editor. He suggested that I move to France, seek sponsors there, or marry someone who would support me, live off my parents, or survive by other cunning means. He ended by telling me to get a job.

I did move to France where sponsors made it possible for me to develop my talent. I did marry a woman who, bless her heart, took up the financial slack sponsors could not fulfill. This proves yet again that Yvon is a visionary. But when I invited him to give me a job, he declined the "honor."

I HURT,

THEREFORE I AM

There is no such thing as exaggerated art. There is salvation only in extremes.

Paul Gauguin

Two failures on the South Pillar of Nuptse caused me to quit alpinism cold turkey in February 1987. I was afraid. When I lost my courage, I lost everything. Without the sustenance and self-actualization of extreme climbing, my life collapsed. Personal relationships were the first to go. My parents tried to check me into a chemical-dependency clinic after reading "Kiss or Kill." They decided drugs were the only possible explanation for my "strange behavior." I left Seattle and never turned back.

During my respite from climbing, memories of it protected me. Hope for a happier future comforted me. Memories and hope are not so different; one is "having done" the other is "to do." Neither constitutes action. You are what you do; thus, if you do nothing, you are nobody. If you once did great things, you think you are great. You coast along on dead, preserved laurels, lifeless and wasting away.

I spent 12 weeks on crutches after knee surgery. During recovery I surrounded myself with wannabes, pretend-to-bes, has-beens, and never-will-bes. I met people who wasted their talent or were afraid of it. They taught me why I hadn't become a good climber. Like them, I was afraid to succeed, scared to commit. I didn't want to be any better than anyone else. Eventually, I sickened of people, myself included, who don't think enough of themselves to make something of themselves—people who did only what they had to and never what they could have done. I learned from them the infected loneliness that comes at the end of every misspent day. I knew I could do better.

The progress I made during physical therapy blossomed into drive. I began training the softness out of myself. I worked to become hard. I vocally put down mediocrity. I pushed myself to extremes and set off on a series of trips.

John Bouchard and I flew to Argentina. We watched the Yugoslav Route on the south face of Aconcagua avalanche every afternoon for two weeks. We flew on to Patagonia, hoping against probability for better weather on Cerro Torre. After a short wait, the rising barometer impelled us onto the Maestri Route, but Patagonian weather can frustrate the greatest skill and effort. We ran toward the mountain. We climbed as fast as we could. Ten pitches up, rain and wind drove us down. I didn't like the place.

Six weeks in the Canadian Rockies with Randy Rackliff temporarily sated the jackal inside. Our first ascent of "The Reality Bath," a difficult and dangerous waterfall, was the most nourishing. The full-course meal included soloing Professor's in 28 minutes, Polar Circus in three hours, and Slipstream in two hours and four minutes. Total damage: seven broken tools and a ruined differential on the van.

A "vacation" in the Alps proved embarrassing when a helicopter plucked my client and me off the Matterhorn. A storm trapped us 800 feet below the summit for 70 hours. When the sky cleared, he thought it too dangerous to descend on foot. He figured playing Superman on the cable beneath the chopper worth the price of admission.

I raced from Pennsylvania to Seattle on my motorcycle in three days. It was like an alpine climb where once on, I could not get off. I simul-soloed the north face of Mount Temple with Ward Robinson. I scavenged for sensation, sought my self in the rewards of being out there, across the Border. I had to go harder, higher, and longer. When I recognized it as addiction, I stopped having fun, but I couldn't stop altogether. I let the jackal take control and wound up in Pakistan.

I might have learned something from Muslim culture had the prospect of the 15,000-foot-high Rupal Face left me in peace. My American passport kept me from relaxing when I saw graffiti saying, "Kill to USA." A Shiite-Suni conflict in Gilgit left a thousand dead and kept us waiting in Rawalpindi for 10 days. The heat rose to a crippling 122 degrees. Even locals dropped dead in the street. Two-stroke motors and incantations toward Mecca whipped up a cacophony that nonalcoholic beverages could not dull.

The term *expedition* implies some size and gravity. Our four-man team felt puny beneath a mountain that had killed more than 50 men. Barry Blanchard, Kevin Doyle, and Ward Robinson invited me on the basis of reputation alone. I'd never climbed with any of them except Ward, dominant personalities all. The trip could be a social nightmare. I hoped the climbing would be hard enough to put any petty conflicts into perspective.

It was our Liaison Officer's habit to look the other way. A better personality trait could not be asked for from a Ministry of Tourism watchdog. He also carried a shotgun, claiming "there will be no porter strikes." As he minded his own business, I soloed a new route on Laila Peak (20,000 feet). Barry, Kevin, and Ward established the technically severe Rickshaw Wallahs on the north face of Shgiri (22,000 feet). They suffered two unplanned bivouacs—one standing on a small ledge—and a 25-mile return march to base camp after descending the south face into the wrong valley. Ward's homemade boot liners trashed his feet. While he recovered, three of us rushed ropeless up to 7000 meters on Nanga Parbat's Schell Route.

Four Siege-Style attempts on the Messner Route had failed since the three-month campaign succeeded in 1970. Acclimatized, we packed to attempt it. Armed for a protracted and violent struggle, each pack weighed 43 pounds, including all our clothing.

Teased by the promise of good névé, we ascended to find hard water ice covered by four inches of slush instead. We soloed everything. We cruised past sun-bleached fixed ropes and old pickets halfway melted out of the slope. Two empty tents, relics from a Japanese expedition, flapped their rotting nylon in the wind.

The first day we climbed 3000 vertical feet. Day two we put the hammer down and did another 5000. It started to hurt. Some people chase pain harder than others, consciously or subconsciously. Some use it to inflate their sense of self-importance. Others test their will by working through it. Each of us has a threshold someplace short of serious harm. Kevin's different. His definition of pain is more highly evolved than ours. He's willing to hurt himself permanently to get what he wants. In a conversation about calories, he told me that there is always something left to burn, "even if it's brain matter." Kevin is, without question, the best I've ever seen. From watching him, I learned to overcome myself.

Serious rockfall bombarded the Welzenbach Couloir between 21,000 and 22,000 feet. I was imitating the best French climbers by not wearing a helmet. I felt vulnerable, unable to react and move quickly because of the altitude. We traversed onto steeper, safer ground and roped up.

At 22,500 feet on the Merkl Icefield, we climbed the seracs directly to avoid a monstrous windslab. Barry led a 140-foot pitch, 85 to 95 degrees at the crux. Above it we all traded leads through knee-deep wet snow. Sometimes crawling, sometimes actually climbing, we always heaved for air.

At night, Ward moaned continually due to increasingly painful headaches. I tried to get used to his rhythmic groaning, unwilling to intrude on his private suffering. Kevin attacked, "Shut up man. It's making me crazy." Ward said it made him feel better when he moaned. "Yeah? Well it doesn't make us feel any better. And there's three of us."

The difficulties of the route began at 24,000 feet in the Merkl Gully. Avalanches, rockfall, or death had thwarted all recent attempts. Messner claimed it was as hard as the north face of the Matterhorn.

I led the first four pitches. The slope varied from 60 to 90 degrees, from hard snow to ridiculously brittle water ice. Blunt tools rebounded. Crampons skated off.

The potential of a huge fall wore me down. Emotionally wasted by two hours on the sharp end, I turned the lead over to Barry. Ward held back, altitude sick but still going for it.

The work absorbed us. We were deep in the gully and no one noticed a storm had broken until an avalanche of spindrift forced me back down to the belay. We looked at each other and up into the cumulus with the eyes of cornered animals. At 25,800 feet, having surmounted all of the technical problems, a thousand feet of comparatively easy snow separated us from the summit, but we were going down, the fast way or the slow way.

Two huge bowls above us collected snow. Wind spit it down the gully. Barry and Kevin tried to dig a cave, but the snow avalanched away. Lightning uncoiled across the ridge every two minutes. The summit glowed dully. There was no explosive punctuation of thunder, just the constant sound of something tearing.

Beside me, Ward was slowly dying. He fought to keep his soul from leaving his body. Waist-deep avalanches constantly washed the face.

"Hey Bubba!" I shouted at Barry. "We have to get Ward down. Now!"

Eyes half-shut, Ward's face twisted painfully, his breath ripped from suppurating lungs. Barry shouted back that there was no place to hide, that we should take refuge below the overhangs protecting the Merkl Icefield. Seven raps and we would be out of the shit.

Barry went first to set up the rappels, Kevin next to chop stances, then Ward. Being the lightest, I rapped last, pulling any backup anchors beforehand. Halfway down the second rappel, a surge in spindrift flow flipped me upside down. My goggles flew off and my hood filled with debris. The snow fell harder until visibility was less than 40 feet.

At the bottom of the third rap, we all clipped into a skinny sewn sling girth-hitched through the eye of a Snarg. We pulled the ropes. Several tons of snow emptied into the gully. It hit us like an express train and swept us off the 60-degree ice. I couldn't force my hand up to the screw or get a tool off my harness. I knew I had to unweight the Snarg. My imagination ran wild. I saw the screw pop or the runner fail, dumping the four of us into a Himalayan-scale Cuisinart. Eight ice tools, eight cramponed boots, four packs and bodies dropped into a blender, chewed up, spewed out, dead in a hole. I didn't want to die like that.

Light faded to black. I felt the dark, shapelessness of death ripping at me. "Fuck off!" I screamed. "It's not time yet! You can't kill me, motherfucker!"

My animal howl brought peace, complete resignation. Calmly, I forced my hand up through the raging sloughs, pulled on the sling, and drilled my frontpoints into the ice. I sank a tool. The slide subsided.

Ward's face pointed upward, streaked with snot. His eyes were frozen shut. Without inflection he stated, "I was just going to unclip and get it over with." In the middle of the next rappel, he passed out. His head bounced off the ice. We jerked on the ropes, shaking him awake.

"Keep it together man!" I shouted.

A wordless scream crossed his face in a final submission to terror. He looked right into my eyes for help and croaked, "I can't breathe." But he continued down. An average man would not have survived this long.

We reached the Merkl Icefield at 9 P.M., feeling like we still had a firm grip on the controls. I dug a ledge for Ward, who was now hypothermic. I got him into his sleeping bag and fired up a stove. Barry and Kevin were cleaning the last rappel. Barry planned to downclimb because the knot looked like it would jam in the jagged rocks if he pulled the ropes from below. One hundred and fifty feet away, in a storm, Barry shouted "Kevin, I'm letting go of the ropes!"

"OK. I let go," answered Kevin.

I suppose that's when we actually lost control. No one registered its departure or bid farewell to our only two ropes. Because we had the two tents, Barry and I downclimbed to our last bivy ledge at 23,000 feet. Kevin took care of Ward. They'd join us later.

Forcing a pole into our Gore-Tex tent, I lost my grip and pushed it off the ledge. I listened dumbly to the fabric slithering away. I didn't chase after it. Instead, I threw the pole off too, saying, "I don't have to carry that anymore," and started digging a snow cave. I finished as the others arrived.

It stormed through the night. Morning brought flat light and a sky streaked black as an airport runway. Messner had written, "It is impossible to descend the face in a storm so keep the high camps well stocked." We ate our last food that morning.

Packing up, Ward asked about the yellow rope, which he'd usually carried. We tasted the horror of understanding. We were 12,000 feet up the biggest wall in the world without any ropes. Death served up on a plain pewter plate. I looked into my friends' knowing eyes and wondered which of us would survive.

We thought there might be enough old rope fixed in the Welzenbach Couloir to tie together some pieces for rappels and began climbing down. One by one I watched the blue and yellow suits disappear into the storm. A team to be sure, but of lone animals, each fighting for survival. We climbed straight down the windslab, unable to descend by way of the serac. "What's the difference?" I thought. "I die in this avalanche or I die when the four-year-old fixed rope breaks, or I just sit down too exhausted to go on. What's it matter?"

We found a tattered pack clipped to a piton at 22,000 feet. Barry cut it open without expectation. Sixty pitons spilled out, followed by a dozen ice screws, some chocolate bars, and at the bottom, two brand new 50-meter ropes. At 6 P.M. the next day we walked into base camp. The storm lasted 12 days—we'd have died trying to sit it out. Time to start lighting candles in churches.

In base camp I drank the lukewarm cocktail of despair, watching ambition wane. I dwelled on the mountain still. Books didn't distract me. I was 100 percent present: festering, rotting, sinking. Throw me a rope.

On day 13 the jackal inside woke me. Sunrise. Good God—the sun. This time our packs weighed nothing. We took three days of food, five days of fuel, two ropes, six pins, two screws, and ten slings. Since I'd dug caves at 19,000 and 23,000 feet, the tents stayed behind. We smoked up the face, soloing every pitch. We climbed from 11,500 feet to 24,000 feet in two and a half days. Ward turned back at 23,000 feet because he was getting sick again. Barry, Kevin, and I reached the base of the Merkl Gully. A lenticular cloud settled over the summit and smothered our drive. None of us would climb in there again with the possibility of another storm. We fled downward, descending from 24,000 feet to base camp in 13 hours.

When friends ask what we would have done without the pack, I say we might not have made it. But we'd have died trying. When the Ministry of Tourism asked us about Nanga Parbat, Barry answered, "It was like having sex with death."

I spent a month in Chamonix recovering. I climbed two good alpine routes with my fiancée, slept a lot, and then left for Everest. Nanga Parbat had been a training route. Kevin and Ward were done with the Himalayas, leaving Barry and me alone to attempt a new route without oxygen, ropes, or support.

I used to think Katmandu a depressing place. It's a circus compared to Beijing's monotonous, gray, and sickeningly oppressive atmosphere. Everywhere people wear drab green or dead blue clothing. Life under communism has shaped their faces into flat, blank expressions. The sky's the color of pavement and unfinished, mono-chromatic buildings wall the streets. The same company manufactured each of the 12 million bicycles in the city, all painted the same flat black. The penalty for bicycle theft is execution.

In Lhasa I saw toilets built from Tibetan prayer stones. Chinese soldiers had machine-gunned thousands of unarmed monks and bombed temples, which had stood for three thousand years. The Chinese had the audacity to advertise to tourists that Tibet actually had something to do with Chinese culture. They walk the world's political corridors pretending Tibet is not an occupied nation.

I hated China. I was disgusted by the reconstructed monuments and the falsely aged tourist attractions. I hated them for extorting huge sums of money from climbers in return for nothing and for kicking me out of three Chengdu nightclubs because they didn't issue permits for their "Western friends." I despised the inherent laziness that attends any communist economic structure. I promise that I will never, ever go back.

The Chinese Mountaineering Association (CMA) tried to prevent us from climbing Everest. Our cargo was held up in port for six weeks. One hundred fuel canisters air-shipped from Canada were confiscated in Beijing. The "Gang of Four" airways refused to airfreight them inside China. We were allowed to buy a supply from the CMA at grossly inflated prices. They forced us to use a six-ton capacity truck to transport our 600 pounds of gear to base camp. We asked for three yaks to carry loads up to advance base camp; nine showed up because that was standard practice. We were obliged to pay for the superfluous six to stand idle for five days while the others worked. There are three prices in China: one for locals, one for Westerners, and a special price levied on mountaineering expeditions. The expedition rate runs 500 percent higher than the average tourist rate. The CMA skims 5 percent from every hotel, plane ticket, or jeep ride they arrange, and they viciously exploit the Tibetans.

We made three attempts on the north face of the Northeast Ridge in early October. My cold toes turned us back at 23,000 feet on our first try. Our second attempt ended when Barry began coughing up pink fluid at 24,500 feet.

After a week of rest at 16,000 feet, we tried again, leaving the advance base camp (21,000 feet) just after 10 P.M. At 5 P.M. the following day I stopped on a ledge at 26,500 feet. Above me, steep rock barred easy access into the Pinnacles. When Barry caught up, he looked worried.

"I've been out of my body for the last half-hour, just watching myself climb and not really paying attention."

I assumed it was a benign hypoxic hallucination, remembering a story in which Ed Webster saw a taco truck pull up next to him on the South Summit.

"It feels like spikes are being driven into my temples and I've lost peripheral vision. It might be cerebral edema."

I consulted another team's doctor by radio. He ordered us to descend immediately unless Barry wished to leave Tibet in a box. Our route was too difficult to downclimb. Without rope, we couldn't rappel. We traversed a half-mile to the North Ridge, cresting it at 25,800 feet. I gave Barry 10 milligrams of Dexamethazone to reduce cranial swelling and forced him to drink a liter of hot cocoa. We poached a bottle of oxygen from Mack Ellerby and Carl Coy at the North Col. Our supply of oxygen was with our medical gear at advance base camp. On four liters a minute, Barry raced down fixed ropes placed by a team from Wyoming. Four of their climbers met us below the Col and shepherded us into advance base camp. We'd been on the mountain for 23 hours.

Barry spent two hours in a Gamow pressure chamber and slept the night on oxygen attended by Doctor Bob Bohus. Two days later he hiked out to base camp.

The French had left. Three different American teams went home. We shared base camp with three Japanese climbers on a winter permit. The team leader, Tsuneo Hasegawa, had been on Nanga Parbat. In 1984 he'd left the bag that saved us on the Rupal Face. Three of his partners disappeared during a summit bid. Efforts to locate them were fruitless. Prior to returning to Japan, the team clipped the gear necessary to survive at the top of the Welzenbach Couloir—a spot their friends could not avoid should they manage to descend the Rupal Face. Barry and I told Hasegawa our story, and thanked him for having left the cache. It was clear from his reaction that he'd rather his friends had survived than us. Frankly, I'd have felt the same way in his place.

We decided to opt for an easier route owing to our condition. I'd lost 15 pounds off my 145-pound frame and vomited every meal I'd eaten over the last five days. Barry headed for advance base camp. I passed out on the trail at 19,000 feet. Twenty-four hours of potassium tablets and electrolyte drinks cured me.

From 16,000 feet I hiked the 20 kilometers to advance base camp in five hours. I met Barry there, and after resting eight hours, we climbed to the North Col. We rested another 10 hours, then hiked up the North Ridge to 25,800 feet and traversed into the Great Couloir. We spent six hours rehydrating at 26,500 feet.

I followed. I led. Despite Barry, I felt completely alone. I'd left base camp 50 hours before, and I was wasted. I fell asleep standing. I forced step after deceptively difficult step. I strung 25 in a row before collapsing. I was slowly suffocating. The poisonous air killed me cell by cell. We climbed to 27,500 feet by sunrise on day two.

My drive ebbed. I realized I might make it to the summit but there'd be nothing left to get down. A year of extreme climbing had stripped away the final blast of motivation needed to succeed and survive. Just a little more; so easy to say, so hard to turn into action. That "little more" distinguishes the victors from the vanquished.

I leaned my forehead on the snow and tried to decide between up and down. Will had driven me upward when muscle alone could not. It had kept me warm. As I favored descent, I began shivering. Muscles cramped. Altitude consumed my ability to care.

This is how they die, I thought. They pass out or freeze without caring. They die as spectators, believing it's all happening to someone else. I'd rather be fully alive and awake when I die. I want to be terrified. The last place I want to snuff it is on a slope no steeper than a beginner's ski hill.

I backed down our steps. Barry climbed 200 steps higher but realized he'd probably perish. Many friends had disappeared in the last four years, and we didn't want to join them.

A week after coming off Everest I climbed a route in the Alps with my fiancée. We ran hills together and climbed waterfalls. We took the night train to Paris and bought our wedding rings. I finished the year by enchaining the north face of the Aiguille du Midi to the Gabarrou Couloir on Mont Blanc du Tacul, followed by Mont Maudit and Mont Blanc. I descended to Les Houches on foot. Nine thousand feet up and 11,500 feet down in 26 hours. It was New Year's Eve.

My pain used to define me. It convinced me I was alive. However, a year in the crucible turned the black hearses of the past into the bright, white veils of the present. While those climbs didn't cure me, I traversed a border few men return from, crossed to a place where pain and fear and suffering are so common they mean nothing. Risking one's existence may teach the learned man a thing or two, but saving Barry's life on Everest changed my own forever.

2000 AUTHOR'S NOTE

A good story has plenty of action but not too much. Even though I left a few things out so the article would flow better, reading it exhausts me. 1988 exhausted me. I don't think a person has many years like that inside of him. I never experienced another like it.

I primed the pump in 1987 with typical Twight behavior: I quit climbing, I grew frustrated, I exploded. I haven't changed much since, although the explosions aren't as bright now. I realized in 1988 that participation in several potentially lethal sports would probably kill me. I quit paragliding first, then got rid of my motorcycle. Climbing mountains was enough.

The hubris we exercised by attempting Nanga Parbat in Alpine Style is striking. The Rupal Face had been climbed once by a large Austrian/Italian/German team that included Reinhold Messner and his brother, Gunther. They fixed ropes, set camps, and ferried supplies for months. The Messners topped out 12 weeks after arriving in base camp. Where had we come up with the idea we could climb up the face in five days and down in another two? It was pure folly, but we almost did it. Following acclimatization during the first attempt and the rest afterward, the climb from 11,500 feet to 24,000 feet in two-plus days opened my eyes to great possibility in the Himalayas. I never capitalized on the experience at high altitude, but I applied the speed I learned on Nanga Parbat to mountains in Russia, the Alps, and Alaska.

The avalanche in the Merkl Gully didn't affect me the way it probably should have. I was so driven back then I was blind to the utter randomness with which the storm and slides struck. Predictable perhaps, but I didn't understand how out of control the situation had been until years later. Had I recognized the full meaning, I wouldn't have gone to Everest so soon afterward or continued climbing in the Himalayas at all for that matter. The same indiscriminate mountain chaos expressed itself with Barry's cerebral edema on Everest. Predictable again, but the ambitious mind sees it differently. Through the distorted lens of youthful determination, these are simply problems to be resolved by more scientific training, improved weather forecasting, longer acclimatization, or better psychic connection to the mountain environment. The underlying suggestion posed by all resolutions is one of being in control, which, I realize now, is not at all the case. I think we may train ourselves to be as adaptable as possible, to respond appropriately in each situation, but the ideal of controlling the outcome or steering events as they occur must be relinquished. Chaos rules it all.

THE ABATTOIR

On

Goulotte

Cheré,

Mont Blanc

du Tacul,

Chamonix,

France

(Photo by Ace Kvale)

It was an hour before I could move my legs. The rock hit so hard I thought it broke my spine. Tears burst from my eyes with the impact. I saw every dream and hope vanish with the rock. I began to fall. I said bitter, acid good-byes in my head, convinced my life would end splattered obscenely across the talus. The black thoughts pulled up short as I came onto the wrist leash of my ice tool. It stopped the plunge. My shoulder didn't separate but I could tell it was bad.

For a moment I felt elated. I'd saved myself. I retained control of the situation. Seconds later the blood drained out of my head. My face was the color of concrete—the color of a corpse. I was in trouble; thousands of feet up in the winter quiet all alone on 80-degree ice. The pain arrested my breath. Snow fell blithely from the leaden sky. The wind lectured me about the futility of my future. I heard the primitive voice of the masses saying that I could not succeed, another prodigy whose life is attenuated by circumstance. I didn't want to die. I climbed up this north face to suffer, to experience the masochistic pleasure of fighting for my life, but I hadn't intended to lose. The need for risk always lurked inside of me, threatening. If I don't satisfy the impulses, if I let them build up untreated, they'll explode with finality. I'd kill myself trying to handle it.

I wondered how long the pick might hold with all of my weight on it. I'd given my precious ice tools more attention than I gave most of my friends. I felt guilty when the picks rusted or remained blunt after some epic drove me out of the mountains. I could feel the tools despise me when I ignored them. I despised them, too, for allowing me to fulfill my obsession. Often I threw them into the basement as punishment for letting me get in too deep. On days like today I praised them for their greatness. I loved them for being good enough to let me push this hard. The rock hit hard enough to rip the holster and my favorite hammer off my harness. A grievous loss but not as awful as seeing my Chacal firmly placed above me—out of reach.

The missile was huge, the size of a milk crate I think. I didn't hear any bones break. I tried moving immediately after the concussive blow. My legs jerked uselessly. They felt like a fish's tail, waving back and forth in front of the blood-dyed-terracotta ice. A 10-inch rent gaped in my Gore-Tex suit. As the stain dried, the fabric stuck to my skin. I couldn't see the bruise swelling on the back of my thigh.

More rocks winged by with the shriek of living things. The air warmed as the sun rose and the ice began to flow with water. Fear washed over me in rivulets, then torrents. My right hand groped for something solid to pull up on. Sinuous forearm muscles cramped until they too were paralyzed. No experience or training had prepared me for the anxious torment of dying slowly and knowing it inevitable. I always thought it would come as quick as a bullet. I could never face the creeping certainty of a terminal illness. As it was, my bloodshot eyes were overwhelmed by tears. I groaned. I was giving up on life surely, willfully, and the tape hadn't ended yet. I'd chosen the blackest music for this route—it would have been the hardest climb I'd ever done.

> We burned and burned, I was a cinder body and soul . . . comfort is treachery
> so pound nails in tight eyes screaming out of sight against a grain like curtain—
> unbearably alive.
>
> **Skinny Puppy**

"Alive?" I thought. "Until today I was hardly alive at all. But I'm too much so now, and I want more." I used to be afraid that I would die young. After living for a while though, I got scared that I wouldn't.

My toes burned. I wiggled them one by one. Pain shot through my leg and hip as life returned to deadened limbs. I fought to move the whole leg. I chased hope down and tackled it. Something inside screamed that it was time to fight back: "Don't give in." It reminded me of the physical therapy after doctors rebuilt my knee. I remember trying as hard as I could to bend my leg and not being able to. The frustration was infinite, quitting so very seductive. Disillusions followed setbacks but I finally bent it. Once I lifted some weights, I regained the hope that I might climb again.

The first time I tried to rest weight on my crampons my left leg collapsed. I fell, wincing, back onto my ice tool—imploring it to save me. My thigh kept swelling; it pulsed and stiffened. I tried again. I was determined to stand on it. After I stabilized myself on the frontpoints, putting as little weight on them as I could, I stared up at the spare tool. It was the key to survival, and it was out of reach. Lactic acid poisoned my contracted biceps and it began to jump with the strain.

I couldn't remove the tool in my left hand to re-place it higher without falling off. I tried half-heartedly to lock off on it and grab the hammer above. I couldn't. I worked my feet up the ice inch by agonizing inch. Pain carved through my legs every time I flexed them. I closed in. Breath heaved out of my lungs. I coughed. It felt like something tearing. I roared with frustration, enraged with my own weakness. In a rally of effort, I muscled up, ignoring the cramps, and lunged for the Chacal's wrist leash, but the Barracuda ripped through the ice. The milliseconds wound by cruelly, taking their own sweet time.

The adze chopped into the bridge of my nose, splattering blood across the ice. I fell, knocked backwards by the impact. I did one backflip before my crampons caught a rock—shattering my ankle—and catapulted me out over the soulless, battered slope. I plunged into the end. Music wailed through my headphones. What was once "the last ride" mused about in barrooms became the real and horrifying truth. I knew I wouldn't hit anything on the way down, just the talus that was lightly dusted with snow.

> *Magnified fear stares back the mirror . . . sweet pain douse the ecstasy, the imagination drained away. Perpetual reverie abruptly fades, heaven's soothing some say. Injured plea—crushed destiny.*
>
> **Skinny Puppy**

THE END, obviously.

1988 AUTHOR'S NOTE

Abattoir means "slaughterhouse." I used to think of hard soloing in those terms, a "place" I went to measure myself. From there I looked within and cut away what I didn't like; the rotten flesh, the wasting thoughts. Anything that was a liability became painfully clear in life-threatening circumstances. I got rid of everything that held me back. Sometimes the experience was not so calculated. Some routes destroyed me emotionally without my being able to prevent it. I discovered the darkness. My best performances often developed out of depression when I used climbing as a tool to forestall suicide rather than a method of achieving it. Despair inspired three years of "crazy" soloing.

I need something from climbing that most do not feel. From climbing I learned to suffer and to surpass myself. I explored the dark despair of failure and acceptance of extreme risk. I dissected the choice between living and dying, between hanging on or letting go. I pushed physical and emotional limits in the most savage environment on earth. I have been splashed with the blood of a friend killed by rockfall. All this leaves scars.

I learned to deal with the proximity of death, of the 24-hour-a-day threat. Without confronting it, my life was meaningless. Others avoid or trivialize it so they *can* deal with it. First I learned how not to die. From death I learned to live, to want to live, to be capable of doing so without making a mess or mockery of living. I learned to love.

I explored the darkness carefully, while my peers, the other kids who grew up bound tightly to a straitjacket future or no future at all, simply dabbled in it. They shot heroin or drank themselves into oblivion. Some wore all black clothing to communicate their desperation. I looked into that same pit and asked "Why?" We are told what is negative; we are told that the "negative" is wrong. We are all responsible to find out who we are, to discover what is right or wrong *for us*. I found out that what some consider beautiful I find bilious, and I happen to think some very nasty things are works of art.

I know it sounds melodramatic and trashy, but from climbing I learned how to love—to love completely with 100 percent of myself, to give everything to another person. To be willing to unselfishly die for or—harder still—live for another. I'm still tortured by the jackal that drives me to climb. That's why I'm here. It chews on me, insomniac and ulcerous. But this relationship makes me stronger. For once it is not an unfair exchange, not parasitic and draining. I have more power because I am in love. Heart and lungs and muscles united at last, with no part of the system sabotaging another.

"The Abattoir" is the combination and extension of several events that actually happened to me. Autobiographical fiction, first-person posthumous. A period of self-discovery died with the conclusion of this work. I've moved on, continued to grow. I don't gain much power from anger anymore. Deep black recesses in me warm in the light. I've climbed out of the basement, off the dark north face and into the sun.

2000 AUTHOR'S NOTE

I didn't have a copy of the *Rock & Ice* (#29) this appeared in and I had not read the piece for several years. I signed a copy at a slideshow and asked the owner to photocopy it and send it to me. I recalled the actual story accurately, and that *Rock & Ice* had wanted to run it but required an addendum because the story was too horrible on its own. Hence, the original Author's Note. Reviewing this "disclaimer" years afterward made me laugh uneasily.

I wrote a draft of "The Abattoir" while living in the Wild Things factory in New Hampshire in 1987. Life was bad. I didn't have anywhere to call my own, just a foam pad and a sleeping bag rolled up next to my duffel bags in the third floor attic. I broke the tip off my femur in a paragliding accident and spent 12 weeks on crutches. This allowed plenty of introspection, too much. I'd split from a woman I truly loved, unable to accept her eccentricities but less able to help her resolve them. The succession of bedmates I took in her place left me unfulfilled, though I pretended otherwise. I convinced myself that one woman was *the* woman, but a hard solo on Cathedral Ledge with water running down the crux clarified the difference between my fantasies and reality. I left her, badly.

In March 1988 I traveled to the Alps to guide a man on the Matterhorn. We trained in Chamonix before heading to Zermatt. During that week I reconnected with the woman I'd been interviewing substitutes for. I lamented the year we'd lost in between, and vowed to marry her, but life intervened again, and we did not see each other for four months.

First, my friend Dave and I failed on the Matterhorn after sitting out a three-day storm in the Solvay Hut high on the Hornli Ridge. Then I traveled to the Canadian Rockies, and eventually Nanga Parbat. When Anne and I got together in Chamonix again, I wrote the Author's Note, convinced she and I would be together forever. I was certain I knew how to love her well enough to overcome whatever obstacles we came up against. During the next three years together we grew apart. I was dissatisfied with something in my life and I thought it was her. So again, I left, badly.

The anger returned. Depression snuck deeper and deeper. I'd finished with soloing but undertook harder and harder routes with partners. And I test-drove more substitutes. Eventually, a bright light showed through the anger and I discovered happiness with another woman. It didn't last either. I went back into the cycle of anger and frustration but stayed because I said I would—punishing her for it.

Then the light again, brighter than ever.

See the pattern? Me too, once I read the 1988 Author's Note. Ugly. But I'm certain I've broken it now. Whether I'm just old, or I've earned some wisdom, I have truthfully climbed off of that shadowed wall. The light I feel comes from within.

In the 1988 Author's Note, I wrote that the story was the logical extension of two separate events that actually happened to me, had they been combined. People ask about them.

In 1984, as I raced a storm to the summit of the Grands Charmoz, the ice my frontpoints were in sheared off the wall and one of my tools ripped. I did the one arm pull-up, sank the errant tool, and continued.

In February 1987 I was nearing the top of Les Droites, having soloed the Boivin-Gabarrou Route. A rock the size of a milk crate fell and grazed the back of my thigh, paralyzing my leg momentarily. I managed to hobble to the top and down the Lagarde Couloir. For "The Abattoir" I pieced the events together and wrote what probably should have happened if I weren't so lucky.

HEAVEN NEVER LAUGHED

I missed the funeral. They told me it was sunny, but the *foehn* blew and made every-one edgy. Very different from the hour I spent paying my respects, kneeling behind the church as a cruel wind beat the rain down, mashing clouds against the moun-tains. The threat of thunder suited an afternoon visit with the dead. Crows loitered in a nearby square. Too weak to attack anything living, they feed on the deceased and discarded. Just like we feed on our memories to nourish us. As more crows landed, their wings beat hard, as taut as the flags on a speeding hearse.

I learned about the accident while celebrating the holidays with my wife's fam-ily in Seattle. A friend from Chamonix telephoned us there. The thousands of cable and satellite miles did little to soften the impact as Anne held me and repeated the details relayed from France:

"Philippe was climbing with Francois Marsigny. They were 400 meters below the summit of the Aiguille Sans Nom. They weren't roped. He fell 700 meters. Francois launched a flare and was helicoptered off. The funeral is tomorrow. That's all I know."

I worked through it in my head, looking for the mistake I hoped was there. I couldn't sleep or eat. I was content to spend a few days in the States getting used to my own loss before seeing Philippe's family and friends in Chamonix.

Over the next few days I heard the undertones around me. People said "I told you so" to each other with smug self-satisfaction. Spectators cautioned one another against getting too close to anyone involved in high-level alpinism.

Back home I avoided Gislaine, Philippe's mother, for the first week she was in Chamonix. I didn't want to see her. I could not bear to witness the sorrow she was submerged in nor answer her questions. I couldn't face her "Why?" and her "How?" and her tears. I stayed clear of Philippe's lover, Miriam, as well.

Philippe was my climbing partner, and not the first to have lost his life in the mountains. I tried not to harden myself against it. I studied his accident as thoroughly as the other ones. I dwelled on it because I want to live. Grief is allowed but a small toehold here.

Eventually I met Gislaine and Miriam together over supper, imagining somehow it would be easier as a threesome. Gislaine asked why Francois didn't arrest Philippe's fall. I explained that they were not roped together. Incredulous, she needed to know what compelled us to climb alone or without protection systems. I had no answers.

I could not satisfactorily explain Philippe's motivations, as I understood them, to his deeply wounded mother. A piano teacher who had lived much of her life in Paris, she did not have the *montagnard's* intuitive awareness and understanding of voluntarily accepted risk. How could I admit that we are often like drug addicts— we need to push harder, higher, and faster on each successive climb? Or that Philippe and I often climbed together without a rope?

She sipped her whiskey and fidgeted with a stack of photos given to her by his friends. Most of the pictures showed Philippe full of life, thrilling to the risk and the beauty of the Alps, to a life of action. In the photos Francois took on the Aiguille Sans Nom, Philippe looked as though he was already dead, as if his spirit had been sucked out of him.

One night a gathering at the Café de la Plage turned into an impromptu wake for Philippe, and other absent partners. The hours passed almost silently. Each climber's physical and emotional scars expressed themselves in action and bearing without the need for words. We drank. Some smoked. But we all knew because we've seen it. We can see in the eyes and mannerisms of a man that he alone survived a storm while others did not. We feel the hardened heart of a "northwall man" in his handshake or his gestures. We are the current survivors. Some of our friends didn't make it, but we don't ask each other why. We reserve that morsel of bitterness for ourselves.

Outsiders ask us why we encourage death, why we act like we want to die young. When I'm especially cynical, I play devil's advocate and counter, "Why prolong life? Why imagine what I'm doing is anything special, that I'm contributing rather than breathing air and eating food another might need? Everyone dies, equalized by it. At least the dead are spared the embarrassing antics of those left behind groping for some meaning." I use those words to antagonize, but I don't believe in them. I'm as interested as the outsiders are.

The telephone rang at odd hours and I grew afraid to answer. Friends and family, searching for a final statement or truth to cherish, believed my *sang froid* over Philippe's death disguised a deeper knowledge and understanding. I spoke with each until I couldn't stand the frustration, then remained on the line politely, saying yes or no or repeating what they had just said. Some found justice in religion, choosing a particular god to suit the situation best. They consigned Philippe's spirit to an invisible universe from which his bright light illuminates us 24 hours a day.

Others preferred the peace of stinking rationalizations, "He was ready for it," or "It was his destiny," or still worse, "He died doing what he loved." Do these convenient phrases color reality differently than if he'd been run down by a drunk driver? Surely no one finds solace in "destiny" after a friend dies on the highway. Meaning and rationale are digestive agents. They make it easier to be a survivor.

It took more than one such conversation to teach me how to get by. At first I turned away from the pain or secreted it deep inside. Then I tried blowing it out of proportion. I imagined it was I who got the short end of the stick, and I begged everyone I met for sympathy. I tried being emotional. I tried being objective. Later I realized that to grow and learn from a fatality, I had to embrace rather than evade it. I accepted it, no matter how much it hurt.

I looked at events and experiences through every available lens—even religion—which, for a soloist, is the most delicate corrective lens of all. Proper use can lead a man to enlightenment, but misuse is cheating. I needed to assign Philippe's death value at a human level; turning it into an act of god cheapens it, absolves him of any responsibility. In Philippe's case it was 100 percent his act. He was human. He failed. He paid.

Failed? Absolutely! His goal was to climb the Aiguille Sans Nom in winter and return safely, in short, to survive. He didn't.

There is risk, known and unknown, in all aspects of life. We often consider the loss of life the only serious risk. Unless we are genuinely aware, we calculate the danger arising from our own physical and emotional states and from external conditions based on incomplete information. If we believe we can manage those risks, we accept them. Whether these choices are born of delusion or reality comes out in the end.

To wisely undertake the risks involved in high-level alpinism or soloing, the climber needs an attitude I don't think Philippe possessed. The soloist must realize that he is 100 percent responsible. There is "I can" and "I can't"; there is no "I will try." Ninety-eight percent means hitting the ground.

Every cell must believe the situation serious. If you think you can survive a fall, you will take that fall. If you think you're going to heaven or will become a bright light illuminating your friends from a parallel universe, you won't fight hard enough to live through the shit. If you believe dying is an act of fate, you cede control over both your life and your death. You put someone or something else behind the wheel. But if you're convinced that once you die, it is all over, you'll fight with every last calorie to keep hold of what you have now. You'll do whatever it takes to stay alive— alive in the present.

Philippe was a good climber, not a great one. Inspired by routes I had soloed, he wanted to do great things. He pushed himself hard to make up for lost time because at 28, he had only been alpine climbing for two years. Philippe also believed in his dreams, in a mystical voice that spoke and seduced and promised. He was not always a happy man, and his emotional pain was susceptible to a quick cure from the outside, from religion or philosophy. He lived inside of himself. Imagination is deadly without the audit of practical feedback. It's easy to believe yourself to be someone else and to let that someone assume risks you might not otherwise take.

The mountains have teeth. Nothing is more certain to set you up as a meal for them than emotional distraction. Nothing can be allowed to interfere with your judgment about what is correct for you. In this game, fantasies kill, which is why an unequal pair, climbing as an unroped team of two, is so dangerous.

Francois was talented, with much experience, and hard enough to climb the route alone. Philippe did not want to rope up with him if it meant holding him back. The pressure Philippe put on himself was difficult to live up to. Laboring under it, he wasn't aware of the information he was receiving about his own performance. The pressure paralyzed his judgment.

Well off the ground, Philippe probably realized he shouldn't have been there in that style, although Francois could be. They were not truly friends—not the kind who listen to each other's advice. Philippe never learned that soloing means self-sufficiency, independence, and the strict refusal to let other people influence decisions.

I think often of Philippe; less though of Francois, who was standing 12 feet above Philippe when he heard *"Merde!"* and turned to see Philippe cartwheeling away. I wonder what kind of scars he'll have. How many nights will he wake up screaming over the next few years? How many people will ask how he could keep climbing after something like that? Will he give them the real answer, tell them about being addicted? Or about how he lets anger build toward an explosive outburst? I'm glad he has climbing as an outlet.

I live in Chamonix because I don't have to justify myself here. I hated the States, where I constantly had to explain to outsiders how the passion for alpinism drives me, a passion that dresses itself up as hate, as fear, as fatigue. It's a demon that won't leave me alone. It always comes back no matter how bad the last experience was. Sometimes I believe in a fantasy where I've freed myself from the cycle. I pretend I don't need to climb, but the need always comes back, and I always give myself to it.

I struggle with my passion for the mountains, the need for risk and self-knowledge. I contend with it because climbing forces me to think and think, never to act without calculation and consideration, leaving little room in myself for others. I fight the obsession because I cannot run from it. I oppose it because it hurts me and those around me. Opposition binds me more tightly to it. I watch Francois

PHILIPPE MOHR'S
GRAVE,
ARGENTIERE,
FRANCE

battle similar fears and desires. He is as addicted to alpinism and its effects as I am. We are tied forever to the thing which may eventually kill us.

Philippe was not the first partner Francois has lost. I wonder whether he'll admit to himself or to me that he might have prevented the accident. Inherent peer pressure exists between climbers. Whether using the rope or not, each member of a partnership must accept responsibility for the influence they have on their teammate. If you are psychologically stronger, you help your partner. If, by choice or circumstance, you assume the role of leader, two lives depend on your decisions. You are unroped but not alone.

Francois later said he recognized Philippe wasn't able to do the route safely without a belay. Francois offered to tie in several times, though both knew that climbing ropeless would be faster. Philippe wanted to play in the big league, so he refused the offer. Francois never went the distance by giving Philippe a way out.

Philippe considered Francois a legend. This was their first route together. He used Francois as a professor and role model, imitating him, hitch-hiking on his psychological power. Neither wanted to turn back. They'd both been working in Paris and were motivated to do an important winter ascent. They had been out of the "lab" for a while and sensed outside pressure to perform, to do something big to regain their places in the Chamonix scene.

On insomniac nights I lie in bed and wish Francois had contrived some pretext to descend, like dropping the stove or pulling a muscle. He could have gone back alone the following day.

I understand now that what happened to Philippe could happen to me. This writing wouldn't mean much then. I used to believe that it could never happen to me. This accident taught me that the way to have a hand in what does befall me is to realize that anything *can* happen—good, bad, and ugly. I learned that freedom of decision, freedom from pressure, is an essential component of going from choice to choice up there.

More than six weeks after the accident I bumped into Francois. He looked like he had crawled out of a grave. We talked woodenly in front of the Weather Office for a few moments.

"How's it going?" I asked.

"Better."

"I'm glad . . ."

"You OK? Been climbing?"

"Yes, and no. Have you done any routes?"

"No. I haven't touched my tools in a long time."

"That's the way it is with me too . . ."

I walked away and haven't seen Francois in Chamonix since. He's living in Paris, working as an architect and spending the weekends bouldering at Fontainbleau. I know he'll be back though.

There's still no monument over Philippe's grave, just an obscene mound of dirt with a wooden cross bearing his name at the head of it. Every time I've visited I've seen fresh flowers there. I don't know who brings them.

2000 AUTHOR'S NOTE

In 1993 I spent a lot of time on the Aiguille Sans Nom. I went alone once and climbed eight or ten pitches up the Gabarrou-Silvy Route. The ghosts shouted in my head, and after a fitful bivouac, I retreated. Christophe Beaudoin and I returned together. He had been quite tight with Philippe. We repeated the pitches I'd soloed earlier and comforted each other through the bivouac. The next day, while a storm was creeping in, we climbed up and stood at the spot where Philippe had fallen. We chopped a ledge and looked around. I finally held my own service more than three years after he'd died. The storm and our state of mind convinced us to escape via the variant Francois had soloed after the accident. It was hard. I couldn't imagine climbing it alone after watching another man fall to his death. We rested at the spot where the helicopter had whisked Francois away, then climbed up into the blowing snow and clouds.

A few weeks later I went back with Scott Backes. Continuing straight up from the accident site we finished a new route called There Goes the Neighborhood. I ranted a lot about that route in the press. I was confrontational with the French and their complacency. All the loud words cloaked a deeper meaning I had discovered during that summer and autumn.

In the week following my solo attempt, I had the good fortune (synchronicity) to meet Gislaine in Chamonix. She was spending her summer holidays there, hoping to feel a better connection to her lost son. We cried. I told her I had been up there alone—spent the night with him. She said she understood. She held my hand and hugged me. She had learned so much since Philippe's death. Our places were switched. Back then I believed I had all the answers, but my peace was slow in coming. Now I find I still have many questions. Gislaine, on the other hand, seemed so lost back then. That day in 1993 I saw she had found her answers, she made her peace, and was able to give some of it to me.

I haven't climbed hard in Chamonix since the fall of 1993. I've been back of course, and during each visit I spend a little more time with Francois. We have been through a lot without ever having climbed together. Philippe's accident was just the start of it. Today Francois and I are the current survivors, the misunderstandings of our past mean less as our peer group gets smaller and smaller. So many other friends and partners have died since that awful day in January 1990, but Philippe was such an innocent compared to the others. It has taken years for me to realize that I never could have saved him, never could have taught him enough. From that realization I have learned forgiveness.

MY WAY:

A SHORT TALK

WITH TOMO CESEN

Three years ago in March, when Christophe Profit started up the Croz Spur of the Grandes Jorasses under spotlights and TV cameras, nobody noticed the lone climber nearby on the Shroud. It was Tomo Cesen of Yugoslavia, who the day before had soloed the Eigerwand in 12 hours.

From the Jorasses, a chopper flew Profit to the Matterhorn. He judged it out of condition and his Trilogy attempt was finished. Tomo arrived in Zermatt by car the following day, set off up the Matterhorn, and after 10 hours of climbing, became the first man to enchain the Three Great North Faces in winter, alone. It had taken him four days.

There was no media flash, no hype. The 26-year-old Tomo drove back to his wife and two children waiting in Slovenia, the northernmost republic of Yugoslavia, and quietly trained for the Himalayas.

1986 was a foul season in the Baltoro, and Tomo was in the thick of it. After success on Broad Peak Tomo's teammates went on to Gasherbrum II. With the consent of his team leader, Tomo excused himself from G2 and headed toward K2. On the afternoon of August 3, he started up its awesome south face. Without bivy gear or food, he quickly soloed up unknown terrain, reaching the shoulder of the Abruzzi Spur (8100 meters) by 10 A.M. on August 4.

Seven unlucky mountaineers were already above him, pushing toward the summit. But on the shoulder where Tomo sat talking by radio with his leader, strong winds indicated an approaching storm.

"I didn't hold the situation in my own hands, so I chose to go down—and fast," Tomo says. By the time he reached base camp, the seven above him were stumbling into Camp 4, where several were to die.

In September 1988, Tomo made what he calls his finest solo ascent—"up until last April, that is." He claimed the second ascent of No Siesta on the Grandes Jorasses in just 14 hours. First climbed by Jan Porvaznik and Stanislav Gledjura on July 21–23, 1986, the route splits the incredibly steep wall separating the Croz and Whymper Spurs. The climbing is consistently difficult from bottom to top. "I used a back rope on the hard rock pitches (the crux is French 6b+—5.11a) because I was in plastic boots and it was very cold," he explains. "The ice was unprotectable, since it was only one or two inches thick; I just got over it as fast as I could." Asked how tough the route was, he said flatly, "Compared to this, the Trilogy was nothing."

In Europe, Tomo's alpine climbing accomplishments are compared with those of Walter Bonatti and Reinhold Messner, Wilo Welzenbach and Paul Preuss. His effect on mountaineering is likely to be similar. On April 27–28, 1989, Tomo soloed a new route on the north face of Jannu (7710 meters) in Nepal. It was an achievement ranking with Bonatti's solo first ascent of the Bonatti Pillar on the Dru, and Messner and Peter Habeler's first Alpine-Style ascent of an 8000-meter peak.

This solo first ascent sent shock waves through the ranks of traditionalists and new wave alike. The face had been attempted several times from the mid-1970s onward and had rejected all efforts. Careful assessment of his own abilities and performance on five previous Himalayan expeditions, combined with an Olympic athlete's training program, allowed one man to quickly overcome what others had labored toward—and failed on.

Passing sections of UIAA 6+ (5.10a/b) and A2 rock, and 90-degree ice, Cesen cruised the 2800-meter face in 23 hours nonstop. Descending the Japanese Route required another 19 hours, including a short bivouac.

I talked with Tomo Cesen in July 1989 in Chamonix, where he was resting, giving interviews, and looking for sponsors.

Are you here for climbing?

No. Mostly for business and to relax. After a very hard route it is important to settle down, to review things. It's dangerous to get caught up in the euphoria of success and become greedy: "now I want this and then that." Jannu was enough for this year.

When I solo I find I don't climb as much—there's so much stress. And I can't let myself get into a routine. Whenever I feel sure of myself, certain that I can solo a route, I quit. It is good to have some fear.

How did you conceive of soloing the north face of Jannu?

In 1985 we did a new route on Yalungkang. Jannu was just a one-day walk from our base camp, so I went to look. I had a sense that the face could be done, if not alone then certainly in Alpine Style.

In some of Pierre Beghin's photos, I saw weaknesses near the center of the headwall that gave me some hope. Those "features" turned out to be shadows. I climbed farther left than I'd originally planned.

After soloing Modern Times on the Marmolada [a route first climbed by Heinz Mariacher with pitches of UIAA 7+, 5.11a/b] and then the Piliér Rouge Directissime on Mont Blanc [pitches to French 7a, 5.11d, and A2], I knew I was psychologically ready for Jannu. The training ended and I went. Luckily, it was a very dry season in Nepal, and a little warmer than I expected.

Why not go Alpine Style with a few friends?

For me it's a choice, an acceptance of extreme responsibility, and it preserves the quality of alpinism I enjoy most—uncertainty, the thing that large teams and fixed ropes destroy.

Also, I can never have 100 percent belief in my partners; I don't want to die as a result of someone else's mistake. I just climb better when I'm alone.

From my own experience, I knew I'd have to get up and down very quickly before I got weak, and two guys with a rope take three times as long. To account for extra days, you have to take more food and clothes. Of course, there's the rope itself and all the hardware to go with it. You risk a change in the weather, you spend longer in the danger zone. To do something like this, it is necessary to carry as little as possible.

I knew from Yalungkang that I could go for three to four days without food and two or more days without sleep. You couldn't climb the headwall directly, even with rock shoes. It's far too cold, and it would take too long. I mean, out in the center of the face I saw a roof that was more than 40 meters long. If you fixed ropes they'd probably be cut by rockfall. The whole lower face is concave and suicidal for seracs and rockfall; you wouldn't want to go through it more than twice. It's where two Dutch climbers were killed in 1984. I climbed that section in less than four hours.

What were your first impressions of the wall, knowing that you were there to climb it alone?

When I first saw the face, it looked plenty safe. I didn't see any avalanches. Only when we got closer did we hear stones ricocheting down. I could never determine where they were, but they fell all day long. Seeing the headwall made me feel awful. As we approached, it began to lie back from a perceived 110 degrees to a mere 80 or 90 degrees.

It's like the Grandes Jorasses, very imposing. I don't think you could find a wall so steep and sustained at this altitude [7100 to 7700 meters] anywhere in the mountains. After several days at the bottom of the face, I was in perfect tune with the mountain.

What did you carry on the climb?

Apart from the clothes I was wearing (I borrowed a Gore-Tex suit from Xavier Murillo, a photographer in Chamonix), crampons, and tools, I took a spare pick, some pitons and screws, and 50 meters of 6-millimeter rope.

In my pack I had a sleeping bag and bivy sack—heavy, sure, but I figured I could always throw it off if it was too much. I took spare sunglasses, a headlamp, mittens, and a balaclava. I carried 500 grams of food: some granola bars, two cans of sardines, and two cheese chapatis. I had one liter of water. The pack didn't weigh more than six kilograms, including the rope, which I trailed behind me most of the time.

The climbing itself?

You can't compare it with anything. Technically, the hardest free section was UIAA 6+ [5.10a/b]; fine when you are on a crag wearing tights and rock shoes, but at 7200 meters, it's another story. I climbed some passages on 90-degree ice in the seracs and such, but it wasn't a problem. The difficulty was climbing the two-to-five-centimeter-thick ice on steep slabs.

At one point the ice ran out, and there was nothing but a smaller-than-finger crack cutting the near-vertical wall. It was absolutely too hard to free climb those six meters separating me from where the ice tongue continued. I drove a pin and pendulumed left [laughs at the memory of himself swinging sideways in crampons and with ice tools dangling from his wrists] into another ice system and it worked out. It was the one time I let my guard down enough to ask myself exactly what I thought I was doing up there.

I was totally committed to going up, though—with 10 pins and a 50-meter rope, 1000 meters of rappelling was impossible. The feeling of engagement was never clearer than when I cut the rope after back-roping the A2 pitch. The act of cutting was symbolic because I'd passed the point of no return long before.

Were you worried about losing the way, making a routefinding mistake that might cost several hours and rappel anchors?

Not really. Even though the way wasn't always obvious, I had a very good feeling.

I don't know how to explain it exactly, but when I am faced with two possibilities—right or left—I am rarely wrong. When I first began climbing, I learned that one's tendency is to choose the easy way. Of course, this is not always correct.

What did you feel like on the summit?

I arrived at 3:30 P.M. The wind was violent and a storm was coming. There was no sense of relief because I wasn't even close to being finished. I knew descending the Japanese Route would not be easy. Faced with continuing as fast as possible without chance for rest, I said to myself, "I've had enough of this kind of torture."

The storm worsened until I was compelled to bivouac in a crevasse at 6500 meters. The wind-whipped snow made it impossible to see or move. I was hoping the pattern of the last few days would apply and the storm would slack off near 2 A.M. It did and I immediately headed down.

In the dark I climbed down through the seracs until I arrived at the edge of an overhanging wall. I was not sure of its height. I chopped a bollard, fixed the rope, and rapped off into the dark.

Fifteen meters down and firmly established on a 50-degree ice slope, I cut the rope again. That left 20 meters for the rest of the descent. Forty-two hours after I began, I returned to base camp.

How do you think that this climb will affect Himalayan climbing?

I won't say that "since I did this others must do the same." For me, at my level, it is simply a sign, the shape of things to come.

In the future, I think that climbers will regularly climb in Alpine Style in the Himalayas. I believe that every face can be done in Alpine Style. Now that the pseudo-mythical 8000-meter barrier has been destroyed, people will begin to open new, technical routes on the highest mountains. I'm not saying that Alpine Style is the only way, but it is progress.

Lots of guys choose objectives because they are popular or easier for sponsorship, but it's not the right way. To be satisfied in the Himalayas, you have to know exactly what you want to do. If you want to reach 8000 meters, then OK. But if you want to do something good, you won't find it on the normal routes.

It reminds me of the French scene.

Yes, many of the French climbers are searching for adventure with a helicopter. Most are going to the Himalayas to set or break records on existing routes. Myself, I want to go to Canada where the mountains are isolated and real adventure still exists.

How are you supported morally and financially in Yugoslavia?

Climbing is accepted very well in my town, and nearly everyone skis. The climbing scene is agreeable. Everybody knows each other, and we all see one another on weekends. There are 40 climbing clubs in my republic alone. None of them are professional. In fact, there are no professional guides or instructors in Yugoslavia. Instructors volunteer for a club and their expenses are paid, but they do not make a profit.

As far as sponsorship goes, it's complicated, but I'll explain. Jannu cost $7000 for my doctor, Jani Kokalj, and myself. Not much in the States, I suppose, but here [in Yugoslavia] the average salary per year is $300 to $400.

Of course, I needed help. Each republic has a Sport Association that receives money from the state to sponsor all kinds of sports. Out of the three classes of athletes in these associations only the International Class receives money. My award from them covered about 10 percent of my expenses for 1989.

My mountaineering club has an Expedition Commission that collects money from all kinds of different factories—not from the state. The money goes toward "worthy projects." The club contributed 60 percent of my Jannu budget. Each town has a Sport Association as well, but to profit from these, one must be very good and lucky enough to have educated people on the board; ones who know the difference between a good and bad project.

Now money is not such a problem. After the Trilogy in 1986, things began to go well. But the first 10 years were grim. As well, I have one of the few private businesses in Yugoslavia. We work on bridges, clean tall buildings, etc. We do any job that requires the special skills of the climber. And one day each week I write a page on mountain sports for our newspaper. I'd like to work as a journalist.

Is there an experience in the mountains that you learned from or were dramatically affected by?

Perhaps the most striking memory is Yalungkang in 1985. It was my first Himalayan expedition—before I'd been to the Pamirs and Peru—and I was 25 years old.

Two of us had gone to the 8505-meter summit and encountered some unexpected Grade 5 rock and 70-degree ice at 8350 meters. We were late, and my partner was completely wasted and not emotionally prepared to continue working at the level necessary to survive. He had psyched up only to reach the top. Afterwards, others said he was like that in the Alps as well. He always had a problem on the descent. He just let himself relax too much.

Anyway, I had to set up his rappel for him, tie him in and all. Near the bottom of the first rap through the rock band he just stopped and waited. I told him to go farther down, but he insisted that we could downclimb from there. I joined him on a small ledge and began driving a piton for the next rappel. It was indeed too steep to climb down.

We didn't have harnesses, so we were just standing there in the night. I heard a noise and looked over my shoulder to see my partner lean back like he was going to sit down. I don't think he even knew he fell.

I was too shaken to continue and bivouacked at 8300 meters without gear. I chopped a ledge out of the ice and walked back and forth along it all night. In the morning I climbed down. I had a retinal hemorrhage but no frostbite.

In the days afterward I felt stronger and stronger. It was a very grave lesson; that standing on the summit doesn't mean it's over, especially soloing.

I also like to remember the Piliér Rouge Directissime that I soloed last winter. It was a very long approach up the Inominata Ridge, and the climbing was hard for me because it's granite and I'm used to limestone. Even in winter it was warm enough to free climb [7a, 5.11d] in rock shoes. The pillar is on a very remote side of Mont Blanc and I was completely alone. It was a special trip for me.

What projects do you have for the future?

[Tomo becomes rather reticent.] Of course, there is Gasherbrum IV, this is a very fine face. Maybe I will go to Alaska next year, or to North Twin [in Canada] . . . Makalu, back to Lhotse, there are so many things to do.

One last thing. When you took the permit for Jannu I know you had offers from others to go with you, in an expedition style. How did you answer?

I gave them a simple "No." I told them that first I would try it my way, and that if I couldn't do it on my own, I'd leave it for someone else. When they responded by telling me what I proposed was impossible, I didn't argue. I never said, though, that I would do it. I said I'd try, and afterwards we would see.

2000 AUTHOR'S NOTE

Better men than I claim to have been duped by Tomo Cesen. When we as a climbing community first heard of his achievement on Jannu, we dearly wanted to believe it to be true. Convinced of the transcendent ability of the human spirit, Tomo's success indicated the potential for great triumph of our own, that we too might overcome. I have always believed Tomo Cesen. Transcribing this interview, rereading the articles and words attacking him, and exchanging notes with the talented Slovenian climber Marko Prezelj caused me to review my position.

The detractors come from too many nations to consider jealousy and nationalism the sole motivation. Initially, I wrote off French complaints because Tomo claimed prizes to which French climbers considered themselves entitled. I disregarded Italian protestations because Tomo dipped his hand into their sponsorship pie. I ignored the Slovenian cry of "foul" because as a national hero Tomo was an easy target of local envy. Objections issued by Reinhold Messner and Greg Child made me take notice. In the end, however, I suggest that all detractors suffer from an inherent conflict of interest. And despite the painstaking research and emotion, there is reasonable doubt, which, if this were a criminal case, is all that's needed to declare Tomo "not guilty."

The Trilogy: Cesen's claim is defective in the first place because he climbed the Shroud on the Grandes Jorasses rather than the Walker Spur, which is considered *the* route to be done when claiming ascents of the Three Great North Faces. But Christophe Profit got away with the Shroud when he did the Trilogy in summer, so why can't Tomo? No one saw him on these routes, but I don't consider this unlikely. I've been on the Matterhorn, the Eiger, and the Jorasses in winter. While the approach up—or down—the Vallée Blanche to the Jorasses sees heavy traffic, I have been alone from the Leschaux Glacier cut-off onward in winter. I didn't see anyone but my partner on the Matterhorn during four days in March 1988. I've been twice to the Eiger in winter and saw no other suitors. Ivano Ghirardini claims it was too stormy to have posted such fast times on each of the faces. But the times are within reason, much slower than the records on every route. Profit climbed the Eiger in winter, taking 10 hours. Tomo claims a 12-hour climb. The Trilogy could easily be done in the way Tomo maintains.

Broad Peak: Tomo made an undisputed 19-hour solo ascent of the normal route prior to attempting K2.

K2: Tomo sped up the south face to the shoulder of the Abruzzi Ridge where, according to Greg Child, Tomaz Jamnick saw him (through a spotting scope I presume) and spoke with him by radio. How Tomo dodged other climbers while descending is unclear. Still, he was seen on the shoulder, which confirms a lightning-fast climb to over 8000 meters.

No Siesta on the Grandes Jorasses: Tomo claims a 14-hour solo ascent, the second overall of the route. Ropeless on 5.11 in plastic boots? Why not? Just because I can't, doesn't mean another is also unable. After making the third ascent, Francois Marsigny insisted Tomo lied because it took Francois, arguably one of France's best alpine climbers, three days to complete the climb, in what he considered better conditions. But two years later, a Russian pair climbed No Siesta in a day and a half as part of an alpine climbing competition during which teams vie for the greatest number of quality ascents in a week-long period. The team did not climb the Jorasses "fresh." Again, it is not unreasonable for a fit climber to climb No Siesta alone in 14 hours, given great talent, motivation, and the right conditions. However, it took Patrice Glairon-Rappaz three days to solo the route in June 2000. Sadly, no one witnessed Tomo on the face.

Piliér Rouge Directissime on the Broulliard Face of Mont Blanc: This is a good choice if one is going to fabricate an ascent owing to its isolation, which also explains a lack of spectators. Italians, active in the area after Tomo, during the same period of good weather, aroused suspicion by claiming there were no tracks on the glacier approaching the climb. Perhaps the glacier was frozen hard when he traversed from the Eccles Hut to the face, a probable state of affairs at daybreak in winter.

Modern Times on the south face of the Marmolada: Respected Italian guide Maurizio Giaordani insists there was too much ice on the face during the season Tomo claimed his ascent to have posted such a fast time, or climbed it at all. I don't know enough about this incident to comment.

Jannu (Kumbhakarna): Tomo's account of this climb (described in his article "My Way," recently published again in John Long's collection of soloing stories, *The High Lonesome*) is alarmingly vague. I achieved such a state of heightened awareness during some of my hard solo climbs that I recalled individual crystals in the granite and could draw accurate topos long after the fact. Tomo's climb on Jannu was at high altitude, some of it done at night. Personally, I must admit to great blanks in my memory of soloing Peak Communism due, I suspect, to the altitude. I interviewed Tomo about this climb. If he sat there, looking into my eyes and lied to me for two hours straight, then I'm a fool for taking the bait. His description lacks detail, but I find no outright lies. Based on the Single-Push ascents undertaken today, Tomo's 23-hour time on the route is not unreasonable. Proof of the climb could be uncovered; the piton left for the pendulum and the remnant of 6-millimeter cord left after he cut his back-rope belay above the A2 pitch. While these clues might not prove a visit to the summit, they would substantiate Tomo's passage up the most difficult part of the face.

Pierre Beghin gave me a very clear photo of Jannu's north face. Reviewing it today, I think Tomo's line of ascent quite logical. His descent of the Japanese Route, although dangerous because of exposure to seracs, is feasible and again, a rational choice.

Lhotse: It is not unheard of to climb a great Himalayan face alone. Nicolas Jaeger climbed to 26,500 feet on Lhotse Shar prior to disappearing during an eight-day storm. Pierre Beghin climbed Kangchenjunga and finished the south face of Makalu unaccompanied. Hermann Buhl summited Nanga Parbat by himself and Messner climbed Everest solo. When Tomo claimed a 46-hour solo dash to the summit of Lhotse via the massive south face, a route on which the best of the best had failed, shock waves crashed through the climbing community. Tomo was awarded sponsorship contracts, $10,000 in cash by Reinhold Messner, and a Slovenian national medal. Tomo was flavor-of-the-month for longer than that.

Russians voiced the first suspicions regarding Tomo's solo ascent of Lhotse. They climbed a new direct route to the top seven months after Tomo and declared it the first ascent of the wall. Twenty-five climbers fixed ropes, placed camps, and used oxygen above 23,000 feet to put two members on the summit. They insisted that if it required this much manpower and technology for them to climb Lhotse, surely no man could have done it alone. Using this flawed logic, I can prove no man has run a four-minute mile. Sergei Bershov said the heavily corniced ridge between the top of the wall and the summit proper was unbelievably difficult, that Tomo is a "superman" to have climbed across it twice. But the Russians climbed Lhotse after the annual monsoon period of heavy snowfall. Tomo was on Lhotse during the pre-monsoon season. I have been on neighboring Nuptse before the monsoon and in winter; some of my friends have attempted it post-monsoon. We experienced vastly different snow conditions during our respective attempts. Perhaps the cornices that plagued the Russians were little ice-cream rolls for Tomo. They also asserted that the Western Cwm is hidden from the summit of Lhotse, casting doubt on photos produced by Tomo.

Tomo's lack of photographic evidence shot him down in the eyes of many. Ivano Ghirardini claimed he always carried two cameras on his important solo ascents. Perhaps that's why he was so slow. But his questions and those of French journalists demanded answers. Tomo presented photos as his own that later turned out to be the property of Viki Groselj. Perhaps he feared that lack of proof would emasculate his claim. This could be the behavior of a true innocent, unaccustomed to the prickly attacks of skeptical media, searching for a way to get people off his back. While this action is suspicious, I do not find it altogether damning. Instead I find the photos and film showing a chipper Tomo returning from the face indicative of a possible hoax. I've been to over 8000 meters and seen plenty of other guys after they returned from high altitude. We all shared an unforgettable burnt-out-shell-of-our-former-self look. Tomo appeared to have been for a walk in the park. But he may well be the "superman" the Russians allege.

Slovenia: Back home, Tomo is not the national hero he once was. A Slovenian magazine (*Fokus*) called the Lhotse episode "a swindle." However, Marko Prezelj and Andrej Stremfelj, who climbed the awesome south ridge of Kangchenjunga on-sight and unsupported in 1991, believe Tomo's position.

Many of Tomo's climbs in Slovenia's Julian Alps are disputed despite lack of evidence supporting these contentions. For example, Tomo says he soloed a route on Travinik called Crna Zajeda, or The Black Dihedral. The rock on the 1800-foot-high climb is not consistently solid. Moves of UIAA VIII- or 5.11c are mandatory and protection is sparse. Tomo climbed it in summer, then repeated his solo effort in winter, claiming a time of eight hours. Because no one witnessed either climb and Tomo did not produce a very detailed topo following his ascents, doubt raised its head again. Tomo's were the second and third ascents of the route. Marko Prezelj made the fourth ascent, free and on-sight, leading every pitch. While he considers it a "serious climb," Prezelj said, "I proved to myself that physically it is possible to climb Crna Zajeda without problems." However, he added, "To solo it twice would take a very strong mind. I feel like really poor climber when I think Tomo climbed it alone—once in winter—because I didn't find it so nice that I want to climb it again in its entirety. The lower part requires a lot of discipline."

Prezelj's statement hints that Tomo should be considerably stronger than he, which may or may not be true. I think this is the motivation behind many of Tomo's critics: they cannot imagine another climber who is so much stronger than they are. It is common to encounter climbers who are 10 to 15 percent better than the rest. Alex Lowe was amazing, but not off the scale. Some of us could keep up when he was having a bad day. Frank Jourdan, on the other hand, was climbing at least 30 percent better than the best guys in the world when he soloed The Andromeda Strain, The Beast Within, and the northeast ridge of Mount Alberta (among others) in a 10-day visit to the Canadian Rockies. Tomo's ascents were off the charts, perhaps too far for anyone to get their mind around. Which begs the question, is he really that good?

Methods: To accomplish the routes in the style he alleges, Tomo would have had to use some very clever systems for hauling, self-belaying, and rappelling. My own limitations make me struggle to imagine going up on Jannu or Lhotse with a standard 6-millimeter static nylon rope. I might use a 5.5-millimeter rope with a Spectra core for rappels or pendulums today, but these were not in common use in 1989 or 1990. Falling on any static rope transmits tremendous shock to the anchors, so any safety derived from self-belaying with such is dubious.

According to my experience and that of my peers, the 40-pound pack on Lhotse was too heavy to move as quickly as he did. But maybe he exaggerated the weight.

He also claimed to have carried three liters of coffee and no stove on Lhotse. Trading a stove, fuel, and pan weighing two pounds in favor of six pounds of liquid, probably in thermoses to keep it hot, is not rational. The stove offers the opportunity to stop for a rest. Coffee is a diuretic and would have dehydrated Tomo over the course of the 66 hours he spent on Lhotse. Staying hydrated is essential for extreme athletic performance, especially at high altitude. But many climbers have gone for long periods without adequate liquid and come through just fine.

At the end of it all, I have to ask, how stupid is Tomo Cesen? If I were to claim an important solo ascent such as Lhotse, I'd write the script, fabricate the pictures, and stick to my story no matter what. I'd train visibly and fanatically beforehand, laying an apparent foundation for success. A little advance planning goes a long way toward fooling the public, especially if they *want* to believe you. These are the actions of the premeditating, cynical storyteller cast by Ivano Ghirardini, but Tomo's actions suggest a hip-shooter, or a man overtaken by events. I interviewed Tomo in Chamonix in 1989 and maintained intermittent contact with him until 1993. I did not and do not think him a stupid man, one who would plan an elaborate, ongoing fraud and then execute it like such a simpleton.

In my opinion, to refute a climber's word requires more substantial evidence than Tomo Cesen's detractors have supplied. In a similar story, with even fewer facts available, folks still contend George Mallory climbed Everest. Based on what I know and what I've read, I believe it a lot more likely that Tomo climbed what he says he did than that Mallory summited Everest in 1923. If Tomo did lie, he paid a terrible price for such a fleeting moment in the spotlight. Much of the fractured Slovenian climbing community blamed him for breaking up their "family." A more cynical voice suggested he was responsible for the death of Slavko Sveticic, perhaps the greatest climber in the history of alpinism. He disappeared while soloing Gasherbrum IV— an attempt that was outrageous enough to steal some of Tomo's thunder.

Marko Prezelj concludes, "I'm aware that I may sound quite naive. When climbers publicize their climbs, our belief is based on trust and respect, especially solo climbs where no evidence is offered in support. I could disbelieve Tomo, but then I would have to suspect many others who have no evidence either. I don't want to do that. Like you, I believe him, but I have no proof for that and I don't want to convince anybody."

PERESTROIKA

CARPET RIDE

Three feet of razor wire ran through my guts. For the 107th morning in a row I woke up hating myself. Punching the fogged mirror, I screamed, "What's wrong with you!" It was a statement, not a question. I knew what was wrong. For four months I'd made a concerted effort to be nice to people. I sought and sucked up to their approval because I had no self-confidence. To make a good impression, I disguised my hate. When it reemerged, the hated object was me. Still, hate beat me onward.

I hadn't climbed in months because I was scared. My partner Philippe was dead. I was out of shape. I drank too much beer. I put away Mishima and Bukowski and turned my brain into pulp. I quit learning. I wasted my time and that of anyone I met.

I pushed off from the mirror and walked across the cold basement floor. I made a strong cup of coffee. No sugar, no cream. While it cooled, I pulled a beige metal file-box from under the table. Under "Projects—Sponsors" I found the Russian folder. I copied the telex number carefully and answered an invitation of three months previous. The coffee went down lukewarm and fast. Salvation.

As I considered the Union of Soviet Socialist Republic, my stomach churned uneasily. I had no idea what to expect, but I knew that whatever came of the trip would be exciting.

Problems arose at the Russian consulate in Paris. The flight Ace Kvale and I needed left on Sunday; however, our visas were promised for Monday. The Consular Attaché demanded why I assumed they'd issue visas to travel freely in the beloved motherland so quickly. I replied that a voice on the phone claimed the process could be accelerated for a fee. "You're wrong!" he shrieked. "You Americans can't do or buy whatever you please!" He tossed our passports and applications onto a pile, saying he didn't want to see us before Monday. We stared incredulously through the bulletproof glass. The waiting room was silent.

A friend knew the Soviet Press Attaché in Paris. After a series of phone calls, a Soviet Embassy official pressured the Consulate into issuing the visas before Saturday noon. Although ordered to play ball with the bad-boy Americans, the Consular official didn't have to be nice about it. We were told to expect some abuse.

We arrived Friday as they were unlocking the doors and calmly joined the line. I was set to eat crow but determined to walk away with the visas that day. When I reached the window, the blood drained from the clerk's face. He physically shook while he raged at me, "I told you not to come back here until Monday, there's nothing I can do for you! Now get out of here so I can help more important people!" Flecks of spittle dotted the inside of the glass. I smiled amiably. Ace and I backed into the humid streets.

Saturday's reduced office hours represented our last chance before we would eat the plane tickets. The clerk told us to come back at noon. We did, and by 12:15 P.M. we were through the line. Without emotion he instructed us to return to the end of the line. After another 20 minutes, I faced our friend across the counter. He motioned us to the back again. The Consulate had been officially closed for 50 minutes. Another five passed while he ignored us. At precisely one o'clock, he acknowledged us with a tap on the window. He slid our passports and visas beneath it in exchange for 284 francs. We didn't thank him.

Leningrad whirled by outside the dirty windows of a four-hour car tour. I bought the watch off our cab driver. That night Aeroflot efficiently packed us into Tupolev's 737 copy and flew us across the motherland toward Tajikistan. I found no Flight Safety Card in the seat pocket. There were no oxygen masks, no pre-flight safety lecture. My knees jammed through the unpadded seat back into the spine of whomever sat in front of me. Flight attendants served an in-flight meal of hard-boiled eggs. Ace said it was just like a bus ride in India, minus the goats and chickens.

Five days later I woke up without a blinding headache for the first time in a week. A helicopter flew us from practically sea level to the 12,000-foot Moskvina Glacier Base Camp in the Pamirs. The instant altitude gain laid us out on our backs. During the following 10 days, we bouldered, hiked, and learned about Soviet-style ice climbing on the seracs next to base camp. Feeling well rested, Ace climbed the south face of Peak Vorobyova (17,400 feet) with a girl from Kiev. Later he told me he'd seen a direct line on the north face, all ice, never more than 70 degrees. The base camp topos and history book showed it virgin.

We woke at 4 A.M. and left our Polish circus tent in the dark. I carried a light pack. Ace was laden with camera gear. Below the face I scanned the line. Two huge bands of seracs overhung the lower half of the face. I began climbing quickly, intending to get above the seracs before the sun warmed them. Up to the rock band guarding the summit, the route never exceeded 60 degrees. The slope above it looked

65 to 70 degrees. An intervening 20-foot column of vertical ice pissed me off. I wasn't psyched for it, but I had to climb it.

I snuck through, lack of acclimatization and fear driving the picks of my tools deeply. My mushy brain failed to register the ensuing 65-degree mixed climbing and the parade of loose flakes I sent to the bottom. Three and a half pleasant hours and 30 epic minutes after crossing the bergschrund, I belly-rolled over the cornice into the sun. I called Ace on the radio and rasped how I didn't appreciate the sandbag. The route is named Suicidal Misfit to honor Doctor Bob Yoho's diagnosis.

After a rest day, Ace and I organized our ski gear and headed for Peak Fourth (20,140 feet). We intended to slake our egotistical thirst on a first telemark ski descent. The slope looked good; almost 5000 feet of southwest-facing corn snow, but the minutiae nearly stopped us. Our packs were enormous, the tent cramped and moist. We drank liter after liter of liquid to help us acclimatize, but forgot the peebottles. Overnight, the tails of our skis froze in a pool of meltwater. A Canadian team discovered us chopping our skis out of the ice and laughed. Fucking right, we're professional mountaineers.

We finally got away from the tent at 11 A.M., climbing in tele-boots, prepared with all the mountain gear: rope, crampons, the Ten Essentials. At 19,200 feet, Ace was heaving. I prodded him up to 19,500 feet where, all cells in revolt, he U-turned. I, too, conceded defeat. We skied. God it was good. A lung-full doesn't go far at that altitude, so we never linked more than eight turns before flopping over with veins bulging. At the tent, we inventoried our food and realized we had enough to try again the next day.

We carried only cameras and water. By 1 P.M. we were on top. Steep rock and blue ice dictated we descend the top 300 feet with crampons. As a ski descent I suppose it doesn't "count," but I don't much care because it was the best run of my life.

Fourteen members of the Leningrad Alpinist Cooperative arrived for a selection competition. Of the fourteen, eight would go to Lhotse the following spring. These were our hosts, so we went with them to Peak Korjenyevska (22,700 feet). They intended to climb the Romanov Pillar. The Soviet climbing scene is similar to that of the Alps 30 years ago; all the major ridges and faces have been climbed, but because of the lack of either modern ice gear or outside influence, the couloir and waterfall routes spilling off the vast limestone faces have not. Ace and I set off to correct an omission on Korjenyevska.

We climbed easy snow to a bivouac at 18,200 feet. The Russians camped at the same height on their route. The weather worsened overnight, so Ace and I retreated. Our Soviet friends climbed through it. They summited, returning to base camp three days later. Their tactics reinforced what I'd surmised about Russian alpinism: they'd rather go to the top and die than fail.

My schizophrenic Alpine-Style dartings in and out of the mountains piqued their curiosity, too. I explained that I carry little margin for error in my pack. If the weather gets bad, I go down. I pick routes where I can move quickly. If anything goes wrong, I run away because surviving is succeeding, standing on top a bonus. I taught them Roger Baxter-Jones' golden rule, "Come back alive, come back as friends, get to the top—in that order." They said climbing my way would be a luxury for them, that they felt a pressure to succeed that no Westerner would ever feel. I said climbing any other way than my way wasn't worth it to me.

I wanted to solo the north wall of Peak Communism (24,000 feet). I'd tried an obvious and difficult line a few days earlier. The route had little objective hazard, but I failed anyway. I was weak. I had too much weight. I climbed 1800 feet in the oppressive half-light of dawn. I wasn't moving well and was preoccupied with fear. The ice ribbon I targeted turned out to be nothing but powder snow plastered onto vertical rock. The sun never touched it, so it could never metamorphose into ice. I was too stupid to notice. I downclimbed and rappelled, defeated inside and out.

While Ace accompanied four Russians to the Borodkin Pillar, I found resolve in solitude. The months of being disingenuously friendly and the resulting self-hatred taught me that self-confidence cannot be based on the approval of others. Somewhere inside me I found the courage to stand alone, believing in myself without needing an audience. My reluctance to let myself be influenced by others is (mis)understood as antisocial. Alone in base camp, and comfortable with it, I began listing my assets and liabilities. I applied this transparent overlay on each potential route up the north face. I would go where I found a match.

Liabilities: I am not Tomo Cesen. I cannot solo 5.11 in plastic boots. I hate loose rock and weird descents. I dislike the weight of a rope and rappel rack in my pack. I do not have the balls to go up on a Himalayan route alone with one liter of water, some sardines, and no stove.

Assets: I am Mark Twight. I have a good head for ropeless climbing on moderately technical ground. I am fast. I know when to go and when to quit. I am willing.

I picked the Czech Route. Although 10,000 feet high, only the first 6000 feet are difficult. It is not dangerous by modern Himalayan standards. There is a 150-foot-high serac at about 19,000 feet, but I didn't intend to linger under it for more than five hours. At ease with my choice, I set my alarm for a 2 A.M. departure and began packing my gear.

I didn't carry a spare tool but slipped in an extra pick. I brought no sleeping bag, tent, or rope. I decided to pack extra Walkman batteries, a stove with three days of gas, my shovel, compass, and altimeter. All of the above could be counted as either assets or liabilities.

I opted for continuous ascent and descent; thus, the sleeping bag could stay behind. I planned to climb the lower wall at night, rest and rehydrate during the heat of the day, and continue to the summit the following night. Unfortunately,

ICE BOULDERING
ON THE MOSKVINA
GLACIER BELOW
PEAK COMMUNISM
IN THE SOVIET
PAMIRS

(Photo by Ace Kvale)

acclimatization didn't fall under either list. It was an unknown. I'd spent two nights at 15,200 feet and one at 18,200 feet, and I contemplated blasting up to 24,000 feet and back. At least I wasn't exhausted from climbing too high earlier.

I was half-awake when the alarm startled me. I lit the stove. Two cups of Cossack Brand Instant Coffee is like a mixture of speed, rat poison, and a roller-coaster ride in a Fellini film. Within 15 minutes I was wide-awake and feeling mean. My mouth tasted like drywall. I stretched, laced my boots, and began jogging toward the face.

Debris littered the flat area below the bergschrund, proving that seracs tumbled off occasionally. The 45-degree slope was peppered by stones flung from the wall above. Deep craters indicated they'd fallen into wet, late afternoon snow. I wasn't worried. The calm, confident feeling in my stomach assured me that "today is the day."

A crumbling rock band reared up malevolent and yellow in the halogen light, but an ice vein pumped through it. It was thin. I searched with my tools for patches thick enough to pull on. When they rebounded off rock, I swung them elsewhere. Sometimes when they bottomed out, I moved on them anyway.

The sun rose. Curious popping noises wafted down from the serac. Around 7 A.M. my calves gave a last flaming effort and cramped. Damn. At least 1800 feet of hard ice remained. I hadn't disciplined myself to drink enough. Instead of chopping a ledge, I traversed to a decomposing rock spur to rest and drink, then continued.

Ace and I shook hands at 10 A.M. He was still in his tent at 19,500 feet, unable to keep up with the ferociously motivated Soviets. I stayed in his tent eating and drinking all day. While I repacked to continue up that evening, our friends from Leningrad relayed disturbing news. Terrible winds had lashed the upper elevations.

79

They'd climbed to the summit wearing thick down jackets—a luxury I had denied myself. Certain I'd have a better chance in the daylight, I settled in for a bitter, ugly night.

The shivering woke me at 3, 4, then finally at 5 A.M. After coffee, Ace said he felt strong enough to go to the top. I was too wasted by the night out with no bag to try a new direct finish alone. By 10 A.M. the sun warmed the tent enough to coax us out. With bad weather tinging the horizon's edge, we simul-sooled up the moderate slopes of the normal route. We passed a Swedish girl left behind by her partners (she got the tent, they got the stove). We passed Boris, a Russian guide who wasn't fast enough to keep up with his Dutch client. In fact, Boris looked totally out of control. Ace took his picture and we continued. Moments later Boris slipped while downclimbing the last 50-degree patch of ice above his tent and fell to his death.

At 23,000 feet, Ace turned back while he was still strong enough to get down on his own. He passed his camera to me, wishing me luck.

My neoprene mask iced up. I tore it off and threw it away. Whipped on by the howl of the wind, with the threat of a whiteout imminent, I sprinted toward the top.

Summit of the USSR. 24,000 feet. 5:05 P.M. Crosses and plaques commemorated the mountain's many victims. I photographed myself several times before the sky erupted and hail beat down from blackening clouds. I descended cautiously at first and then with total abandon as I was overcome by the fear that falling snow would bury my tracks. Disconnected, half-time images paced me as I ran: a 10-man team barely able to descend, the Dutch climber with his head in his hands, the Swedish girl offering me dried apricots, whiteout, overexposed views of the ridge—steep on the left, less so on the right—greasy, evil sweat trickling down my back. There was a half-memorized crevasse pattern from the morning, someone's dinner puked up in the snow, Ace's fresh footprints, and then the tent.

We were both spent. I tread nervously on the slender edge between fatigue and too much caffeine. If it snowed a foot in the night the only way we were going to descend the normal route was in an avalanche. We postponed the decision by eating the last of the food and burning the last of the fuel. Thunder and distant flashes fluttered at the edge of consciousness and then faded. The hiss of the stove slowly overpowered the sound of snow hitting the tent. I unzipped the door and looked out at the sky—clear and brittle as glass. We both sighed in acknowledgment of the reprieve. Not quite safe, but we hadn't died yet either. Perhaps the Cold War really was over.

2000 AUTHOR'S NOTE

Despite some logistical hassles in Paris and Leningrad, this trip was one of the most fun I'd ever been on. Neither of us had any preconceptions, each experience was fresh. For having turned out so well, it began ominously, especially once we arrived in Tajikistan.

We traveled to Russia with little Western food because the weight limit on luggage between European destinations was 20 kilograms per person. We scammed two 70-pound bags each onto the flight, but our supplies were skeletal for a month in the mountains.

At the Alpinist Cooperative "hotel" in Dushanbe, we ran into British climbers Mark Miller and Andrew Broom. They'd been guiding clients on Peak Lenin. Upon reaching one of the high camps, the pair assessed an avalanche slope threatening the heavily populated site and pitched their tents away from the danger zone. Miller's sixth sense—and his obedience to it—saved their lives. Seracs calved, triggering a huge avalanche. It swept through the main camp killing 43 people. Only two survived.

After aiding the rescuers, Andrew, Mark, and their clients descended, psychologically emptied. Our conversation at the hotel was stilted. They were in a very different world. As we made small talk, Ace and I naively asked where we might buy some more base camp food. Broom asked how much we'd brought. Hearing our list, Miller said, "You're going to die on that diet." We bought some of their extra supplies, feeling especially good about the Scottish crackers and dense cakes laced with liquor. Despite the curfew, Ace and I located a "tourist" hotel, which happily exchanged dollars for warm cans of Heineken. Any car in town became a taxi by waving one U.S. dollar toward the street. We felt like kings and carried our plunder back to the hotel, but no one there felt like having a party.

AGAINST THE GRAIN

MICHEL
FAUQUET
RETREATS
FROM THE
SOUTH FACE
OF KHAN-
TENGRI IN
KAZAKHSTAN.

I stood alone on top of Peak Communism. As I snapped photos of the wastes falling away toward Afghanistan, I realized I still hadn't achieved anything. Others would think I had. They'd congratulate me with unreciprocated camaraderie. The parasites would gather around, growing fat on a diet of vicarious little calories. I wouldn't object. I would nourish them in return for being told I was a great man. Empty, I turned toward base camp. I was content to have stood on top and returned with my life.

Back in Chamonix, I wore my achievements in the Pamirs proudly, but my pleasure rotted faster than fruit left on the ground. Ace Kvale and I had made the first telemark ski descent of Peak Fourth (20,140 feet), 5000 feet of perfect corn snow. I had soloed a new route on the north face of Peak Vorobyova (17,400 feet). After that I extracted a promise from myself not to climb below seracs as often in the future. I soloed the 10,000-foot-high Czech Route on the north face of Peak Communism (24,000 feet) as a consolation prize for failing to climb a new route on the same face.

I wrote friends about the two new routes I had attempted and the vast potential of the region. The trumpeting hollowed me out. I lowered my defenses long enough for the worms of doubt to squirm in. I realized I had let myself be satisfied with second best.

Having seen the opportunities, I planned to return to the Soviet Union. I invited Michel Fauquet, a Chamonix Guide known as "Tchouky," to climb with me predominantly because I was too apprehensive to try the route alone. Our climbing resumés bespoke similar motivations and ambitions. We'd worked together on a film crew and spent the down time with small talk. He'd climbed some hard routes in the Alps in exceptionally fast times. We brashly discussed trying the direct south face of Lhotse together before the Russians sieged it into submission, but we eventually agreed that plucking Khan-Tengri in winter, using light and fast tactics, would serve our ambitions.

The allure of the unclimbed south face of Khan-Tengri (22,500 feet) in the Tien Shan region bordering China blinded me to the problems of sharing hardship and risk with a man I hardly knew. My hindsight was too dull to dissect lessons learned on five previous expeditions.

I wanted to disappear like I did in the Pamirs, but I allowed myself to become entangled because this trip cost more, and our egos needed recognition. Every time sponsors are involved in a project, the external pressure increases. Each boast binds me further.

Going away alone without broadcasting my intentions beforehand protects my freedom, leaving only private dreams and goals to live up to. The Khan-Tengri trip wasn't my show. It took on its own life, complete with the bureaucratic hassles attending larger Himalayan endeavors. I couldn't back out at the last minute when the premonition of failure colored the blank spots in every day. I toned down my aggressive attitude, I became a diplomat, and I promised to be considerate of others. I even listened to their opinions, whether or not they were relevant to climbing Khan-Tengri in winter. I told myself the concept looked good on paper.

Eight Soviet climbers joined our two-man team. Ace Kvale and John Falkiner came as photographers. The Soviets would attempt the first winter ascent of Khan-Tengri by any route, act as interpreters, and provide inspiration against the fierce Russian winter.

There were no internal flights remaining for tourists. The quota had been filled for the year. We could wait a week, until 1991, or take the train. The prospect of a four-day ride from Moscow to Alma Ata, across the Russian countryside seemed romantic until day two when the toilet backed up with frozen feces and bits of newspaper. I grew sick of peering at filthy, opaque windows. We rode the tired Russian rails at an average speed of 27 kilometers per hour with our breath coiling above us in the subfreezing, "hard class" compartment.

Three helicopter flights ferried us and all the gear 140 miles from the small village of Kegan to base camp. As we flew over two 11,500-foot cols and threaded our way up the 45-mile-long Inylchek Glacier, my sense of dread grew. If things went bad, escaping on foot would be ugly indeed.

On the glacier we worked like demons to put the tents up before the sun went down. I felt the temperature's sharp point inside me. Skins wouldn't stick to skis unless we heated both first, and duct tape shattered like sun-rotted Tupperware. The feeling in our toes came and went with howls of pain and the scrupulously observed fear of never feeling them again. Sweat-soaked fleece froze solid immediately when removed. Had our Soviet compatriots not brought propane heaters for

the triple-walled kitchen tent, we'd have paid dearly for errors of overexertion.

A mile from base camp, Trident Peak (16,300 feet) erupts from the relatively flat South Inylchek Glacier. I convinced Tchouky we could climb its north face in a day if we didn't use the rope too much. At 9 A.M. we began tiptoeing anxiously up the windslab below a triple bergschrund. We ate altitude quickly, slowing on the steeper pitches but never stopping. We moved at roughly the same pace and made routefinding decisions without too many words.

At noon I confronted a horror show of overhanging blocks. I tied in and lowered the rack to Tchouky, who led around a corner without placing any gear to protect my creaking belay. I was furious. No matter how easy the terrain, I place protection whenever possible on hard alpine routes because when I want it, often I can't get it. I always place more than one piece to keep me from going to the ground. There's no excuse for not protecting the belay.

My anger built as minutes ticked by. Tchouky was taking too long. We'd never get close to the top before dark at this speed. Short of lowering off to let me lead through, nothing Tchouky might have done could appease me. For his sake, I hoped the pitch was hard to follow. Our slim margin of safety held me on edge. After two hours and fifteen minutes Tchouky belayed off two pins and a nut hammered into suspect rock.

I unfroze myself from the belay and followed the pitch thinking more about my partner than the climbing. He'd done Yosemite Big Walls, was a hot free climber, and had ticked some good routes in the Himalayas. Trident Peak was easy compared to Khan-Tengri, so two hours for one pitch was unacceptable. Fifteen minutes later I grabbed the rest of the rack from him without bothering to say "nice lead." I rode my tantrum up past a tied-off screw, a horizontal nut placement, a runner around a none-too-solid flake, and a tipped-out Friend. At the end of the rope I sank a three-quarter-inch angle, and my ears were still ringing merrily when Tchouky cramponed across to me saying, *"Chapeau, par-ce-que c'etait pas facile."* The pitch had not been easy, I reflected, but neither was it difficult.

Tchouky and I had climbed together only once before. I was getting a closer look at a trait I'd observed in many French alpinists. Most can't frig protection into weird features because they cut their teeth on limestone clip-ups or the nearly perfect cracks of the Mont Blanc massif. Fixed gear litters most routes. Without question, Tchouky is very, very fast when the climbing is straightforward. Indeed, he sprinted away up a 60-degree ice gully. Paying out rope, I weighed the words I'd say at the next belay.

Ace and John came on the radio, postponing my talk with Tchouky. They carefully described our situation. Looking through the 600-millimeter lens, they figured we had two more hard pitches. Then, an easy traverse on ice might allow us to avoid the overhanging rock guarding the summit. It was 4:30 P.M. and minus 20 degrees Fahrenheit, two weeks after the shortest day of the year. Routefinding was problematic in the daylight. I didn't care to try it by headlamp. We hadn't brought bivy gear.

It was obvious we should descend. I didn't even want to discuss it, but we spent 20 minutes doing just that. When I climb alone, I am the dictator. Democracy in the mountains is a waste of time, but Tchouky wanted to vote. At 10 P.M. we walked into base camp after nine scary rappels off marginal pins and hastily chopped bollards. Exhaustion deprived me of the energy needed to express my anger, so I said nothing.

Khan-Tengri dominates all surrounding summits except Peak Victory (23,800 feet). Its 8700-foot-high south face makes the 6000-foot wall on neighboring Peak Chapayev (20,200 feet) appear reasonable. The photo I'd seen of Khan-Tengri in August 1990 stopped my breath. The mountain was a hidden treasure, the soul-illuminating jewel I needed. Its beauty caused me to put aside my differences with Tchouky. I recalled having said in print that "as long as climbing is the most important consideration, petty squabbles remain just that." I tried to live up to my words.

After climbing to 18,500 feet on Khan-Tengri's normal route, Tchouky and I began psyching ourselves up for the face. We tried to dig a snow cave to cache gear or sleep in at the base of the route. The ceiling of one collapsed. I bent an ice tool hacking at the rocks on the floor of another. As tension built between us, I spent more and more time alone.

Tchouky was cocky about the face and treated it like a classic route in the Alps. He acted certain that no difficulty could stand against his talent. His cavalier attitude made me very conscious of my own paranoid concerns blossoming unashamedly in my head. I'm not pessimistic, but I've been thrashed by mountains so many times that I'm wary of what appears to be a giveaway. Above all, I detest being pressured to perform according to schedules or to please peers. That's how alpine climbers get the chop.

When I'm on my own, and my body and soul agree that "today is the day," the world is mine to take. Tchouky and I would never reach that point because we weren't as strong or wise together as I would have been alone. I didn't love him; I didn't trust him and I never would. My goal was to survive an attempt on the face, to learn something useful for the future.

We intended to climb the face in one push, with a daytime bivy at about 19,800 feet. This naked style meant that an ordinary mishap would kill us. I don't think I'm so good I can always get away with taking such enormous risk. No one gets away with it for long. Acceptance of this risk offered a way to climb the face. We'd spend as little time in the danger zone as possible, applying our resources prudently, not spending energy too quickly, nor holding anything back.

We left our tent at 7 P.M. The full moon allowed us to move without headlamps. Ace and John waited in the tent listening to the walkie-talkie. We muscled past the bergschrund and then squeezed into a narrow couloir separating the rock wall from a menacing cascade of seracs. They popped, creaked, and occasionally fell down. My stomach twisted into a psychotic macramé. Above, the straight white lines we hoped were bands of tender névé offering easy passage up the hard, black ice proved to be powder snow fantasies. Our tools and crampons made slight scratch marks on the ice's surface. The climbing was slow and insecure.

As we moved higher, a facet of the wall hidden during our reconnaissance re-vealed itself. Ice gargoyles perched on the southwest ridge, and a freakish tongue of seracs licked its way down the face. We stopped, stunned. I stared up into the moon-light, searching for a feature that might protect us.

We felt a muffled vibration, like dynamite exploding underwater followed by the screech of jets taking off overhead. I frantically sank my tools as if it would help and pointed my helmetless head at the descending cloud. The heaving mass passed by 50 meters away. In the dead silent aftermath Tchouky blinded me with his headlamp as he searched my face for a sign.

We climbed on, both knowing we hadn't tried hard enough yet, that turning back now would be a waste. Twenty minutes later I cocked an ear skyward, hoping I'd heard my heavy breathing resonating inside my hood. Another avalanche swooped down, ruthlessly polishing the ice beneath. I sensed it would be close. We sprinted rightwards, driving our tools in when further motion seemed pointless. Powder snow rushing ahead of the tumbling ice dusted our downturned faces. I took a breath and sucked my head down between my shoulders. The atomized blocks missed us by 10 meters. I started dry heaving in the cold night air.

I wished I were alone, that the choice between up and down was solely mine. Tchouky's presence intruded on the intensely personal decisions affecting my survival. We were not a team, but I continued climbing partially because of him and because I'd survived worse situations. I didn't want to give up without a defensible reason.

At 18,200 feet we stopped. The last 900 feet had gone faster. Black ice had given way to névé. By 2 A.M. we stood halfway up the face. We had climbed above the windbreak provided by the southwest ridge. The upper face was exposed to the jet stream. Furious gusts whipped at the snow, threatening to knock us off our minute steps. It was minus 17 degrees Fahrenheit in Ace and John's tent 5000 feet below. We were already bundled into all the clothes we brought. Climbing higher was lunacy. Staying put until sunrise might be suicidal. After chopping just enough ledge to comfortably stand on we rested for 30 minutes, willing the wind to calm down.

Uncontrollable shivering forced a decision. To make a ledge big enough for our tiny wall tent would take three hours. The work, although a waste, would keep us warm. Spending the remaining dark hours motionless required the sleeping bags we'd sacrificed to reduce weight. We needed the sun if we were to stop moving. Climbing ropeless in the fierce wind involved great risk.

I wanted to go down. I knew I was not equal to the challenge. It was too cold, the wind was intensifying, and the face was too dangerous. I'm often weak. When intuition says "no," I dare not disobey. I listened to that small voice, shivering inside and out. I thought perhaps Tchouky wasn't frightened, that maybe he could continue climbing for 36 more hours nonstop in these conditions. I hated myself for being petty enough to consider how he would present his view in the media and to his colleagues.

When Tchouky describes a route as deadly, he implies that his skill kept him alive, that he's a cool guy to have been there at all. He never admits to weakness or fear. This has not always been the case. During an Alpine-Style attempt on Lhotse with Vincent Fine in 1985, Tchouky freaked after seeing a Polish climber fall past them and insisted on descent. Conditions were perfect, and Vincent wanted to continue. They went down. Tchouky took the blame for failure. He never wanted that to happen again so his motivation to continue up Khan-Tengri wasn't as simple as it appeared.

Nor was mine. The helicopter was to return in four days, so this was our only chance to do the route. I had invested much time, money, and posturing in this trip, but I didn't want it to kill me. I didn't mind being responsible for failure. After weighing the costs versus benefits, the risks against rewards, I insisted on descending.

To avoid traversing below the ice gargoyles, we rapped straight onto the hanging glacier. The sun rose, warming the concave face. Seracs cut loose with alarming frequency. Ace and John coached us down because they could see the terrain below us better than we could. "It looks like you'll have to traverse to your right into the couloir you climbed last night."

"There must be another solution," I shouted, "because look what's coming now!" Tchouky and I slammed in our tools and crouched behind a protective hump of snow. It split the avalanche, which shot by on both sides and emptied into the couloir.

There was no other way out. I was willing to postpone flight until nightfall. Tchouky reminded me that seracs fall 24 hours a day. Immediately after the next slide we raced for the gully and downclimbed with total abandon. We might survive a fall but not an avalanche. As Tchouky rappelled over the bergschrund, another huge serac tumbled down, but crevasses swallowed it before it reached us. We covered the remaining distance to our tent in comparative safety. I was happy to be alive.

The helicopter was six days late retrieving us from the glacier. Tchouky, Alexai Shustrov, and I made a lightning stab up the normal route, skiing and climbing from the 13,000-foot base camp to 20,500 feet in 12 hours. Again, wind beat us back and we gave up on Khan-Tengri at 5 A.M. on January 30.

In my quiet little chalet, I painstakingly dissected the expedition. The house is hidden in the forest on a dead-end road outside of Chamonix, a perfect operating room for the introspective pathologist.

I appreciated the futility of our efforts. The trip to the Pamirs had been ideal. I hoped to achieve the impossible by re-creating the same thing in the Tien Shan, but we were not a team. We were four guys in the same place at the same time with a similar goal. No one picked up the slack left by another's weakness. We could not work together, so we couldn't succeed. It devolved into an expensive reconnaissance.

Tchouky said he won't return to the Soviet Union because the bureaucratic problems cannot be solved with money as in Nepal or Pakistan. John returned this summer to tour a new national park and study permafrost. Ace says he won't go again in winter, two trips to Russia were enough for a while anyway.

I can't look at it as failure because we never had a chance. The trip was wrong from the start. The bad taste of my experience with Tchouky remained in my mouth for weeks. I believe I was right, that my decisions were correct. That may just be the rationale I use to justify my childish need to have it my way all the time. I'll get it, too, because I survived. And that's enough for now.

2000 AUTHOR'S NOTE

I'd never thought it appropriate to air "dirty laundry" following a climb or expedition and never did so until this article. I'd had several "memorable" experiences with partners and clients in the mountains, but none affected me like the winter trip to Russia did. I am still unsure why.

I was angry enough after the trip to follow through with this critical article, even though my pettiness was evident, and I made Tchouky look bad. It was printed in the USA and Spain, but word reached Tchouky and we never spoke much again. I was also reviled by American readers who did not know me. The letters received by the magazine made it clear that I should not have written about the problems we had. I hoped that my own self-castigation would balance the criticism leveled at Tchouky. Yes, I behaved like an adolescent. So what? I invited the guy on the resumé to Russia forgetting that reality is often much different than legend.

Looking back, I don't hate Tchouky or even dislike him. Given an opportunity, I wouldn't climb or socialize with him, but I feel little toward him. I suppose I am indifferent. I am sad and angry to have failed on Khan-Tengri though. Despite conditions being less than ideal, we had an opportunity that won't be available again. We didn't understand how important the wind's effect would prove. With more research, we might have chosen a better period, perhaps later in the winter.

That period in history was rife with change. We listened to the entire Gulf War on a shortwave radio in base camp, wondering each day what Israel would do if a Scud carrying a chemical warhead exploded in downtown Tel Aviv. During our trip, the USSR crumbled a little more as well. Our companions learned from the shortwave that 50, 100, and 500 ruble notes were being pulled from the system. One might exchange any notes he had at a bank if he could prove the money was not earned on the black market. The exchange period lasted for three days during the expedition. Several of the Russians watched their savings, earned from "illegal" work done repairing and cleaning high buildings, disappear virtually overnight. The value of the ruble dropped from 40 to the dollar to 85 during our six-week stay.

Khan-Tengri heralded a change in my climbing career. It was the last big mountain I ever attempted overseas. This was due in part to the cost of expeditions and my unwillingness to allow too much commercial influence on future trips. I had reached a point in life where a two-month absence was not as attractive as it used to be. I climbed instead in Alaska and Bolivia, both ranges being considerably less expensive and more user-friendly to a resident of the Lower 48.

HOUSE OF PAIN

Daniel saw him squatting perpetually on some north wall, enduring the
storms and terrors of the great faces, a contemptuous eye cocked at his malig-
nant gods. You cannot starve me, he would say to them, more than I've always
starved—nor cause me greater pain than I've always suffered—nor make me
any lonelier. And there he would preside forever.

Roger Hubank, *North Wall*, 1977

After a hot summer season and a little autumn snowfall, the north face of Les
Droites is a disaster zone. The remaining ice is thin, black, and as hard as the deck
of a battleship. The rocks that didn't shriek off the face during the summer are
frozen stubbornly together, hibernating, waiting for the spring thaw and the next
wave of summer alpinists. The sunless northwest face offers a hostile invitation to
those remaining after the "season" is finished. No one talks about the wall much,
lest word gets around that a new route still waits to be climbed. Complacency and
fear mix a cocktail of inactivity, disguised by the rationalization that conditions
are no good, that it will be an easier line when there's more ice on it, that the cable
car is closed and the bars are still open. No one goes near the wall. No one men-
tions it. Instead, they pretend that considering the climb an impossibility makes
it one and makes it so for everyone.

I really don't care what anyone thinks. I do what I want. I succeed. I fail. Sometimes I'm so lazy I do neither. I live and breathe along with my problems and my
work and my self-inflicted pain. I live in France because the mountains are high
and beautiful, and the air is cold; but sometimes it's not enough, and days arrive
with an ugliness even I can't support. By the time October rolled in, I had had it up
to my neck with kissing people's faces in greeting and stores that close from noon
'til three. I was sick of the snotty chauvinism that reassures the French their past

glory still counts for something. They were pissing me off with their mountaineering narcissism and their nouvelle cuisine. I had five feet, nine inches of hate hidden under my coat and decided to get a bit of payback by poaching the route on Les Droites. I'm no different than any other prejudiced bigot; sooner or later I feel a little nationalism and xenophobia. If I stay in one place for too long, I see only the bad things while the good fades, glossed over and unrecognized.

Barry Blanchard was at my house with Jim Scott, preparing for another go at the Eiger. After two inspired attempts with less than cooperative autumn weather, Jim gave up the grail and returned to the USA. My flight for Katmandu left in four days. Barry sharpened his tools, and with every beer we drank took a little more hardware off the rack. Bubba and I purposefully waded through my supply of alcohol. We broke the windshield out of my wife's car, threw up across the lawn in a weird male bonding ritual, and with that out of the way agreed to go climbing. We hadn't climbed together since 1988 when we gave our (insufficient) all to Nanga Parbat and Everest.

Barry's a reformed asshole and cynic. He's a pleasant version of me, better adapted to the social niceties required of men in the 1990s. He is considerate of other people, or at least when he's not and he recognizes it, he tries to do something about it. I am not and I don't. I am willing to cut it all away in order to have my way, to live how I want, and for only as long as I want.

Our climbing talents differ too; Barry is the master of the Canadian Rockies style of alpine masochism, with several truly sick first ascents to his credit. I converted to the motorized alpinism flourishing in Chamonix, where climbing is made easier by cable car access or helicopter transport (if at all possible), VHF radios to call in quick rescues, and the modern alpine climber's speed worship.

The cable car was indeed closed (to soup up the motors and increase capacity). I complained about having to walk the 5000 vertical feet to the Argentiere Refuge. Barry admonished me for my attitude, saying that all of the mechanization has soiled alpinism's purity. To be sure, machinery has displaced physical effort in some instances. But just as the development of Friends, and later bolts, has allowed Sport Climbers to concentrate on climbing, the improved accessibility, system of high mountain refuges, and competent rescue services have allowed us to give our full attention to the climbing itself. Modern routes in the Alps reflect these resources.

The rack was anorexic for the route, and we wasted time placing gear. The potential for a big fall was huge. A healthier, heavier rack would have let us go faster. We climbed vigilantly on the thin ice. With a stopper and a knife blade between him and the belay, Barry broke a tool. He placed a nut, hung on it, and changed the pick. Twelve feet higher he broke another. I squirmed at the belay as he swore and screamed and pounded the hammer against the wall. I empathized. Why bother climbing beyond the capacities of the gear?

I followed, grabbed the meager gear sling, and cast off onto the next pitch. Bubba reached my belay breathing heavily and told me I was climbing as good as Doyle does when he's fit. I liked hearing that because Kevin is one of my climbing heroes.

"Mark, let's trade tools so I have two good ones to lead with . . . and maybe we could take the third anchor out to give me a little more gear to protect the pitch."

I agreed to his reasoning. "When I come up, Blanch, keep me tight so I can go faster."

"That's something we do in Canada too," he said, arranging the gear on a sling. "Glad to see full-strength runners on your rack, Twight, it makes me warm all over."

"I'm even more paranoid about gear than before. I've just broken too much or seen other people on the ground after they've broken theirs."

"Except for your ice tools, I notice. You don't even have a spare pick, do you?" Barry's tone said he knew the answer.

"Grivel made these prototypes especially to be 'Mark-proof.'" I shrugged off my oversight with a cavalier turn worthy of the French.

"Well, I want some," and he sped away.

We raced up the face, hunted by the coming night and nagged by our light packs; empty except for the walkie-talkie, headlamps, and a virtually gasless stove. Useless items if we had to bivouac, but sleeping on routes is a very unfashionable practice in Chamonix. At 5 P.M. we started climbing rock two pitches below the summit ridge, and I knew we'd get off before dark. I pulled through the last moves with my crampons screeching across the granite. I watched the sun dip beneath the horizon as I belayed Bubba up. Total blackness fell while we shared the remaining bits of food and frigid water. Barry trundled rocks to prepare a bivy site—sage tactics as he had no idea how to get down off the south face of Les Droites.

"Yo, Bubba, what are you doing?"

"Aren't we going to sleep here? I mean how're we gonna get off this pig in the dark?"

"Blanch, we're in Chamonix, we *can't* sleep here. The Couvercle Refuge is about 3500 feet down complete with blankets and beds, and that's where we're going. Besides, I've got this descent totally rehearsed, with the rap anchors in place and everything ready. 'This is the modern world,' to quote The Jam."

I'd done the descent two years earlier with Philippe Mohr, who died a year afterward on the Aiguille Sans Nom. During the trip down with Barry on that moonless October evening, I thought about Philippe and cried, silently wondering about all of our futures. We were snug and warm inside the Couvercle Refuge before midnight and back at my house packing for Nepal by 10 A.M. the next morning.

We named the route the Richard Cranium Memorial, hoping we had outgrown him. It was the last route Barry and I climbed together for several years. A few months later, life came between us. Our solid bond ruptured and going to the mountains together became a delicate proposition.

Recall that I'm adept at cutting away anything I perceive to be holding me back. I've used the knife on my country, my family, and finally—with no small amount of hesitation and fear—my wife. It wasn't clean; it wasn't pretty. I killed a part of me when I did us in. I slapped convention and everyone who believed in us in the face. I soiled the proud institution of marriage beneath my selfish feet and think about it every single day.

Confessing does not absolve me of guilt or make it easier for anyone affected by my acts. I walked away as I have usually done, leaving Anne, her friends, and family to work out the reasons for themselves. People take my actions personally, whether they were implicated or not, so I let them resolve their problems their way without my presence cluttering the issue. I sort out my difficulties my way—alone. In short, I run. Barry's compassionate nature comforted my not-yet-ex-wife in her time of great pain and need, offering solace with a bit more than his strong arms and understanding. In turn, she helped put him back together hard on the blistered heels of his own divorce. Barry and I distanced ourselves from each other. I watched the trust we shared fade, the fire dim and cool. I began climbing with other men.

> *In all his life he'd never known anything like this. He had never imagined anything like this. Now he realized that the worst of life had always been like this. That always it must be like this for someone, somewhere. And perhaps the time had come for him to suffer what all men must have suffered since the beginning.*

Roger Hubank, *North Wall*, 1977

Barry and Andy Parkin have little in common except me, alpinism, and the painting. Andy painted it and Barry likes it. The painting hangs on my wall, and Barry said that "our lives, rather, your life," pointing at me, "is becoming more and more like it." A man's large, tortured, and searching face demands attention first, and only very slowly figures emerge from behind him. One gestures for him to come back, or pushes him away. It's hard to tell which. A naked woman lies on her stomach with her chin on her hands looking at him boredly, maybe saying, "So long, anyway I've got these others" with her eyes, resigned that she cannot prevent him from leaving. A third man looks on with a curious detachment as Mr. Tortured stares into his clouded future with his back to them all. The lines are hard and harsh, the painting somber blue, gray, and black. Barry casts me in the role of the tormented man and himself and my soon-to-be-ex-wife as figures. I like it. Andy is also, like Blanchard used to be, one of my climbing partners.

He was one of the world's best alpinists of the late seventies and early eighties;

DURING THE FIRST

ASCENT OF

RICHARD CRANIUM

MEMORIAL,

NORTHWEST FACE,

LES DROITES,

CHAMONIX, FRANCE

(Photo by Barry Blanchard)

having soloed the Droites by several lines, the Walker Spur alone in winter (in 19 hours), and the serious Boivin-Vallencant on the Aiguille Sans Nom. In Pakistan Andy climbed Broad Peak and attempted K2 in Alpine Style. A groundfall that nearly killed him in 1984 left his hip in 13 pieces, many of his organs displaced inside his torso, and his left arm shattered along with his future. Today, both the hip and elbow are fused into single, motionless pieces. Despite doctor's predictions to the contrary, Andy has climbed again, and climbed well. In the last three years, Andy has put up five big climbs in the Mont Blanc range, attempted Makalu and Everest, and climbed Shivling. He consistently climbs 5.11 and gets in the occasional waterfall routes when his career as a painter and sculptor allows him the time. Andy is one of the most gifted climbers on mixed terrain that I've ever climbed with. His determination, experience, and willingness to risk it all propelled him up three new, modern alpine routes in the Chamonix Aiguilles last winter. Beyond Good and Evil on the Aiguille des Pelerins is the most serious and difficult of these climbs.

The Aiguille des Pelerins' north face is an austere wall. Its shades of oppressive gray lighten as the sun passes over without touching, but it never warms to red. Great men have left little trace of their presence on this face, accounting for three, seldom-repeated routes. It is a cathartic place, attracting only those few who want to test themselves, to throw the dice, to beat their heads against it. All efforts undertaken in moderation count for nothing up there.

I half-heartedly attempted a new route on the Aiguille des Pelerins with Christophe Beaudoin in 1989. Technical difficulty and slow progress stopped us.

Variations on the same theme and a turn of the weather cut short my effort with Andy a week later. The November days were criminally short. I took a 25-foot upside-down fall out of the big corner on the fifth pitch. Andy shouted enough encouragement that I led through, but at the top of the sixth pitch, the relentless approach of the 14-hour night finally got to us. With too much unknown terrain waiting above us, we retreated, turned our backs, and snowshoed away.

The unfinished climb left a scar time wouldn't heal, and I vowed to acquit myself. I could see the face from the gym where I trained. It taunted me through that window, made me realize the weights I lifted and the hills I sprinted up meant very little to any great north wall.

For two years I wore the route around my neck like a weighted chain. Andy and I both had excuses for not going up again, the same excuses I criticize others for using. It never came into condition, the weather forecast was no good, our work preoccupied us, and the cable car remained closed. We substituted the usual list of rationalizations for laziness and lack of motivation. Neither of us was ready to give what we knew the wall was going to take. In April of 1992 we attempted the route again. It hadn't become any easier in the interim. Conditions were not ideal, and the aid went slowly. We managed to climb seven 60-meter pitches and to get a look at the upper wall before the clouds moved in and snow forced us down.

With failure stuck sideways in my throat I wrote catalog copy for nine days before Andy called and said he was free. I dropped everything and filed my ice tools. We decided to get on the wall and stay on it until we finished. We took bivy gear and a pair of jumars, so the second could follow carrying it. We loaded the packs heavy because experience dictated a rack of hardware larger than anything I had ever taken in the mountains (except for the South Pillar of Nuptse). The size of the rack represented a huge judgment against our ability and confidence, but previous attempts had demonstrated this to be the minimum.

The first pitch was brutal by headlamp, adrenaline on top of coffee and a good chance of seeing breakfast again. The first good piece was a Lost Arrow 30 feet up. "Hmm, the pick's buried about halfway and it only dragged a few inches before it caught on something. Too bad there's nothing for the other one." Looking down, "That Arrow doesn't look as good from above, maybe I'll wiggle a nut in there, yeah, and tap on it with the hammer. Shit, I'm hanging off the hammer. Well, I'll use the pick of the other tool. Andy might have trouble getting it out, but on pitches like this it's 'fuck the second.'" Higher, on easier ground, I ran it out without stopping because I'd taken too long below. The last protection was so far down I couldn't see it. "Hell, if I fall off this I *deserve* the deck. It's only about 100 feet to it and the snow's deep and soft."

Jumars made the whole thing reasonable, since the passage of the leader often left no ice for the second to climb on. The seventh pitch started with some unrea-

AIGUILLE DES PELERINS, CHAMONIX, FRANCE. THE NORTH FACE OF BEYOND GOOD AND EVIL IS THE NARROW RUNNEL OF ICE LEFT OF CENTER.

sonable aid off copperheads and tied-off pins directly above an unprotected belay. I pulled out of the étriers into a 70-degree corner stuffed with just enough ice to mask the crack.

An overhang capped the corner. Andy remembered that he'd found a place for an upside-down three-quarter-inch angle on the last attempt. The latest storm plastered a huge snow mushroom under the roof, and I was afraid to touch it. Instead, I dry-tooled out left onto a slab with my right calf shaking and frontpoints dancing a psychotic, carnival step against the granite. I torqued the shaft of my ax in a flaring crack and locked it off low enough to hook a thin flake with the hammer. I managed to rest by leg-humping a rounded arête. The only hope for gear was an iced-filled horizontal crack. I hand-placed a wide Leeper and welded it with my hammer, fixing it for the next generation. It gave me just enough confidence to reach a small shelf and good ice.

Two exciting pitches higher I made the evening radio call to get the weather report while we dug out a bivy ledge. Things were working in our favor: the bivouac was large enough for two, and the stormy forecast had been modified to call for a just a few snowflakes. We slept as well as one does in these places and woke to broken, timorous clouds with the promise of amelioration during the morning.

Andy fell 15 feet onto the belay as he started the 13th pitch. Of course, it had to be the 13th, and the belay was suspect. I had one hand in the pack searching for some food when the piton popped. I mistakenly gave him a dynamic belay, but it probably saved us from going to the ground. I followed the pitch, warily eyeing the slot clogged with big, loose blocks that gave access to the Col des Pelerins.

The only belay anchors were directly beneath this deadly cavity. It was too steep to avoid pulling on the flakes and teetering bricks. I was quite happy to be absorbed in the process of leading rather than waiting for the sky to fall on me. I fought with every ounce of self-control remaining after 13 hair-raising pitches. I pulled gently and pushed resolutely down and inward on the creaking mess. Tunneling through the cornice, I felt the familiar fear-sweat running from my armpits and the small of my back. It cooled rapidly as I belayed Andy up. I relished the world's greatest remedy (victory) and my second nightfall route-finish of the year.

We rappelled and downclimbed the west side of the col and marched back to the cable car midstation through heavy, wet glop that often sucked us in to the waist. My newly scarred watch showed 2:30 A.M. when we reached the hut's drifted-in doorway. We'd been on the mountain for 45 hours and spent 26 of them actually climbing. My hands were smashed-up and bleeding, I was dehydrated and wasted as badly as I have ever been. The knee I'd broken several years before pulsed dully. I had just enough energy to force the hut door open and collapse inside. I kept my pain to myself because what I felt was certainly trivial in comparison to what Andy must have been going through. I silently admired his drive, his great commitment to the ideal.

> *Only great pain is, as the teacher of great suspicion, the ultimate liberator of the spirit . . . it is only great pain, that slow protracted pain which takes its time and in which we are as it were burned with green wood, that compels us philosophers to descend into our ultimate depths and to put from us all trust, all that is good-hearted, palliated, gentle, average, wherein perhaps our humanity previously reposed. I doubt whether such pain "improves" us—but I do know it deepens us . . .*
>
> **Frederich Nietzsche, *The Gay Science*, 1887**

And we are chained together in the house of pain searching for our truths—beyond good and evil.

2000 AUTHOR'S NOTE

From the end of 1991 through the first half of 1992 I experienced profound change. Barry and I did the route on Les Droites in October. Days later, in Katmandu I ran into Scott Backes. He was returning from an attempt on the still-unclimbed south buttress of Annapurna III. On the street that night he introduced me to a woman who helped shape the following year. Kristen appeared to fill the empty places I had discovered in myself. Strong and independent, she'd just ridden her bike from Katmandu to the Pakistani border, 90 percent of the way alone, and returned to Nepal by train. She was a professional athlete in an alternative sport. We shared much in common. Our meeting was like a high-speed car crash: fast, furious, and damaging.

Trouble had been brewing in Chamonix for a year. Marriage did not fit me well, and the chance encounter with Kristen reminded me I could walk away at any time. Back home, I tried to work things out, but I wasn't serious. I'd seen greener grass, or perhaps just grass painted brighter green. I left my wife to hook up with Kristen briefly. My wife, Anne, entered a similarly brief relationship with Barry. He had the strength and decency to call, "Rather you hear it from me than someone else." Although I'd walked first, their union burned in me. It took years for me to forgive either of them. I thought her action malicious, her intent to destroy my relationship with Barry. She did. I let her.

Back in Europe I moved to Courmayeur, across the Mont Blanc Massif in Italy, so Anne and I would not have to see each other.

The attention I gave to Beyond Good and Evil diverted me. After six weeks in Italy I rented a small studio in Chamonix which offered a view of the route from the bottom of the sixth pitch upward. I paid attention to conditions and trained. I searched myself for clues: what did I want, whom did I love, whom did I trust, why had I caused such pain? Few answers surfaced.

To an extent, Andy stood in for Barry as my partner, although I was never as close to him as I was to Barry. Our partnership was amiable. We liked each other a lot, but this was the only route we ever did together in the mountains. I don't know if we burned out on each other or if our ideals were too dissimilar. His fused hip precluded moving as fast as I preferred, but my God, what a phenomenal climber. Chiefly, I think our different cultural backgrounds betrayed us. We did not share certain fundamental American programming. That said, I respect his determination and motivation immeasurably and promise to retrieve the painting from its French storage area one day.

Salvation did not follow success on the route. I descended with more questions than ever. I was hammered for days afterward, too. Scott came to Chamonix 10 days later. He saw the sun twice in 30 days, but our talk and training, our frustration and striving cemented the future of our partnership. If redemption occurred that spring, Scott was its messenger.

A LIFETIME
BEFORE DEATH

FRED VIMAL
ENJOYING
HIMSELF AT
LE FORON,
FRANCE.
"MORE FUN
THAN
CLIMBING!"
(Photo by

Cathy Beloeil)

17:30, May 21, 1993, Rue Paccard, Chamonix, France (a year after Mugs died):

The nightmarish scene began with a snide comment. Cathy Beloeil and I had been climbing in the south. Back on Chamonix's main street, I told Matty Notlind how safe rock climbing is these days.

"The only risk is that you could be electrocuted on the rim of the Verdon Gorge."

"Ho," Julian Mills piped in, "maybe you shouldn't joke about lightning after what happened to Fred."

Cathy gave Jules a disconcerted look. I knew deep down Fred Vimal had been killed, and I pursed my lips.

Jules continued, "Dédé (Rhem) just came back from a reconnaissance with two other guides and four guys from the PGHM. Fred was on the Grand Cap, trying to do Elixir d'Astaroth alone but didn't return when he said he would. They saw him hanging on the wall today and assume he got hit by lightning. I mean, on the Capucin it wouldn't be stone fall. Too steep."

Cathy hadn't faced death as often as the rest of us, wasn't as jaded either. She'd cooked Fred dinner at our house the night before she and I drove south to visit her parents only one short week ago. She pleaded, "Fred who? Not Vimal?"

"Yes. Fred. Dédé is pretty beat up as you can imagine." Jules checked his watch without urgency. "Well, I've got to get back to work, see you guys later."

Matty, stunned, said, "Wow, first Alain and now Fred . . . and he promised to go climbing with me this summer."

"Alain?" I asked, thinking Ghersen.

"Morouni," answered Matty. "You didn't know him? He was such a cool guy, he even speaks Norwegian." He paused. "Well, *spoke* Norwegian anyway." With the joke, we all separated to go about our business.

I had enjoyed the time Fred, Cathy, and I spent together during the last three weeks, and I missed him already. I felt sick to my stomach. I hated the way we heard the news, set down like an empty beer mug, casually. I preferred to hear quietly from a friend, personally, or on the phone with some chance to prepare. In the end, I guess it's all the same and none of it matters.

It was early still, so I telephoned friends who might know more, guys connected with the Rescue Squad. I started to form a picture. Fred had gone up Sunday afternoon, and when he didn't return on schedule, there was the usual alarm, but a small one. By the time he was 36 hours late, though, Dédé drove down from Paris. He and some friends skied out to search despite the bad weather. I asked for details at the Mountain Rescue office. Fred had fallen about 70 feet and caved in the back of his head. He'd placed three pitons at the belay but no intermediate gear. The self-belay device probably flipped him upside down. Either he died on impact, lost consciousness and froze when the bad weather came, or he simply bled to death.

Dédé explained that they spotted him about eight pitches up the wall, already above the hardest climbing. He was swinging on the end of the rope, encrusted with ice.

"I saw him after they brought the body down—he's not the same. I mean, his face isn't fucked up or anything, but I didn't know him anymore. I barely recognized him and I've been climbing with him for eight years. He just didn't have any luck."

Dédé had taken the biggest dose I've ever seen a guy take and walk away. The previous week he and Jerome Ruby made the first snowboard descent of the north face of the Aiguille du Plan. They watched their partner, Alain Morouni, get swept off it by an avalanche. Then Fred was killed. Dédé and Fred were best friends.

I used to think it a great thing to be this alive and aware, to be doing something that made my nerves so raw. I considered it a valuable way to spend my life; climbing up and down on meaningless heaps of ice and stone. I know it is man and men who give value to the mountains and not the other way around. But to me, the Grand Capucin is worth a lot today. I am sick of determining who my good friends were by analyzing how much I'm affected when they die.

Most mountain climbers and those who love them avoid thinking about and dealing with this aspect of alpinism. Death plays a huge role in why men climb, in the way they climb and why some of them eventually quit climbing in the high mountains. Alpinism often means high risk and the loss of life. Your friends may die up there in the clouds, in storms, swept away by avalanches, or cowering under a volley of stones. Perhaps they'll freeze to death alone at the bottom of a deep, dark crevasse or sit down to rest and never get up again. This is the long fall, where the sky is rose and the mountains have never been as beautiful as they are today. Life bleeds away from a head injury, unnoticed. It's about climbers dying doing what they love and spectators speculating, judging, and maybe having the last word. Alpinism is the story of men and the risks men take, the ones they are equal to, the ones they barely get away with, and those risks that kill them. It is about obsession.

The danger and the glory, the addiction of going harder, higher, longer. Sometimes we get away with it, we survive when others do not. Death in the mountains can be as ugly as a falling stone surprising an innocent hiker on the trail. It can also be as beautiful as seven men struggling through a storm day after day, giving everything they have to life and living it. But one by one, from cold, from exhaustion, from having fought so hard, they die. Until three remain.

I say this is beautiful because the greatest human act is the act of *survival.*

I face death, rather than avoid it. I climb anyway. Somehow I manage to handle the comings and goings of partners and loved ones. I pay homage, but I also move on. I don't know about whatever might come with death. Little by little I understand what it is that comes before: the life we are all living through right now. I see how easy it is to die in those beautiful places. I have lost many friends to the loveliness and horror of ice and stone walls. I still cry for them, for myself. The beauty of the high places is tempered by threat and danger. I remember the struggles won and lost up there. Every situation in life has its black side. Every human being on this planet would love to make that side go away. Wishing it away, ignoring the danger and the consequences, they can make believe it no longer exists. I refuse this option.

I understand my lifestyle may eventually kill me. It is no different than the high-risk lifestyle of the police officer or soldier, the firefighter, the drug dealer and gang leader, or the political revolutionary. I can not turn off my hunger. I demand more and more from myself. Each successful climb waters a small seed of dissatisfaction. It might have been too much, but it could never be enough. Some men have high ideals, which they're willing to die for. Others are willing to try living for them. My hunger helps keep me alive. There is always more.

I live in a town where the cemetery is full of men who died at 20 or 24. They were killed in the mountains. I participated like they did, but I got away with more. I didn't make the mistakes they made. I used to think it made me a superior human being, and I lorded it over everyone. I believed it was natural to die up there because my emotional health depended on the delusion. I couldn't let death and dying poison my precious ambition, so I built walls to prevent close relationships. If I don't know you and you die, it's easier for me. I avoided friendship with my peers. I purposely forsook the few people in the world with whom I did not have to justify my lifestyle. I did it to protect myself from pain.

When I came to Chamonix, I exchanged my American routine of trivial drama passing as sensation for genuine feeling and a true sense of being alive. Over time I had all the feeling I could take, so I traded it for shallow acquaintance and the emptiness of experiences never shared. Fred and I had met one year before his death, but I refused friendship because I was certain he would die climbing. Three weeks before he died, we started hanging out together. I liked him more than I like most men. Now I regret the year we missed together. I wonder what we might have done together had I not been afraid of feeling more pain.

That night I couldn't sleep. I didn't want to go out. I didn't want to drink insomnia away with friends so I uncorked a bottle and drank it alone, tapping at the computer without inspiration. Dead inside, too alive inside, the last thing I wanted was someone touching me or assuring me that they understood.

I crawled between the sheets, but tossed uncomfortably. I couldn't make love with Cathy. *Make love?* Out of what? The necessary components for assembling a physical expression of love were missing. An act that passed for love but was just bodily release in disguise offered nothing in return. Perhaps the next morning—or maybe the one after that. I lay listening to the last song on the CD over and over, hoping the phone would ring. I thought, "Maybe it's a mistake. It hasn't ever been before, so perhaps it is this time . . ." I wished I'd answered when Fred telephoned last Friday. At least I could have called back sooner, motivated him to come south. I left such a stupid message on his answering machine Sunday night, *"J'espere que tu as la forme et tu fais les belles choses . . . a bientot."* Of course he was doing something beautiful. But I'll never see him again, not soon anyway.

I have a list in my head and every year I add more names to it. My list isn't special, other men have longer ones. But most men don't have a list like mine at all because they live life insulated from living and dying. Their acts of courage consist of getting out of bed in the morning, disagreeing with their boss, or using public transportation in the inner city. Perhaps they tempt the unknown by eating in a Vietnamese restaurant, or they travel outside their native country. They have nothing to do with me except to provide contrast. They aren't part of my insulated community of climbers who pull the wagons in a circle to protect themselves from judgment. As closed as the climbing brotherhood is, I am still afraid. Are we careening out of control? The No-Future future is no place to grow old. I add another name.

Steven Strang, Paul Holmes, Chris Stefanich, Becky Davis, Sue Lowe, Ian Kraabel, Dave Kahn, Mugs Stump, Roger Baxter-Jones, Mark Miller, Catherine Freer, Dave Cheesmond, Mark Bebie, Wolfgang Gullich, Alexis Long, Wanda Rutkewicz, Slavko Sveticic, Pierre Beghin, Bruno Cormier, Vincent Fine, Xaver Bongard, Francois Rickard, Philippe Mohr, Benoit Grison, Bruno Gouvy, Jean-Marc Boivin, Patrick Vallecant, Jean-Francois Causse, Bruno Pratt, Jef Lemoine, Gian-Carlo Grassi, Eric Mariaud, Fred Vimal, Tahoe Rowland, Richard Ouairy, Mark Sinclair, Benoit Chamoux, Alison Hargreaves, Trevor Peterson, Scott Fisher, Steve Mascioli, Mike Vanderbeek, Eric Escoffier, Alex Lowe, Seth Shaw.

These men and women, alive in our memories, mustn't be forgotten. We must learn from their lessons instead of ignoring them, swallow the pain to make it part of us rather than pushing it away. It is sometimes difficult to believe in an ideal when

CATHY
BELOEIL
AND FRED
VIMAL, LE
FORON,
FRANCE

so many have died because of it. There is no shame in walking away, passing the torch, as long as we remember.

The world we know is ending. But another's coming hard on its heels. The whole landscape has changed, and whether happy or sad, we remain to live and to tell. Life isn't easy on those of us who survive, especially during the first few weeks. After Fred was killed, there were accidental moments when I thought I could phone him, maybe climb together.

I don't feel sorry for myself. I chose this, or accepted it anyway. I gulped it down whole. I shot the dose. I wish I'd learned the courage to admit to the men and women on the list that I cared about them before they died. I live with the unspoken words inside of me because I can't say them to the people who deserve them anymore.

Fuck your dreams man, this is heaven.

Aftermath: Dédé and Fred's brother went up to recover Fred's equipment and try to understand what happened by doing the climb. The eighth pitch was the easiest on the entire route, 5.9 perhaps, so it was logical that Fred (who'd soloed the Walker Spur in 4 hours 30 minutes and enchained it to the Peuterey Intergrale) didn't put in any gear. If it was cloudy, he might not have seen the huge icicles suspended beneath the summit overhangs. Dédé said, "A few of them fell while I was on the tenth pitch, they exploded all over the eighth . . . maybe that's how it happened." Yes, maybe.

2000 AUTHOR'S NOTE

I've spent a lot of hours thinking about this event since 1993. I have told the story to countless people during my slideshows, trying to learn its lessons myself.

I first met Fred at the film festival in Autrans, and we got along well. I gave him a ride home, and we talked nonstop during the three-hour drive, even promising to get out climbing together, but I never called him. I chose to eliminate the possibility of experience in order to preserve myself from the pain his death might cause. His talent and ambition were on display, and I saw a bit of myself in him when I was 25. While my paranoia allowed me to survive my learning curve, he showed no restraint or fear. I knew he would die young in the mountains and wanted no part of it. I said "Hello" in the street but that was all.

A year later we ran into each other at a local crag. I was there climbing with Cathy and the two of them hit it off instantly. We started Sport Climbing together, trying to get strong for the season. Fred wanted to go to Yosemite again. I wanted to climb, and it didn't matter where. But the spring weather was fickle, so Cathy and I made plans to climb in the south where the weather promised to be better. Fred said he had some things to take care of in Chamonix, but would join us after a few days. He promised to call Cathy's parents' place in Le Cannet to arrange a rendezvous in the Verdon. The next thing I knew, I was there on the Rue Paccard with Jules telling us what happened. There followed many days of aimless walking and regret.

I've been to enough funerals in my life, so I've finally quit going. Some were good, some were awful. People attended the good ones to remember the life of the deceased. The awful services focused on death, while the living bemoaned their own fates rather than honoring one who'd met his. After Fred was killed on the Grand Cap, his service was held in the old stone church in downtown Chamonix. It was the most powerful funeral ceremony I've witnessed. Typically, it began with family members saying pretty things accompanied by beautiful music. I stood in the cold hall, bored, waiting for more, and missing Fred. It was so damn ordinary, and every person there was uncomfortable with their grief. Some fidgeted. Others turned their faces upward toward the stained glass. I hated the superficiality I sensed around me. I wanted to be transformed by spiritual experience.

Once the family was done, the priest spoke. I thought him too well-rehearsed and insincere. The music ended. The brief silence was broken by shuffling feet and whispers. Then Dédé Rhem, Jerome Ruby, and David Ravanel, all friends with Fred since childhood, stood and recited a list of routes Fred had climbed with them or alone. They spoke back and forth, alternately, in staccato bursts. They read some from a piece of paper and spoke other names from memory. The number of climbs, of hard ones, was astounding for a 26-year-old. I let the litany sink into me as I closed my eyes. When they'd finished, one of the three went behind the podium and pressed "play" on a tape deck. The recorded sound of cheering filled the church.

The audience was not at an opera. Familiar bells chimed above the roar and an almost mournful guitar riff clawed its way through the applause. It was beautiful in its own way, and I smiled hugely at the contrast. The live version of AC/DC's "Hells Bells" wasn't quite loud enough for me. Nor for David, who turned it up. Then, accompanied by a fourth whom I didn't recognize, Dédé, Jerome, and David shouldered Fred's casket and carried him out of the church. They placed the box in a waiting hearse, got into their own cars, and sped away at a less-than-solemn clip.

It was a cool spring day, with clouds licking the mountains above us. We stood outside, stunned. No one knew what to do. Fred's friends and his body were gone. The ceremony imitated life perfectly. In the end, the climbers took care of their own.

DISTANT

WARNING

As far as déjà vu goes, the scenario could have been better. Worse too, I suppose. Scott Backes was at the house again, and the rain fell continuously, hard and black. He didn't smoke, and I wasn't drinking as much as the last time he'd been over. That trip, I fell through my self-discipline into the bottom of a bottle, into a hard, wet circle of love and hate and doubt. Nothing new. Another version of the theme I've been living since I can remember. I let it thrive and grow. I kill it and I bury it. Then I resurrect it. Déjà vu: there's a woman, the mountains, and the godforsaken rain.

In September Christophe Beaudoin and I dashed up the Macho Direct on Mont Blanc du Tacul during a 40-hour window of high pressure. We climbed up to the hard pitches on the Aiguille Sans Nom before veering to the Marsigny-Mohr variation, escaping to the Arête Sans Nom in bad weather. We were strong. Body and soul. Work pulled him back to Paris and I still had a month to burn before my flight back to the USA. I planned some parting shots for the French Alps. Conditions were good, but I needed the right partner, so I called Scott and offered to split the plane fare.

I've spent hours eavesdropping on the beer muscles in the bar and know where most of the unclimbed routes are. They're obvious to anyone willing to look. The remaining lines would require some effort, rare conditions, and a willingness to suffer. The climbs come into condition for a few days at a time, often when the cable cars are shut down. So if you have a full-time job or climb in Chamonix as a tourist, you need not apply, but that leaves plenty of talented young bucks who could have and should have snaked those routes ahead of me.

I was supposed to mellow out as adulthood gained a foothold, but I am angrier than I was 10 years ago. It isn't my all-purpose emotion. My anger is more precisely directed now. I grieve for what I've lost or cut away. I recognize what others avoided or didn't do; those same experiences I was allowed in payment for the beatings I've given myself over the years. My life is full of shit and blood and pain but I'll take it all without analgesic or complaint if I get to win big every now and then, especially if I win in the company of a man who I care about. I still solo, but it's not as good as climbing with a peer.

I met Scott in 1985, the night Jonny Blitz fractured his elbow on a wood stove, slam-dancing at the going-away party thrown for my second trip to Chamonix. We didn't talk until 1989. He came to France with Michael Gilbert. Michael further embellished his own legend by asking my wife how she could "deal with me doing what I do." She gave him a blank stare.

Scott introduced himself by saying, "I don't know what happened man, I just fell down the goddamned stairs." I was the only Skinny Puppy fan I knew—he quoted one of their songs titled "Stairs and Flowers."

Destiny opened ahead me. I knew we'd do more than a few casual sport routes together. Scott climbs fast and hard in the mountains. He's intelligent without the weight of institutionalized education chaining him down. And he speaks the special language of modern music. We developed our own verbal shorthand based on those lyrics. We use it to center each other when things get out of control. We use it as social commentary if we don't want bystanders listening in.

"It depends on the dosage."

"Yeah man, but you got to know how to use it."

"It's easy to find."

"It's just in front of the sky."

"Say a little prayer for the motor."

"800 TV Sky."

"I taught the Killing Game first."

"There's no truth."

"There's no lies."

"It's not for glory, it's not for honor."

"It's just something someone said."

"I think you guys are hypocrites and I'd like you to defend yourselves."

"I'm going to hell with the lid off that's definitely true."

"Hey kid, wanna earn 10 bucks?"

"Fuck you, queer."

"It's just the violence buried within."

"If I cut off my head would it be me and my head or me and my body?"

"Is it safe?"

"Give me something skin, something like forever."

"And he can't touch the bottom, but he sinks himself deep."

"All I wanted was a Pepsi."

"Looking California."

"But feeling Minnesota."

"How fortunate the man with none."

"Pushing you too far."

That's three years of climbing together and three different styles of music (with a little cult-film dialogue thrown in). And Scott is from Minnesota.

We went to the Grands Charmoz first. René Desmaison climbed a route on rock there in 1959, and we planned to loosely follow his system of corners and chimneys, staying on ice as much as possible. Andy Parkin and Thierry Renault tried it in 1982, but a front moved in after five pitches. They'd said it was very hard. Routes are possible today that couldn't have been done back then. But as Andy comments about thin ice, "We're starting to fall off things now." And I almost did. An ice tool wedged behind a flake as an afterthought caught me on a hyper-extended arm. Once the adrenaline flood subsided and I'd choked back the puke, I realized I wasn't into it anymore. The blinding spindrift gave me an excuse to lower off. We cached the rack and rope before hiking away.

I used to feel a paralyzing terror when I approached big routes. Now I know how to do them. I know what to expect. Today the apprehension stems from signing contracts, agreeing to the expectations, saluting the motordrive, and posing for full-page photos in European magazines.

On the mountains the fear never changes. Rocks fall. Helmets break. Ice tool picks snap. Ropes cut over edges and are tossed. The harder the routes get, the bigger the packs grow. The more competent I become, the greater my willingness to push the boat way out, the tighter the hands grip the throat. No other game can train me for it. It's a stupid activity, but name one that isn't—to someone somewhere.

Fools ask why, looking for a sound-byte. OK, I'll play. I do it because I can. I climb because it hurts, and the pain gives me perspective. It's difficult, and I can lord my mastery of it over the rest of you. Alpinism is not necessarily about "fun." It won't transform every climber into a better person. I'm just a guy who pays the rent, who checks his shit for Nepali worms, who the tax people want to corral. Except I never watch TV or eat frozen food and I don't own property. I spend my disposable income on compact discs, camera gear, and climbing mountains. I was a "no future" kid, and I hope it comes true because I don't plan ahead for fishing holidays on Social Security. The future will be what it is whether I have insurance or not.

We carried a huge rack because we couldn't expect easy protection as on the "sport" routes sprouting all over the Mont Blanc Massif; bolts next to cracks, fixed belay stations, fast-food alpinism. Homos put 'em up. I don't mean homosexuals, I mean homo-genized men. I mean lame, bloodless snots without any moral character or respect for the environment—climbers willing to climb a route by any means just to be first. These are men who refuse to recognize that other, more capable men will come after them, men who may climb the routes clean. These climbers don't

SCOTT
BACKES ON
THE THINLY-
PLASTERED
SECOND PITCH
OF BIRTH-
RIGHT, GRANDS
CHARMOZ,
CHAMONIX,
FRANCE

realize that homogenized climbs are forgotten by those who repeat them because they can be done without commitment. So they sabotage their own supposed "legacy." I can take Sport Climbing—I participate. Sport Alpinism though? Yeah, Verm, it's neither.

Every time a French alpinist or *telepherique* attendant shakes his finger at the size of my pack I want to shoot him. And his smart-ass countryman who bolted the first seven pitches of the American Direct on the Dru and found sponsors for the project.

There were no giveaways. Belay anchors were solid, so we knew we'd never go all the way to the ground, but the potential falls looked long.

The ice in the big corner was from 1 to 8 centimeters thick. It ran for 90 meters, 85 degrees at the crux. Protection was sparse, three pieces in the first 60 meters. We were breathless and starving as night wrapped around us with no apparent bivy site available. Our headlamps stabbed feebly into the sense-around blanket of silence. Two pitches below we made out a snow patch.

Scott said, "Everything looks flat from above and that 'great ledge' will be 60 degrees and need three hours of chopping. Besides, losing altitude is wrong."

Instead, he led through. Twenty meters higher he hit the dance floor, a lying-down bivy and the barometer hadn't budged. We waited and waited for our stove to give up five liters of water, knowing the homey little scene would be replayed in the morning.

We emptied our packs and used them as pillows. Scott's sleeping bag went by the clever name of "Summer Breeze" (rated to 50 degrees Fahrenheit). I had an insulated bivy sack made in 1987. It had lost most of its loft over the years.

We sleep in all our clothes. We eat a lot of fat. We put Shake-n-Warms in our socks and hot water bottles between our legs. When we wake up we're already dressed. It's a pretty good system, and we look forward to every bivouac.

The next morning I swarmed up an ice-choked chimney with a liter of Earl Grey in my blood. Avoiding an overhanging corner, I paused briefly to pull on some A0 nuts, aided off Camalots—two cams on rock, two on ice—and ran it out to the belay. Scott took the A2 pitch. I jumarred. The photos inspired an acquaintance to tell him, "You looked a lot like Mugs up there."

We arrived on the huge terraces and looked for a way off. The wind slabs weren't enough to slow us down, but every little bit of uphill did. I couldn't face a sleepless bivy or a meal of spiceless potato powder and lukewarm water. Scott could have gone either way. Thankfully, we had the power: four chocolate-covered espresso beans, a Power Bar, and a pint of water each catapulted us 5000 feet down to the house. We sprinted into the sea of clouds. Visibility extended about 15 feet. It rained and hailed. We slipped on wet roots and fell down swearing. The sky unzipped with a parting comment as we hit streets awash with trash and dead leaves. We refused to bow our heads. Tired-blinded and proud, we strode the last three kilometers to the house. We ate pasta. We took baths and slept in beds.

The following morning we drew the topo and named the route Birthright (ED+, 90 degrees, 5.9, A2). "A classic in the modern idiom." "You can't touch this." "*Plein feu*," French slang meaning it's in the limelight and every one can see it from town every day. Every climber can talk about how cool-looking it is, about repeating it. The same as another line on the north face of the Aiguille Sans Nom: visible, talked-about, cool-looking, unclimbed. Poaching we will go.

We modified the stove; Scott changed the picks on his tools. Although brand new, the set had survived only one climb. Their poor performance would probably be excused because of "misuse." The good news is they didn't break. Gear failure's not uncommon anyway. We expected the lead rope to last only two routes. We had to replace some of the nuts after we chopped the cables while hammering them in with the picks of our tools. We push most gear past its design limits, but some is better than the rest.

The cable car had closed for the season and the train to Montenvers was shut down. Approaching the Sans Nom meant 5000 vertical feet on foot, a distasteful and unique situation in the Alps. Keeps the riffraff away, though.

From our bivy on the Rognons des Drus, Scott and I waded through waist-deep snow for 90 minutes to reach the base of the Aiguille Sans Nom. We found no ice on the lower wall, just powder snow and temptation. We'd both been burned by it before. We retreated to check an alternative. Neither of us wanted to fail after the effort we'd made to get up there. Plus, the weather was too perfect.

A consolation line looked possible, but not that day. We imagined a midnight departure would allow us to get it over with in 24 hours. Visualizing, the first three pitches took an hour each, then another one for the 400-meter snow slope below the hard climbing.

"There'll be about six pitches up there and they'll take 10 hours so we'll get to the top at 2 P.M. if we start at midnight. Add four hours for wasted time and it'll just be getting dark. We are so cool."

We didn't eat much that afternoon and saved enough fuel to get us through a bivy on the remote chance we couldn't reach the Charpoua Hut the next night.

We crossed the 'schrund at 4 A.M. Better late than not at all. Sometimes. We "rochambeaued" for the first pitch, and Scott's rock beat my scissors. He shouted that the climbing was "pure fucking joy," 70, 75 to 80 degrees, thin, snow-ice, dragging his picks 'til they caught on something, then a ramp with an overhanging wall above and tolerable anchors. Navigating by headlamps, we couldn't see much. We told ourselves that you can only fall as far as you can see—my argument against halogen bulbs.

An hour and a half later I equalized four Camalots and tied off the stretched 60-meter lead rope. I had plenty of cams left because I'd placed only three tied-off screws, a steel nut, and a good baby angle between the belays. The face tilted 85 to 90 degrees and then 90+ (whether you believe me or not), thin enough that the one pitch blunted my picks. I bent over and threw up. It looked like the dried bananas. At least the oatmeal stayed down.

Night fell as I was following the A3 pitch. We knew it would. It always happens in the most inconvenient place. Night makes most any place inconvenient. The stress was palpable. Neither of us had seen a ledge to bivy on since the night before. Tired and hungry, our skin wore thin.

Scott shouted belay commands, I answered too quietly to be heard. He exploded, "When I say something to you, you better fucking well answer me!" We screamed at our own deficiencies after recognizing them in each other. I wanted to throw him off. I wanted to untie and continue alone. I wanted to crawl under a stone, refusing to accept the man I was. Scott had just led a hard and dangerous pitch. A couple of placements moved under his weight, especially the ice tool adze hammered into a bottoming flare. A fall would have sent him onto a two-meter-high granite spike sticking out of the ice and killed him. Still, there we were, shouting schoolyard taunts helmet to helmet in the dark.

On the
Macho Direct,
Mont Blanc
du Tacul,
Chamonix,
France

I led through angrily, searching for a place to brew up and sleep. From below, every ledge looked bigger than it actually was. I hurried from one tempting false-platform to the next until I ran out of rope. We gave in to reality and spent an hour chopping to fashion a "three-cheek" space to sit on.

Struggling, we shuffled into our bags, feet over the edge, tied-in short, sitting upright with slings wrapped around our shoulders so we couldn't lean over and slip off. Spindrift magically accumulated in our bivy sacks. Despite our bland and thin dinner of milk and potato powder, cheese and lukewarm water, we were content to be together in the middle of the lifeless, menacing wall. We stared at the thousand points of light coming from Chamonix, too tired to be curious about what morning would bring. The night was benign, and after a couple of false starts, we both slept.

Scott woke at dawn, stating flatly, "My ass will never be the same." My feet were numb, and I opted for movement to re-warm them. We enjoyed a breakfast consisting of a pint of watery milk and a Power Bar each. We were already dressed so we saw no point in hanging around. We needed to get over our inertia, to trade one form of pain for another.

WAKE UP! It wasn't really my lead, but I took it and I deserved every inch. I fought to keep the bar down. Pulling on placements that shouldn't have held, I forgot about my feet, climbing up on the sheer will to work it out. The fear-sweat ran. With each movement the ferment of terror and catabolism wafted up from inside my jacket. I used all the Load Limiters and all the screws on that pitch. I hung from the anchors bleeding from the face and knuckles. My muscles cramped, and I let the screams come loud and cathartic when the feeling rushed back into my fingers. A salutation to the mountain.

We belly-flopped into the sun around noon. At 4:30 P.M. we said a few kind words over the chopped lead rope and threw it into a bergschrund. It had done well, but it had given us the last full measure. We tied into the 8 millimeter and walked away.

I talked to Scott the other day. His voice was compressed, shot from a life that didn't have anything to do with me or the francs ticking off the payphone Smart Card. It was 1 A.M. There was a traffic jam outside the phone booth. We screamed back and forth about new bands, about the illness that made me step off a plane headed home to take a job in Paris. I said I missed him. I was missing a woman too. The longing I felt gave the beauty of Paris a fetid white underbelly. I was seeing her whole for the first time, the mysteriousness wiped away.

Suffocating clouds trap the pollution of 12 million cars and trucks beneath them. Standing in one place means breathing the same fumes over and over. The rain turns to snow. In the mountains, snow is unadulterated and white, a purge and renewal, but the city's illness infects my beloved snow, rendering it gray and viscous. There's no biting crunch underfoot, just a slick, liquid stain left over from melting and refreezing and melting again, mixed rudely with mustard-colored poodle shit and whatever runs in the streets when they open the pipes to flush the gutters. The buildings are pitted by history and the rain of industry. The Seine so polluted the homeless dare not fish for a meal.

Arguments erupt over the precious few parking places available. People can afford to shout and gesticulate here, since no one's going to reach under the seat for a 9-millimeter Glock. The real inner-city people take the Metro. "If you don't know the Metro, you don't know Paris," one of my co-workers stated condescendingly, "but I have been attacked twice in the last year." I hail Bernard Goetz every time I hail a cab. A sickening claustrophobia comes over me when I go underground. I hate sharing my intimate space with rushing, shoving imbeciles for whom idle chat is preferable to the loneliness of silence. Under the wet French streets are the sewers and the Metro. They smell about the same.

I ask myself if the routes were really hard, if we actually climbed the 400-meter snow slope that fast, if we didn't lose a day somewhere and whether I've lost my mind in the last two weeks. Scott wonders too. But he assures me that the climbs were difficult. He said, "Somewhere on (mostly) every pitch I thought it would be possible to fall—and there's not many routes where that happens for me. There was only one pitch like it on The Andromeda Strain."

It doesn't make walking to work easier. Harder if anything, since I breathe in a little more illness every day. Every hour in Paris costs me more of the strength and discipline I had a month ago. Being surrounded by people with feeble ambitions and impotent anger contaminates the fortress I have built of myself. Slowly, I allow the job to eat me and possess me just as they do. It is harder and harder to resist. The rewards are few, and knowing I do the work well only goes so far.

I've rented no-future holes before. Basement windows light the one in Paris dimly; it is farther away from wherever home is. I burrow deeper into it each night. Sunday afternoons I crawl out and feed off the commotion and energy glowing in the streets. The Champs Elysées are lit up from the Étoile to the Place Concorde 18 hours a day. The Electricité de France happily provides free Christmas lights to the city for the occasion. The taxes used to pay EDF might be well spent on sheltering some of the homeless dying a little faster than the rest of us each day. On the other hand, the streets do look pretty, and a guy is roasting chestnuts on the corner a few yards away. I think I'll go get some. After all, it is Christmas and even though I don't fit in, there is no reason to complain.

We named the route There Goes the Neighborhood in honor of Ice T, one of the few rap songwriters boasting a triple-digit IQ. We graded it ED+, 1000 meters, 5.9, A3, 90 degrees+ and it's already been mistranslated and misunderstood.

1994 AUTHOR'S NOTE

The fitting postscript to all this is the French climbing community's reaction to our Press Release and our topos. They misinterpreted us when we told the truth about how hard the routes are. *Vertical* magazine published an account where I stated that Birthright is the most difficult ice/mixed route in the Alps. There Goes the Neighborhood is actually harder and may be the most difficult route of its type in the Alps. If it isn't, then Beyond Good and Evil—in its original condition—is. The French prejudice insists that foreigners can not climb as well as the home boys— this is true of all prejudice and it exists in every nation or community in the world.

Other media transgressions include misgrading Birthright in both *Montagnes Magazine* and *High*; we gave it ED+ and they printed TD+. Our grade was conservative in the interest of not going too far. It should probably be EX if we were sticklers.

Difficulty and the commitment required to complete a route change according to conditions anyway. I want to see the truth, not someone else's judgment of what I have accomplished. In fact, since none of my new routes in France have been repeated, thus no confirmation of grade is available, how can anyone justify commenting about the climbs without quoting myself or my partners? On each pitch of the topo for There Goes the Neighborhood where 90 degrees+ is written, the number has been changed to 90 degrees (by publications). *High* wrote that the ice was only "quasi-vertical." So says the man who's never been there. Is it simply because the editor has never seen, much less climbed, more than vertical ice in the mountains that he decides without checking facts that the ice we climbed was not 90 degrees+?

Both *Montagnes Magazine* and *High* changed the name of the route on the Aiguille Sans Nom to "Here Goes the Neighborhood," proving that many of our points, whether sarcastic or simply caustic, were misunderstood.

"There Goes the Neighborhood" is the title of a song by Ice T's metal band, Body Count. It's about blacks moving into the neighborhood and running down the property values, and blacks playing rock music that has been principally white domain for the last 30 years. Kind of like the Americans visiting (or even moving to) France and poaching first ascents. Birthright comments on the general American attitude that it is "our" right to go anywhere and do anything, regardless of local custom or restriction.

I laugh hard at French climbers and their media because there is too much talk and not enough action in France. They spend too much time posing and not enough time training. The common availability of high-quality terrain causes complacency. It makes them wait for perfect conditions, when all the conveniences coincide before attempting a new route, which makes their remaining plums ripe for plucking. It just takes a bit more motivation than the locals possess.

2000 AUTHOR'S NOTE

Finally, Beyond Good and Evil was repeated. My friend Francois Marsigny is making a point of repeating and demystifying my new routes. The set-up was perfect; only the best climbers dared consider attempting the route, and being in the media spotlight, they could not afford to fail. They had to hold off until success was certain. Having waited three years for "perfect" conditions, something Andy Parkin and I never encountered during the three attempts it took to climb the route, Marsigny and Francois Damilano managed to eliminate some of the aid points we used and climbed the route in a day. (We bivouacked once.) During the second and all subsequent ascents, climbers found ice plastered eight inches thick and six feet wide over areas where we found an intermittent, narrow ice runnel interrupted by a thin crack in a corner. Bill Belcourt later said of his ascent that he protected most of the pitches with ice screws. Andy and I found the ice too thin to place even one. Although conditions improved drastically from when the first ascent was made, they were not good enough to tempt anyone onto the last four pitches—which are the most dangerous ones on this climb—so despite numerous claimed "ascents," no one has finished the route. They all traverse off after the 10th pitch.

Even though he did not finish the climb, Patrick Gabarrou claimed that the line

was, in fact, "within the easy reach of mortals," not restricted to Nietzschean su-
permen as I had brashly stated. He traversed off to easier terrain because "it is more
in keeping with the style of the route, and you can do it in a day that way." I wish
my own rationalizations could be so convenient, that my image in the mirror was
not so clear.

Equally abhorrent are the actions of Valerie Babanov, who attempted to solo the
route but failed 9 pitches up. He placed a bolt at every station to rappel from. Fucking
asshole. Andy and I got off "clean" from the top of the seventh pitch and there are
definitely anchors available that do not require drilling all the way to the top. Whatever happened to respecting the ethics of the first ascensionists?

Two years later (1997) Marsigny and Thierry Braguier repeated There Goes the
Neighborhood. They climbed it in February with one bivouac after "dropping in" from
the Grandes Montets cable-car station. Francois, who is a brilliant climber, found a
thin-ice variation to the A3 pitch, making the entire route go free in some conditions.
He said, "It was not as hard as I expected, but you guys made a greater commitment
by hiking up from Chamonix. You were further 'out there' than we were."

The first six pitches of Birthright were climbed in early 1999. The climbers added
a half-pitch variant continuing up the 90-meter corner past where we traversed out
to avoid an overhang. The new variant, which ended below the roof, was christened
Birthleft, and the six and a half pitches of both routes were equipped with permanent rap anchors to accommodate easy retreat. No one has ventured onto the upper pitches.

THE REFERENCE POINT:

JEAN-
CHRISTOPHE
LAFAILLE

INTERVIEW WITH JEAN-CHRISTOPHE LAFAILLE

October 11, 1992

After three days of good weather a storm breaks rapidly. Spindrift makes exiting off the rock wall impossible. Jean-Christophe Lafaille and Pierre Beghin begin retreating off a new route on the enormous south face of Annapurna (8091 meters). At 7200 meters Pierre plants a single, small-sized camming unit in a bottoming crack. He rappels 10 meters down a vertical, ice-choked chimney. Reaching the lower-angled snow-slope below he unweights the anchor. It shifts in the brittle Himalayan rock and then rips when he leans back to continue. Pierre falls 1500 meters. The ropes and rack go with him, leaving Jean-Christophe alone two-thirds of the way up one of the most difficult and dangerous walls in the Himalayas with little equipment. Stunned, motionless, he listens through the hiss of spindrift for any sign of life. He hears nothing.

This is the most important spiritual reference point in his life. It signifies the end of one period and the beginning of another. He doesn't recognize it yet.

Signs distinguishing these transitions matter to Jean-Christophe. Spiritual landmarks punctuate his life. Most relate to mountaineering. Born in Gap, with the Central French Alps looming above, he began climbing with his father at the age of six. This gave him, "the opportunity to progress slowly and accumulate an enormous amount of experience compared to the climber who starts later." They did easy routes at first, climbing occasionally. In 1979, at 14, Jean-Christophe started climbing seriously. Alpinism interested him the most, but he divided time equally between the crag and the mountains.

Jean-Christophe was swept along in the Sport Climbing phenomenon. The area around Gap is isolated from more fashionable Sport Climbing venues (and their fashion victims). Rather than traveling to these, Jean-Christophe developed his own "private" cliffs, such as the Roche des Arnauds. At Ceuse, the Sector Lafaille, which he and several friends developed, is renowned for its very hard but above all very beautiful routes. Jean-Christophe's individualism separated him from the "super-mediatized" course of the French climbing scene. Asked why he didn't want to be part of all that, he answers, "The leading clique among French climbers lacks ideas and initiative, whether they are alpine climbers or sport climbers. In 1985–86, Christophe Profit began his string of enchainments in the Mont Blanc Massif, virtually running up and down several peaks in one day. All the other leading alpinists began copying him."

Today the same self-proclaimed "leaders" copy Jean-Christophe by going to big alpine walls alone, taking their time. Marc Batard spent 19 days on the Dru. Francois Marsigny contrived to be on the French Direct of the Dru during Christmas, perhaps in order to attract more media attention. Jean-Christophe continues, "Many Sport Climbing cliffs came into vogue, then disappeared from sight as activists left their marks and went elsewhere, looking for the new and different area or a style that might attract more media attention." Living away from the "pressure-cooker" lifestyle in Chamonix kept Jean-Christophe from being sucked under by the pathological inertia most resident climbers exhibit. He also managed to avoid the murderous peer-pressure and copycat ascents common to the scene. Jean-Christophe kept to himself and worked on his own projects. In the autumn of 1986, during his military service, he placed well in several competitions held on natural rock, notably at Troubat and Biot. In 1987 he free-soloed Reve de Gosse, 8a+ at the Roche des Arnauds. Starting with a hard bouldering crux, the 18-meter-high route overhangs throughout and becomes "a question of endurance" at the top. The climbing world took notice, but Jean-Christophe returned to his secret projects and unknown cliffs. This period of determined work resulted in many new routes. Perhaps the most important of these is Patience at the Roche des Arnauds. He graded the climb 8c, and although several people have worked on it, the route remains unrepeated.

After weeks in the claustrophobic cave repeating and rehearsing the technical, dynamic movements of Patience, he longed to see the horizon stretching away toward the unknown. He drove four hours to Chamonix where he soloed the Swiss Route on the Grand Capucin (300 meters, 6b, A0). It was like flicking a switch. Recognizing he was saturated with Sport Climbing, he decided to spend more time in the mountains. Alone.

Jean-Christophe closed this period of his career with a reference point. He wanted to hang something on the shutting door. Privilege du Serpent 7c+, solo. As he described it, the 25-meter-high route has "good holds with big dynos between them. There was no way I could have downclimbed if I'd wanted to, and technically, the higher one climbs, the harder the route is." Several friends filmed him soloing it, and every time he walks beneath it now he remembers well his previous life as a Sport Climber.

During the summer of 1989 Jean-Christophe spent five weeks visiting Yosemite, the City of Rocks, and American Fork. He participated in the annual Snowbird Competition, where he placed 23rd or 25th, "like everyone else who happened to be short." He returned to France, picked up his wife, Veronique, and departed for two months in Morocco. The Atlas Mountains made him think about the Mont Blanc Massif and what he wanted to accomplish there.

First, he went to the east face of the Grand Pilier d'Angle on the Italian Face of Mont Blanc. He climbed Divine Providence (900 meters on the pillar, 6b, A3, plus 600 meters of snow and ice to the summit of Mont Blanc). Thierry Renault and Alain Ghersen had just made the first free-ascent (7c+). Conscious of the good conditions at altitude, Jean-Christophe rested briefly and then soloed the Pilier Rouge Directissime on the Broulliard Face of Mont Blanc. The 400-meter route goes mostly free at 6c+/7a, with one A3 pitch. The climbing begins at 3800 meters. After descending the route, he bivouacked in the Eccles Hut, then soloed the Bonatti Route (400 meters, 6a, A2) on the same face the following day. Each climb was self-supported, without helicopter surveillance, gear caches, or assistance "because doing things this way has more integrity." The following winter Jean-Christophe soloed the Bonatti Route on the Grand Capucin, (400 meters, 6b, A1, or 7a), the Harlin Route on the south face of the Fou (300 meters, 6b, A2, or 7b), and the American Direct on the Dru. Bad weather prevented him from continuing past the "jammed block" (600 meters to the block, 6b). "It was a good winter—I did one route per month."

During the years dedicated to Sport Climbing Jean-Christophe trained for the mountains. He ran hills; taught himself to navigate with map, compass, and altimeter; and paid attention to weather patterns. On rest days he slept outside to test bivouac systems. He expressed his commitment to the hard climbs of the future by climbing easier routes in bad weather. Jean-Christophe had a plan and didn't want to confront any surprises along the way. In Gap he worked on his equipment and trained. Studying topos and photographs, he hunted for shadows signifying corners or cracks, lines of weakness. And he found some.

During the brutally hot summer of 1991 Jean-Christophe prepared himself for "something big" by soloing a new route on the east face of Mont Maudit: Ballade pour Melanie. At 650-meters high, it featured a compulsory section of 6c, which is "very exposed," and a pitch of A1. He pared his equipment further, and, carrying enough food to last four days, returned to the Pilier d'Angle. Beginning August 11 he soloed a new route on the east face, right of Divine Providence which he named Un Autre Monde 6c/7a, A3. Jean-Christophe continued up a new route on the Central Freney Pillar. L'Ecume des Jours, 6c, A2, is independent up to the Chandelle where it joins the original route for one pitch. "It was more logical than contriving something independent just to be independent. Besides, I wanted to avoid putting any bolts in the Chandelle. Placing bolts up there is too far away from the spirit of the previous generations. I respect what other men did in the mountains. I try to abide their ethics even though more highly evolved technology is available to me."

The French climbing magazines dedicated several pages of photographs and text to these routes. Jean-Michel Asselin from *Vertical* magazine christened him, "the Mystic of the Extreme," setting the stage for the future. Jean-Christophe signed contracts with Charlet-Moser, Millet, Beal, and Petzl. The French Mountaineering Federation awarded him their annual prize for mountaineering achievement: The Crystal. Philippe Poulet, a photographer for the prestigious Gamma agency, sold articles and pictures, organized helicopters to ensure coverage of future ascents, and sounded the Jean-Christophe trumpet. Jean-Christophe quietly acknowledged all this, knowing it a necessary tool to finance larger expeditions in the years to come.

He planned to visit the Himalayas in the autumn of 1993, believing he needed another year of experience to succeed on something big his first time out. His arduous "preparation" resulted in another important first ascent: Chemin des Etoiles (1000 meters, 6b, A3) on the Grandes Jorasses. The route doesn't solve the problem of the huge El Cap-like wall on the left side of the Croz Spur but is very serious nonetheless. "The worst part was two pitches of 65-degree compact 'dirt' the dry winter had left exposed. Normally it's snow and dead easy, but I had to aid my way up on gear that would barely hold weight."

Jean-Christophe tried the route in March, but bad weather forced retreat 600 meters up the wall. He finished the climb in April, spending four days alone. "The bad part about succeeding was dragging my two haulbags through waist-deep, wet snow down the Italian side." Almost as soon as *Vertical* broke the news, an invitation to the Himalayas changed the course of his life. Another reference point.

Pierre Beghin intended to attempt a new route on the massive south face of Annapurna. He believed the combination of Jean-Christophe's technical expertise and his own vast Himalayan experience would prove crucial for success on the difficult and dangerous line. Jean-Christophe accepted eagerly, advancing his schedule a year or so in the process. They plotted, they planned, and after the monsoon season, they flew to Nepal.

Katmandu didn't faze Jean-Christophe. He'd spent two months in the North African desert, so the Third World was nothing new to him. "It's just like any big city, really," he stated, and then smiling, "as far as big cities go, I liked San Francisco better." He didn't much like the bureaucratic hassles involved with climbing in Nepal, but the people, the countryside, and the feeling of having embarked on a magnificent adventure thrilled Jean-Christophe. He says he'd return today "as much to see the people and the land as to go climbing." Because he'd passed much of his youth hiking and camping, and purposely bivouacked on a number of routes—a rare thing among today's French alpinists—living in a tent was easy for him. He whiled away bad weather listening to classical music on his Walkman, reading, and hiking around to get a better feeling for the mountain.

Pierre Beghin expected the difficult new route, climbed Alpine Style, to be his great Himalayan statement and one of his last expeditions to the big mountains. His previous climbs, the solo of Kangchenjunga, then K2, Dhauligiri, Jannu, and Manaslu in Alpine Style, prepared him for it. Soloing the final 1500 meters of hard, technical terrain on the south face of Makalu may have been his finest achievement.

The pair climbed the lower face at night to avoid the unbelievable stonefall generated by the rockbands. Stonefall rained perpetually during the day but froze silent at night. "It was an impressive bombardment. I've never encountered, or even heard of anything like it." (Alex MacIntyre was killed by stonefall attempting what became the Catalonian Route on this same face.) The initial ice and mixed terrain rose 1500 meters, continuously 55 degrees with passages of 90 degrees. Pierre left 150 meters of fixed rope at 6600 meters to facilitate the descent, but otherwise they climbed in pure Alpine Style; simul-soloing and carrying everything on their backs. The steep wall offered few bivouac sites.

On the third day Jean-Christophe and Pierre reached a band of "curious" Himalayan rock. "It was like bricks, or café trays stacked on top of each other. Not really loose, and surprisingly compact in places." They free-climbed where possible, bypassing overhanging sections on ice and hard mixed ground. An unavoidable roof went at A2/A3. "We got around one nasty-looking wall on a perfect, frozen waterfall, 25 to 30 meters high. Wild." According to their photos, seven pitches up the rockband should have placed them on a ledge above the waterfall, at 7300 meters. Instead, they discovered a 70-degree slope of dense, black ice. They couldn't chop a platform for the tent and had to bivouac hanging in their harnesses. Unable to fire up the stove because of the wind, the night trudged by slowly, foodless and bitter. "It was awful and drained everything out of us. Luckily, we managed to slide most of our bodies into the sleeping bags."

The next morning they climbed to 7500 meters, "within 150 meters of the easy climbing, we could see where the angle eased back." They fought through these final difficulties before the diving barometric pressure developed into a storm. Wind and spindrift stopped them cold. They agreed to descend. Wasted and slightly out of control, the pair took huge risks on every rappel. At one point Pierre was willing to rap off a single tied-off ice screw, but Jean-Christophe hammered in one of his tools to back it up.

After two more rappels, Pierre set the anchor that would allow them to reach lower-angled terrain and arranged the gear over his shoulder. Holstering both ax and hammer was too complicated. Annoyed, he handed his ax to Jean-Christophe who stood on a small ledge, out of reach of the anchor. His years of experience muddled by fatigue, the confusion of the storm, and the need to get down quickly, Pierre leaned back on a single anchor without any backup. It failed and he fell. Jean-Christophe watched, sickened, but certain that "he would stop himself. Even though it was so steep I believed he would self-arrest . . . I won't ever forget thinking that."

He was alone; the storm raged on.

Realizing that "it would have been impossible to go up," Jean-Christophe downclimbed through relatively difficult mixed-terrain to their last bivouac and 20 meters of rope they'd left at 7000 meters. He spent 48 hours cowering there while the storm blew itself out. He ran out of food and there was little gas left for the stove. During those hours, he schemed with the cunning instinct that keeps hunted men alive. He figured, "Once I recover the extra rope, pitons, and fuel left at 6500 meters, it'll be a simple matter of rappelling and staying out of the way of the stonefall."

The following afternoon during intermittent clearings, he retreated, using a combination of downclimbing and rappelling. After Pierre's fall, Jean-Christophe found himself with two carabiners, a sling, and two ice tools. He rapped off whatever he had; the tent poles went first. He hammered in two sections at a time as far as they'd go and called it good. His long experience of soloing up (and down) routes in the Alps allowed him to clinically assess each problem, find the solution, and execute it without freaking out. "The sum of everything I'd done over the last 10 years got me out of that situation—mostly the solo climbing. Still, I had trouble getting myself going. I almost stayed at 7000 meters because I was scared—scared of falling."

About 150 meters above the ramp that led back to the fixed rope, Jean-Christophe lost a crampon. It tumbled away and disappeared from sight. He continued downclimbing, sliding one foot and then stabilizing himself with his tools and the other foot. At the top of the ramp, he discovered the crampon sticking out from behind an ice flute. It had stopped in softer snow. Hanging off his tools, he replaced the crampon. "It was a sign to me that I was going to make it, things were going my way."

He reached the rope, which was fixed in 50-meter sections, and rappelled. As he stood at the first changeover, a falling stone smashed into his right forearm, compound fracturing both bones. It swelled immediately, filling his jacket-sleeve. "My morale was high when I got to the rope because I knew I was going to live. Ten minutes later I was as down as I have ever been . . . I didn't think I could make it off the wall." He continued down to the bivy at 6500 meters and spent a sleepless night. "I'd had it. I was at the end of my reserves. I laid there in my sleeping bag, thinking that I was suffering too much. I had given everything, but I'd lost. It was a cold, cold thought, without judgment. I knew that all I had to do was roll a half-turn toward base camp, tumble off the ledge, and it would be over. I thought this without emotion."

The sun came up bright and hard the next morning. Jean-Christophe spent the

day eating, drinking, and recharging himself. The condition of his arm hadn't worsened during the night and, hope springing eternal, he felt he just might make it. At
nightfall, as the stonefall ceased, Jean-Christophe continued down. "I thought about
Doug Scott and Joe Simpson and figured, those guys gave all they had, and then
gave more. They fought and fought and did not give up. I should at least do the
same—give everything I have. I still had a little left." From 6500 meters he rapped
200 meters, but then left the ropes because they were too hard to pull with only
one hand and his mouth. He downclimbed the 55-degree ice using a single ax.

The rope they'd left to get back over the 'schrund was frozen and no amount of
yanking and chopping and biting would loosen it. "This chipped tooth is from that
incident," he says as he smiles and points it out. So on the morning of the fifth day
after the accident, his eighth on the wall, Jean-Christophe downclimbed into the
bergschrund. Sheltered from stonefall by the overhanging lip, and not far from base
camp, he relaxed. After unfastening his helmet, he threw his pack off and lay down
for 30 minutes. He felt that 10 years had just been subtracted from his life. "I will
never, ever go into the mountains again," he swore.

Before the climb, he and Pierre easily ran from the 'schrund to base camp in half
an hour, but it had snowed half a meter while they were on the face. The tent they'd
left at advance base camp was buried and frozen solid. Jean-Christophe practically
went crazy when he couldn't get at the food cached inside. He took two tubes of
honey from a Slovenian team's tent. "I was scared to take more. Now, I don't know

why," he recalls, and he followed their tracks toward base camp. A helicopter over-
flew the glacier and he realized that others knew something had gone wrong. He
was no longer alone.

Then he saw a figure. Far away on the moraine someone was running toward him
carrying something in his hand. After eight days of virtual slow motion, Jean-
Christophe was amazed at the runner's speed and agility. Five minutes passed before
one of the Nepalese base camp staff, holding a full teapot and a sack of food, wrapped
his arms around Jean-Christophe, and they both burst into tears.

After several operations on his arm, Jean-Christophe climbs well on rock again
and intends to travel to the USA next spring. "I want to do a Big Wall in Yosemite
and work on my English. I never thought it could happen, but I really enjoyed the
western United States and the American people." Although Jean-Christophe's ap-
preciation of wilderness makes him somewhat of an outsider in Chamonix's mechanized, test-lab atmosphere, he appears to have made himself at home with the
American point of view.

"To the French, wilderness, as defined by our mountain magazines, is very different from the American perspective. In France you see photos featuring man in
the foreground, large in the frame, wearing brightly colored clothing—man con-
quering the mountain, man being more important than the mountain. In the USA
the photos are more like Japanese watercolors; man is always small, dwarfed by an
environment which is huge. Man is a visitor; the wilderness is forever." He never
would have guessed that this is the general view Americans have of the mountains.
He assumed the "fast-food attitude" would be directed toward the wilderness as well.

"I was surprised at how open the people were, how concerned they were about
cleaning up after themselves in the mountains, and treating the environment properly. The French are not like that and it's embarrassing to see other French climbers in the mountains—especially in the Third World. We are very colonial in that
regard."

This summer Jean-Christophe is teaching at the Ecole Nationale du Ski et de
l'Alpinisme (ENSA), training future Guides and Aspirant Guides. It pays well and
gives him the chance to impart some of his hard-won knowledge to others. "I want
to help some of the young, less-experienced climbers avoid the modern traps. The
French scene generates tremendous pressure. Guys move quickly from hard rock
climbing to hard alpinism, and then they try to solo big, difficult routes without
adequate experience. It is just poker, and although you can gamble and win one or
two times, luck runs dry quickly. Every future route increases the risk whether you
recognize it or not. What I learned 10 years ago saved my life on Annapurna, but
climbers without the same background will try these things, and they aren't going
to get away with it."

Despite his declaration in the bergschrund beneath Annapurna, Jean-Christophe hasn't given up on Himalayan climbing. He had plans to go to the Shishapangma with the Slovenians who helped evacuate him from Annapurna Base Camp after the accident. "I wanted to go with them because we got along well together, there were no sponsors to please, no last great problem to solve, just a climbing adventure among friends. I need to test my head to see if I've absorbed everything and can actually go on climbing. I also thought it would be a way to get out from under the pressure of the French scene. But the trip fell through, and now I'm going to Cho Oyu having bought a place on a French Commercial Expedition. It's a way to get there," he states with resignation. More eagerly he allows, "I spotted a 1500-meter-high route I can solo if I feel good." Jean-Christophe has other plans as well, but he's keeping quiet about them. "I certainly won't be going to one of the current 'fashionable' walls. It is a joke to me; the fashion passed from the south face of Lhotse to the west face of Makalu and everyone who's anyone will be throwing themselves at it until it gets done. I have different ideas. I mean, they are attractive mountains and all, but those walls are measuring sticks for other men. To remain true to myself, I need to find my own challenges and weave my life around them. Most important at the moment is to close this chapter, to absorb it and put a name on it, build a monument to it and leave it behind. I don't want to wear the weight of Annapurna around my neck for the rest of my life."

2000 AUTHOR'S NOTE

After nearly two years of rest and therapy, Jean-Christophe began climbing again with a vengeance. He climbed Shishapangma in 1994, and made a solo traverse of Gasherbrum I and II in a three-day round-trip in 1996. In April 1999 Jean-Christophe returned to the monolithic wall left of the Croz Spur of the Grandes Jorasses. Overcoming pitches up to A4 on his new line, named Decolage, he eventually joined the late Slavko Sveticic's route Manitua. Climbing this route's crux pitch (A3) brought him to the second névé of the original Croz Spur Route. He called it good at that point and retreated after spending eight days on the wall. During a trip to the USA in January 2000, Jean-Christophe made a quick repeat of Will Gadd's M9 test-piece, Amphibian in Vail, Colorado, and later in the spring he climbed Manaslu (8163 meters), his sixth 8000-meter peak.

Jean-Christophe's reputation in France these days is that of a "media" climber. Reporters for both specialized and *"grande publique"* press pay attention to his exploits. He maintains his relationships with sponsors, earning money by climbing, but he still works with the ENSA training guides, "giving something back." While he is a public figure, and one of the better-known mountain climbers in Europe, I think Annapurna gave him a depth of character rarely seen among climbers made popular by the media.

NO TIME TO

IT'S A COLD,

COLD WORLD.

(Woodcut by

Randy Rackliff)

CRY

It would have been funny if it wasn't happening to me. Other guys had lost lovers and more over an opportunity like this. I weighed the selfishness of their sacrifices against the total self-fulfillment offered in return. No hardcore player ever questioned whether it was worth it or not. She didn't like my going away for two months at a time each spring and fall. This trip, so soon after the last, might ruin our relationship.

We talked over lunch at an outdoor café, neutral territory where neither of us had eaten before. I ordered a spinach and goat cheese salad. She took a large coffee with cream, no sugar. Tension knotted my chest. She fiddled with her engagement ring. Despite my talk of commitment, she knew there was something more important in my life. I began bluntly, asking how she'd respond if I went to Everest in two weeks. She smirked; clearly prepared to deal with the situation. She must have read the faxed invitation.

"This café is no place to discuss these things." Her body language suggested we find more privacy. I knew if we went to the apartment before resolving this, I'd give in. It had never been my place. I never established a male presence in it, and I wasn't comfortable staying there. Its soft lines and light made me feel vulnerable. She had invited me to live with her, but I felt like a trespasser.

Suddenly, playing it by ear felt like a mistake. Walking out first was the only available defense. I could preserve myself by leaving her to pursue my own absorbing and cathartic task. On the other hand, she might walk before I developed the courage. Her maturity was frightening. It made me realize how infantile climbing mountains might be in comparison.

"Look, Allan, you just returned from an expedition. You've been home three weeks and haven't been strong enough to give me anything—'recovering' you said. I thought we were making progress, but leaving again . . . I don't know."

She was rightfully jealous of the attention I pay to mountains. I certainly don't give her very much when I lay insomniac at night wishing I loved her as well as I love them. She used to provoke the same humility that climbing does. Lately she can't. I don't hold it against her. She comes second to Everest and my career.

I lost another close friend on the last expedition. His fall off Kangchenjunga tore open old scars that time won't heal. There's an ache where he used to be that isolates me so I don't fit in anymore. But experience earned from climbing can't quell the fear of her walking out on me forever. I thought I had prepared myself for this confrontation, but if she leaves first, I'll be lost—possessed by her, not self-possessed. So I attack, solving the problem the way I always have, because my delusion says the outcome is inevitable anyway. It's a bad habit, but I flex my muscles.

"I'm going anyway, whether you agree to stay involved with me or not. I don't want to lose you, Monique, but Everest matters more. It could make my career."

I am frank and think it's a good effort. Lighting a cigarette, I signal the waiter for an ashtray and continue, "What I need to know, I guess, is whether I should leave my things at our place or ship them back to the States . . ."

She removes one of her own Dunhills from her bag and leans forward to light it off of mine. She exhales her first lungful into my face, something I had never had the courage to do to anyone.

"I'll take care of shipping it for you, since you'll be busy with sponsors and organization. I'll send it to your mother's place, or is there another address I should use?"

She stabbed appropriately low. I'm 26 years old, no job to speak of, and no permanent address. I spend all of my time climbing mountains or writing about climbing them. A dysfunctional family in the States is my safety net, so I'd pinned my hope to a future with her. But I can't give up a small chance at the world's highest mountain in order to preserve our relationship. Everest called, and despite my obstinate love for her, I answered. I accepted the pain as a penalty due for surviving when others did not.

I considered blowing off Kangchenjunga because of her. For the first time in my life, I almost put another human being before climbing. I went, but it had been difficult to justify. Ignoring Everest is out of the question though. If I climb it without using supplementary oxygen, do it alone, or by a new route, I'll be set for life with sponsors and a yearly corporate lecture tour. Sometimes I ask, why can't I climb simply because I like it? Why is it always business these days? I'm too far along the path to ever go back to zero. Success breeds the taste for more success. I reject any sensations weaker than those provoked by climbing on the greatest mountains of the world. I cut things away. I do without the things other people take for granted. I can make the cut again. I know I will because if I quit climbing, I'll be nobody.

Holding both coffee and cigarette in one hand, she continued fingering the ring I gave her and smiled cynically.

"Allan, I told you I needed someone with me and you promised to stay."

"No, I said I loved you and would do what I could to help you, that the mountains around here would be enough for me. But I qualified the phrase by saying 'for a while.'"

"My career is at a critical point and it's hard. I need support and help and if you can't straighten your spine to give me what I'm asking for, then I guess I'll have to find someone who can."

"You knew who I was when you fell in love with me."

"What I see now is a man who breaks his promises. You're scared to make the 'total commitment' you claim you made to the mountains to a mere human relationship. Allan, you can't give me what I need."

I'm used to having my own way all the time and never imagined she'd react so strongly. Her conditional dismissal sank in, but as I started to respond, she continued.

"Don't interrupt, this is disagreeable enough already. When you decided to go, why didn't you just do it? You don't even have the balls to tell me one way or the other. I'll help you pack your things. Use my airline contacts to make the departure go more smoothly if you need to. You can stay in the apartment too, and I may even let you make love to me. But once you are gone, it's over. For good."

Her clinical practicality surprised me. I wasn't sure how to handle it. I wanted her hate. I wanted her to despise me so I could walk away with no remorse. If she threw me out and kicked me when I was down I could pity myself. There's climbing motivation to be found in that. Instead, she simply showed me the door. I'd accept the offer of a roof and her help, which was more opportunistic than practical. I'd probably sleep with her too.

I had thought we'd found some stability with each other. I'd come to enjoy being able to count on her, and us. I invited chaos to join us by applying my pragmatic, black-and-white, high-altitude values to our flat, social world. Up there everything is bright and obvious, choosing right means winning, survival. The wrong decision often ends in suffering, and perhaps death. Down here I won't die, but I wondered at that moment whether living could actually be worse.

I once laughed as my friends struggled to leave their homes without breaking them so there remained some structure and support to return to. They were shocked by my mechanical rejection of home and city. I impressed them by exercising my singular dedication to mountaineering at someone else's expense. I lived for it back then. I seized every possible chance to display my commitment and ferociously put down whatever obstructed my path.

Now I play with less resolve. Singular desire doesn't drive me up mountains. Instead, my investment chains me to them. The selfish gestures I made for climbing wounded other people, binding me further. I love climbing. I love her too and choosing between them was not as clear-cut as it once would have been. I wished the doctrine of black and white didn't dog my heels and that I hadn't educated her with it. I never anticipated she might turn my all-or-nothing theories against me. I tired of the conflict and wondered why this one trip couldn't just slide by unnoticed. I avoided the detail in her words. A dose of denial could make the relationship wonderful again.

I could tell the strong words felt good on her tongue. She was willing to push, but couldn't tell how much I would accept. There was a point to be made and a point at which to turn back from the edge. The longer I maintained silence, the less determined she looked.

"Allan, say something. If I honestly mean something to you, say so. It might not change things, but I'll have heard you and it will help me get through the rest."

Then, tenderly, "How I've wished you'd say you loved me. You never understood how much I needed that from you. I don't think it's too much to ask for every now and then. I wanted you once. I used to believe in you . . . you make it hard for me to do that these days."

I stared blankly, eyes straying inward to the picture of an elegant line traced on a mountain wall. It was direct and simple, not at all like this.

After waiting for a response, she said, "Look, let's do away with the posturing and the resentment. I know you're angry with me and with yourself—but let go of it. It shouldn't have to be like this. The silence scares me."

The cigarette smoke stung my eyes. Tears formed. Below the table edge, I fingered a fold of skin through my shirt and pinched until a dull ache spread. I removed my sunglasses. I became brightly aware that if I touched her cheek lightly or if she extended her hand, we might reach an understanding. I had an opportunity to give in, to admit my love and my desire to continue. I hesitated, but I couldn't do it. It was tough to tell whether too much really had come between us or if I was pretending so I could walk away. I wanted to alienate her enough that if I died on this expedition, it wouldn't be a problem for her. I pinched hard enough to leave a bruise and then put the glasses back on. I knew the formula.

"I guess I still resent the fact that you want to change me and bring me to the whip."

"You know that's not true anymore. You know I've changed."

Hardening, "You still have your agenda—the house, the cars, a family just like your own—and you believe I can fulfill some part of it. I have a plan too, and it doesn't involve making any concessions or taking any direction." I looked into her eyes as I said it, watching her realize what was coming.

"Stop, Allan. We still have a chance if you can hold back now. I know you. If you go on, you'll wreck everything just to prove you're strong enough to do it and to stand alone afterwards."

"Monique, we've gotten too good at hurting each other."

EVEREST,

8848 METERS,

TIBET

"I'm leaning on you because I want you to realize how much this means and to show you how hard it is on me when you reject me and go away to the mountains. I need to know I've done everything I can to save us."

Her self-control proved her belief in what she said. The profiteer in me argued that I could eat the cake too, if I was willing to work and fake it a little. I considered caring for the wounds instead of salting them, but there was no going back without looking wishy-washy. My ego depends on an appearance of strength and decisiveness, it insists I do only those things I do very well. I'm good at choosing what's important in my life—as long as it's climbing. I'm especially adept at hurting people who do not deserve to be hurt.

"Maybe we can live together and maybe we can't, but to remain lovers would take greater compromise than I am willing to make. You might not forgive me for leaving, ever. We might never be friends again and that will cut me hard and deep. But I know I have the capacity to forget emotional pain. I can get over it. I'm going to walk away. I'm going to the mountains because they give me something you could never replace."

I rose deliberately from the chair, crushed the cigarette underfoot, and pushed my sunglasses up. I paid the bill with some crumpled francs, leaving a ludicrous tip because I didn't want to stand around while the waiter made change. I stared at her, resigned. Her face was a silent shriek of anguish. Her shoulders sagged under the weight. I ignored her pain.

"I'll pick up my gear tomorrow while you're at work and stay with Jean-Luc until

I leave. I'll be out of touch for a while. I don't want to know what kind of man you end up with . . . good-bye, Monique. It was good between us."

My hangover is awful. Hindsight is brutally clear. I see the burning bridge and my future in flames. Is this what I really want? No. But I made it happen. I couldn't break my habits. I was too scared to show tenderness, so I responded with all-purpose anger instead. I couldn't level the wall of resentment and fear I used to protect myself. Maybe someday I'll find a woman for whom I will. But this morning I relive yesterday and try to classify the subjects objectively: should Everest head the list in terms of importance or the woman I sacrificed for a chance to climb it? With a pounding head, I open the first beer of the new day. Forgetting my mistakes might be enough as a start. All I have to do is get through this moment. Then the next. It'll be easier after that.

2000 AUTHOR'S NOTE

Rewriting this was tough. The original style was odd and I'm not certain why I chose it. I wrote in the *Bright Lights, Big City* method where all the "I"s were "you"s. For example:

"It would have been funny if it wasn't happening to you. The other guys had lost a lover, some more, over an opportunity like this. You weighed the selfishness of their sacrifices against the total self-fulfillment offered in return. None of the hardcore ever questioned whether it was worth it or not. Eventually it had to happen to you. She didn't like you going away for two months at a time each spring and fall. You suspected that this trip, so soon after the last, might ruin your relationship."

But the point of view got in the way of the story, so for this collection I rewrote it in first person. I think it stronger this way.

The piece is a rendition of every conversation I had with every woman I ever left to go climbing. I remember many of these talks, but have blocked others. I behaved terribly to people if they stepped between fulfillment of my ambition and myself. I always figured they could be easily replaced. And I was right as long as I maintained shallow relationships.

I changed with time, opening myself to diverse experiences. I also learned to compromise more often. Intimacy improved with women, of course, but most powerfully between my climbing partners and myself. I learned I could love them. Love translated into trust and we became stronger in the mountains, which is not as mercenary as it sounds. No one taught me better than Scott Backes. We loved so hard we transcended the making of mistakes.

The article helped me recognize some of my own behavior. I did not necessarily resolve the bad habits, but I noticed them. Monique represents many women. The protagonist represents me, as well as many other men. I saw such cruelty over the years as men exercised their selfishness. I can't condemn them. Those egocentric acts resulted in quite an evolution in both the alpine climbing and the climbers themselves. Although everyone hurt equally in the end, it is easiest to blame pain on those who act in their own self-interest.

More often than not, however, climbers involved themselves with women who had no idea what they were getting into. Many women had never taken second place to anything, much less the mountains. I loved several despite the fact they were not conscious of their own plans to rein me in. Monique confronted her programming. Few I met managed the same.

When I wrote the first draft, I listened a lot to a band called Opposition. In particular, a line in the song titled "Five Minutes" seemed relevant: "She wants five minutes, maybe a lifetime." We grow up believing in the sanctity of one relationship that lasts "forever." Those who break the pattern are vilified. But when the right man finds the absolutely right woman, neither makes huge concessions to appease the other. Coexistence is not effortless, but it can be graceful nonetheless.

THIS IS WHAT YOU WANT,

DURING
THE FIRST
ASCENT OF
DEPRIVATION,
MOUNT
HUNTER,
ALASKA

(Photo by

Scott Backes)

THIS IS WHAT
YOU GET

What we do is never understood but always merely praised and blamed.
Frederich Nietzsche, *The Gay Science,* 1882

I used to live in the Alps. Their hard lines and hard routes defined me as a man. Although there's more pollution and more hypocrisy, Salt Lake City is soft. Here, it is easy to settle for less, and easy to hate myself for doing so. I had to get out, to recover the self-respect I'd lost in the city.

Another mountain adventure rife with escape and denial. I read accounts of Alaskan climbing and convinced myself I could apply my lightweight, speed-dependent ethic up there. I liked talking about my plans with other people. I showed cavalier confidence in my ability and the certainty of success. I used the ruse of shy understatement and casual affinity with failure to make my ego appear smaller than it is.

Scott Backes and I lasciviously paged through *High Alaska*, the Playmate Calendar of high, hard mountains. We underlined phrases and drew our own routes onto the walls depicted in Washburn's revealing photographs. The whole idea was more seductive than it should have been. The simple fact is this: when you go to Alaska, you get your ass kicked. I'd been beaten up by those mountains once, so I *should* have known. Other climbers gave me free advice based on their asses having been whipped up there and I *could* have listened. But, romantic that I am, I still believe in breaking karmic chains, in going against the grain and defining my own limits myself. With our fantasy complete, we planned to do a new route on each of the three big peaks in the Alaska Range during a six-week stay.

In the city I pretended to myself that sleeping in a portaledge night after night wouldn't be so bad. I fantasized that I could lead pitches quickly with an enormous pack. I said I didn't mind hauling, following with jumars, or chopping ledges out of the ice for every bivouac. I loudly insisted that I wouldn't mind aid climbing when we had to—I ruled the sub-zero aid belaying out of my mind. I even convinced myself that the routes would be so hard that we'd need at least 15 cams and dozens of pitons on the rack, new ropes for every climb, and a selection of stoves and sleeping bags to choose from. I allowed the gear I own and the quest for pure technical difficulty to get in the way of sensible route choices. All the gear we dragged up to Talkeetna barely fit into one airplane. I flew into the mountains with a Black Hole Bag on my lap and one numbed arm pressed hard against the rear window. The view wasn't what it's cracked up to be.

> *Dear Diary—I have the same song going around and around. It doesn't improve my state of mind, no matter how appropriate the lyrics are. John Lydon's screeching vocals can't compete with the howl of the airplanes, and it grates my nerve endings raw. I keep my head down. I keep my mind turned off. I watch dumbly as the hordes disembark, load their sleds and packs, and march purposefully toward their objective. Invariably, they disappear knee-deep into "the trench" and trudge on snowshoes, or with skins attached to their skis down Heartbreak Hill. So far, none of them have had the vision to actually ski down, or better yet, ride their sleds, as they make their way toward the West Buttress of McKinley. The entertainment value of this parade is meager.*

The song has six different words, only two of which are verbs. These are organized into two repetitive five-word phrases that go on for 5 minutes and 15 seconds. Its monotonous peal describes my Alaskan experience perfectly: "This is what you want, this is what you get."

I learned a long time ago not to trust anyone else's weather forecast. Since then I've usually gone by my own nose instead of bowing to another's "expertise." After all, I've been in the mountains enough to figure it out myself . . . but we missed a bunch of good days while we sat at base camp listening to the NOAA weather channel forecast disaster.

On the other hand, maybe we weren't desperate enough to go up there yet. And for what we intended, we had to be desperate and insane, to want it badly enough that all the lame excuses couldn't stand in our way. We hadn't been in the BIG mountains for a awhile, and it takes time to reassure ourselves that we do know how to do this.

> *Yo Diary—Snow white and we suffocate with our dreams wrapped around us, with the days ticking by. Inch by inch it deepens, trapping ambition beneath the familiar face, a clock, the wall, the face where we would play out our drama, spend our selves and spend our power in tribute to our gods given one half*

of one chance. But here, down here the pitter-patter silence of snow wraps up our dreams in a box of its own, ties us in ribbons of defeat and desire. The silent waves of weak fronts and weakness push us down until the mundane, the hopeless routine and the futurelessness becomes worth living for.

I live without purpose, neck-deep in the mire of futile hope. I have a goal, but it is so vague that it's hard even for me to put my hands on it. The hordes are still striving toward the West Buttress with their hard resolve and headbanging intensity—the weather is what it is, the packs are as heavy as they are, conditions do not matter. They just keep hitting it again and again and making a little progress (or not) toward their goal each day. For them there are no confusing options, just the one way of doing the one thing. For us there is second-guessing and doubt, double-talk and speculation. We're supposed to be the experts too, so there's no one to tell us what to do or how to do it—much less when. We're inventing a new game and there aren't any rules yet. We depend on our frail, sometimes insufficient but often adequate experience to tell us how to go about climbing something.

We tried the route to the left of the Moonflower. The white stuff wasn't ice. Scott almost fell. We weren't climbing well enough to do the route "my way"; too heavy to go fast, too light to go slow. I knew we were going to fail as soon as I lifted the pack, but we had to try as long as the weather was okay and we didn't find a pitch that could stop us. Scott found it though, so we turned back. The day was annoying enough to let us know that our strategy was wrong; therefore, we were wrong.

We marched back to our tent platform in the middle of the glacier; each man alone dragging a rope in the silence, each carrying the burden of his aggravation and his questions. We sat among the previous night's pissholes watching Steve Mascioli and Joe Josephson continue up Mugs' route. We hated ourselves and wished it would storm so they'd fail too. We were small, pitiful men. I broke the wearing silence, "Look, let's do the thing we're good at—let's do something we can run on. Let's carry the light packs. No one can go lighter than we can. I'd rather climb something easier in three days than struggle day after day with a few hard pitches at a time and sit out the storms and ration our food and all that *High Alaska* rulebook bullshit." The words squirted out in the best manic-depressive style. The wonderful smile Scott sometimes shares kept getting bigger and bigger until we were both laughing in agreement. After all, that's what we came up here to do.

Michael Kennedy and Greg Child arrived in base camp. We told them we'd tried "their" line and wouldn't be going back. I invited them to go up and get punished in our place. They were ready to go after it Big-Wall style and stay on it for days, prepared to do whatever it took. I was still asking myself if I was ready for Mount Hunter in any style.

Dear Useless Diary, I want to move! I want to do a route that I can get up and down fast. To go and go and go until it's done. I don't want to have to chop a ledge to sleep on. Fuck the huge packs. Fuck the haulbag. Ditch all that food and fuel. Forget hard, psycho-climbing; leave it for someplace where the weather is good and can be trusted to last for a while, or survived if it does go bad.

I need an exercise in competence to do away with self-doubt. What is this doubt shit anyway? Why am I doing it? Why am I holding myself back, afraid of success again? Frightened of my own talent and where it could take me?

Doubt, self-doubt and no reason for it. No time to spend alone with it, to look at it and handle it with care or hatred or anger, whatever it takes. Just Scott there beside me, in front of me, behind me, reminding me that my self-doubt is there too. "Hey," I say, "leave me the fuck alone so I can deal with it. Give me the chance to beat it instead of reminding me that it exists and I've allowed it to get inside me, between us and the prize." I've whipped this before, I have turned this into power before. I haven't lost my talent, I know where it is: subverted, repressed, disguised beneath and behind, the PUBLIC Mark, the SLIDESHOW Mark, the Mark that can't be allowed a foothold here.

Something snapped inside me. I suppose it was seeing Michael and Greg's organized persistence, how professional they were about going after their new route, the spotting scope and the early morning starts. Their years of experience reminded me that I have a decade of my own and the voice said I could and should climb this wall, instead of doubting my ability.

Dear Mark, you'd do well to read your own writing sometimes.

Hey, put IT away instead of giving IT away. Sharpen the power and direct it precisely, instead of giving the shotgun blast to everyone who will listen. If you don't shine it then they can't bask in it. Besides, every one of them just wants what he believes is his or her share, to hold any fucking way they please.

Say this instead, "Here asshole, hold it like this, it's how I think you should hold it."

Don't patronize me. Leave me alone with my weakness. I'm not giving you my best, which makes me detest me. My sickness insists I take your small portions of praise, your interest and your joviality as nourishment. But I don't need you. I can get over needing you to help me feel worthy of you. I'll take this doubt and transparency and I'll armor myself against you with it, I'll wrap it around me to keep me warm. I'll turn it into drive. Because self-doubt is harsh I can sharpen my tools with it; because self-doubt is the bottom, I can only climb upwards; because being frightened of talent makes a man waste his talent—and that is wasting life. I want instead to use my time.

I crawled out of the tent early that morning because Scott was raving. He shouted just enough for it to register subconsciously, but not so loud that anyone would know what was being said. His technique is superb, I knew they'd be dreaming it later, "Hey fuck-up, instead of measuring those calories, instead of labeling your food bags and organizing all that gear, rather than planning and studying pictures— You Could Have Been Training."

He was laughing cynically at another planeload of "trudge-lodytes," and I joined in the game. I cocked an eye at him and said, "What would you say if I told you we should strip some more gear off the rack, that we can climb this wall with two bivouacs, and that one quart of fuel will be enough? What would you say if I told you we shouldn't take a tent?" In his best Henry Rollins imitation, Scott shouted, "I'd say, 'Well, ALRIGHT!'" And I continued, "Go ahead, hit me—you can't hurt me. Make me run out of food—you can't starve me. Tell me those pitches are steep— you can't stop me. Hit me!" We slapped hands and Scott smiled, "Welcome back, I guess you're finally ready to go climbing." I looked back at the departing horde and considered that our superior posturing teetered on the foundation of future achievement more than anything else.

I knew future achievement was largely contingent on stripping away as much weight as we dared. Ours would be the guerilla strike; supernaturally fast, with little margin for error, fragile in the extreme. We'd already packed and repacked five times, but we loaded and unloaded the packs one last time. In the end, they weighed around 27 pounds each without the ropes and rack. Scott suggested we add more fuel, but I goose-stepped over his apprehension with wild-eyed determination. I had had "The Vision." I knew exactly how far we could push it, what a fine, sharp line we were able to tread.

Propelled by fear and inspiration, and the despair of having waited so long for conditions to be this "right," we crossed the bergschrund at 2:30 A.M. We climbed 2500 feet by 7 P.M. Several pitches were quite hard. Our ledge below the Third Rockband required a mere hour of chopping into blue ice. Since we slept head to head in our bivy sacks, the ledge was long and shallow rather than the deep, wide, four-hour platform a tent requires. We calculated every risk in terms of saving time and energy, in terms of speed.

Our line up the buttress linked weaknesses together, rather than forcing its way through direct but time-consuming passages. We completely avoided the difficulties of the Third Rockband. We sprinted up through afternoon clouds, through a burning 10 P.M. sunset, plodded through a bitter night that froze carabiners open and ice screw cores solid. At 5 A.M. we collapsed on top of the North Buttress of Mount Hunter. We brewed and ate, closed our eyes a little, and three hours later continued upward.

Interdependency was total, our metaphysical connection with each other and the mountain a potent synergistic cocktail. A storm was brewing, but neither of us proposed descent. For us, sanctuary waited at the end of long, punishing effort. We simul-climbed all the way to the top, running on perfect sastrugi, launching ourselves onto the 80-degree serac walls knowing full well that an error would kill us both. Knowing with equal certainty that we had transcended the commission of errors.

I was wasted and stumbling when the storm hit. The "safety drugs" kicked in, survival instinct, a second wind. More jogging. There was no more food, but an inch of gas sloshed in the fuel bottle. We were sure we could get through the night with what was left, but preferred the fight downward instead. The storm whipped our faces raw, and I was glad to have my goggles. We dropped into the Northwest Basin where we'd helped rescue two avalanche victims earlier in the month and were not surprised to see their high camp had been utterly destroyed. The memory of that long night out lay crushed under several tons of serac debris.

We ran. We were out of it in 30 minutes, and through the Alaska dusk I made out figures on the glacier about a mile away. Scott and I were far beyond the borders of casual human experience, living inside ourselves and living off the transcendent mind link we'd forged between us. I hoped the figures skiing toward us wouldn't break that connection and bring us back to earth too roughly. Scott and I strode toward them together.

My tears ran freely as Michael and Greg skied up along with Joe-Joe and Ken Wiley. They'd brought our skis, food, and a thermos full of hot cocoa. The thick, visceral camaraderie broke over me, broke me down onto the snow. I'd never felt anything like it. I was too strung out to resist feeling close to these men. I let myself be carried away on the strong bonds that form between men when we allow them to. I don't know who said it, "You guys look like shit, when did you last sleep?" The question hurled me back to the ledge where we'd woken up and begun climbing 39 1/2 hours ago. Greg and Michael snapped a few pictures and took our packs. As we skied toward base camp I realized that we were roped together appropriately: our four friends on one, and Scott and I tied into our own. The bond between us was that strong.

Dear Diary, I hear the manic engines and what could be gunfire in someone else's life, the rocks winging by with a killing sound. I see the pitiful men playing out their fantasies on these pitiless walls where so many lives are taken. It doesn't hurt when it doesn't touch you personally, it kind of makes you feel tough to know you survived and others did not. But I watched a man break the frozen arm of a corpse so he could zip it into the bag. I saw the bruises sustained in a fall showing through the make-up at an open casket burial and I lowered that steel box six feet into the ground. The shovelfuls of dirt hitting its lid are still ringing in my ears. I helped rescue the living and shouldered the dead. I watched a man break down when the memories of 27 Vietnam burial details piled up on the one he was speaking at. I watched that same man reach deep inside and get a hold of his shit and be as heroic as man can possibly be. I went to The Last Frontier and I climbed a mountain, I tried myself against some others, but I failed. I laughed about it some and I cried myself to sleep. I bared my soul to other men. I shared their exhaustion, their joy, and their grief. That was what I wanted. That's exactly what I got.

2000 AUTHOR'S NOTE

This trip was another turning point in my career. During the climb on Mount Hunter, which Scott and I named Deprivation, I finally understood the sacredness of the partnership, the power that can come from it. I haven't soloed a hard route since, preferring instead to climb with good, close friends like Scott and Steve House, Jonny Blitz, and Bill Belcourt. Other friends and partners have faded toward the edges of my life, time and circumstance forcing us apart.

I have only experienced the psychic connection Scott and I enjoyed on Deprivation on one other route, also with Scott. I haven't been on any routes that required it since then either. I take care, these days, not to waste any precious time by climbing with someone whom I do not love or respect. More than once I have felt the mystical connection to the mountain that I learned on Mount Hunter. It is always there, if I am open to it.

Deprivation taught me about the existence of this mystic path in the mountains. It made me ask myself, "How can I be tired while climbing on the mountain when I have become the mountain?" I have searched within myself, through both passive and active meditation, for the tools to open this "door" whenever I will it. I still search.

Originally, my idea for the route's name was Depravation, something to do with the depravity of the drug addict going for the big binge: the harder, higher, faster, longer that all good alpine climbers struggle to experience and/or avoid. But we decided it would take too much explanation. Settling for Deprivation was fine because it communicates the experience with equal clarity.

This climb opened eyes, some of them youthful, to the possibilities that the Alaska Range offers. Steve House's Single-Push efforts were the logical extension of what Scott and I managed on Mount Hunter. And there is a lot more to come.

TWITCHING
WITH TWIGHT

AT EVEREST
BASE CAMP IN
TIBET (CHINA,
IF YOU MUST).

(Photo by Barry

Blanchard)

What's your problem? I think I know. You see it in the mirror every morning. Temptation and doubt hip to hip inside your head. You know it's not supposed to be like this. But you drank the Kool-Aid and dressed yourself up in someone else's life.

You're haunted because you remember having something more. With each drag of the razor you ask yourself why you piss your blood into another man's cup. Working at the job he offered, your future is between his thumb and forefinger. And the necessary accessories, the proclamations of success you thought gave you stability provide your boss security. Your debt encourages acquiescence, the heavy mortgage makes you polite.

Aren't you sick of being tempted by an alternative lifestyle, but bound by chains of your own choosing? Of the gnawing doubt that the college graduate, path of least resistance is the right way for you—forever? Each weekend you prepare for the two weeks each summer when you wake up each day and really ride, or climb; the only imperative being to go to bed tired. When booming thermals shoot you full of juice and your Vario shrieks 7m/sec, you wonder if the lines will pop. The risk pares away life's trivia. Up there, sucking down the thin cumulus, the earth looks small, the boss even smaller, and you wish it could go on forever. But a wish is all it will ever be.

Because the ground is hard, Monday morning is harsh. You wear the hangover of your weekend rush under a strict and proper suit and tie. You listen to NPR because it's inoffensive, PFC: Politically Fucking Correct. Where's the counter-cultural righteousness that had you flirting with Bad Religion and the vintage Pistols tape over the weekend? On Monday you eat frozen food and live the homogenized city experience. But Sunday you thought about cutting your hair very short. You wanted a little more volume and wondered how out of place you looked in the Sub Pop Music Store. Flipping through the import section, you didn't recognize any of the bands. KMFDM? It stands for Kill Mother Fucking Depeche Mode. Didn't you know? How could you not?

Tuesday you look at the face in the mirror again. It stares back, accusing. How can you get by on that one weekly dose? How can you be satisfied by the artifice of these experiences? Why should your words mean anything? They aren't learned by heart and written in blood. If you can not grasp the consciousness-altering experience that real mastery of these disciplines proposes, of what value is your participation? The truth is pointless when it is shallow. Do you have the courage to live with the integrity that stabs deep?

Use the mirror to cut to the heart of things and uncover your true self. Use the razor to cut away what you don't need. The life you want to live has no recipe. Following the recipe got you here in the first place:

Mix one high school diploma with an undergrad degree and a college sweetheart. With a whisk (or a whip) blend two cars, a poorly built house in a cul de sac, and 50 hours a week working for a board that doesn't give a shit about you. Reproduce once. Then again. Place all ingredients in a rut, or a grave. One is a bit longer than the other. Bake thoroughly until the resulting life is set. Rigid. With no way out. Serve and enjoy.

But there is a way out. Live the lifestyle instead of paying lip service to the lifestyle. Live with commitment. With emotional content. Live whatever life you choose honestly. Give up this renaissance man, dilettante bullshit of doing a lot of different things (and none of them very well by real standards). Get to the guts of one thing; accept, without casuistry, the responsibility of making a choice. When you live honestly, you can not separate your mind from your body, or your thoughts from your actions.

> *If you really want to hurt them and their children not yet born tell them the truth always.*
>
> **Henry Rollins, *See a Grown Man Cry,* 1992**

Tell the truth. First, to yourself. Say it until it hurts. Learn the reality of your own selfishness. Quit living for other people at the expense of your own self, you're not really alive. You live in the land of denial—and they say the view is pretty as long as you remain asleep.

Well it's time to WAKE THE FUCK UP!

So do it. Wake up. When you drink the coffee tomorrow, take it black and notice it. Feel the caffeine surge through you. Don't take it for granted. Use it for something. Burn the Grisham books. Sell the bad CDs. Mariah Carey, Dave Mathews, and 'N Sync aren't part of the soundtrack where you're going.

Cut your hair. Don't worry about the gray. If you're good at what you do, no

RIGGED OUT FOR A PRACTICAL SHOOTING COMPETITION, PROVO CANYON, UTAH

one cares what you look like. Go to the weight room. Learn the difference between actually working out and what you've been doing. Live for the Iron and the fresh air. Punish your body to perfect your soul. Kick the habit of being nice to everyone you meet. Do they deserve it? Say "no" more often.

Quit posturing at the weekly parties. Your high pulse rate, your 5.12s and quick time on the Slickrock Trail don't mean shit to anybody else. These numbers are the measuring sticks of your own progress; show, don't tell. Don't react to the itch with a scratch. Instead, learn it. Honor the necessity of both the itch and the scratch.

But a haircut and a new soundtrack do not a modern man make. As long as you have a safety net you act without commitment. You'll go back to your old habits once you meet a little resistance. You need the samurai's desperateness and his insanity.

Burn the bridge. Nuke the foundation. Back yourself up against a wall. Have an opinion one way or the other, get off the fence and rip it up. Cut yourself off so there is no going back. Once you're committed the truth will come out.

You ask about security? What you need is uncertainty. What you need is confusion. Something which forces you to reinvent yourself, a whip to drive you harder.

I never try anything—I just do it. Want to try me?

White Zombie

In *Dune*, Frank Herbert called it "the attitude of the knife," cut off what's incomplete and say "now it has finished, for it has ended there."

To carve out your place in the world of Gravity, you must make a commitment. All you have to be is good at your chosen discipline. It's a Meritocracy out there, with gravity as the auditor. Inconsistency, incompetence, and lies are all cut short by the ground. It will stop you if you can't stop yourself.

SOUNDTRACK FOR PERSONAL REINVENTION

BAND	ALBUM
The Clash	London Calling
	Give 'em Enough Rope
Treponem Pal	Excess and Overdrive
Tool	Aenima
Murder Inc.	Murder Inc.
The Young Gods	T.V. Sky
Iggy and the Stooges	Raw Power
The Wipers	Youth of America
N Factor	Vibes From No Go Area
Bad Religion	Against The Grain
New Model Army	The Ghost of Cain
Rollins Band	The End of Silence
Die Cheerleader	Son of Filth
The Gun Club	Miami
Skinny Puppy	Remission
	The Process
Fugazi	Steady Diet of Nothing
Sisters of Mercy	Floodland
Social Distortion	White Light, White Heat, White Trash
Wayne Kramer	Citizen Wayne
Sonic Youth	Daydream Nation
Joy Division	Closer
Catherine Wheel	Happy Days
Killing Joke	What's This For?
Sex Pistols	Never Mind the Bollocks . . .

2000 AUTHOR'S NOTE

This piece was meant to be way over the top. It was written in late 1996 at the behest of Will Gadd. As an associate editor for *Gravity* magazine, he asked me to download my attitude toward "posturing weekend-warrior" types, inviting me to "be as bad as you want."

I had retired from climbing to begin a career as a photographer, but I could not escape from the Dr. Doom persona. The marketing construct affected the way people dealt with me in other arenas. I was sick of the pigeonhole I'd carved out for myself. I was equally angry with myself for finding it difficult to walk away from the notoriety I earned in the climbing world. I'd grown comfortable with the "legend." I was stagnant and repeated myself.

I needed a cathartic experience to break myself free, so I decided to write "Twitching with Twight" in the voice Dr. Doom would use if everything readers—who knew only what I had sold them—believed were true. Seeing it in print allowed me to separate the good doctor from Mark Twight in my own head. It took a few more years and the publication of *Extreme Alpinism* before similar severance occurred in the minds of the climbing public.

"Twitching" affected several people close to me in a positive way. It allowed them to recognize their adherence to the recipe, that they were trying to fulfill other people's expectations, but not their own. Some have done the necessary work to break the pattern. That the article helped far fewer than it offended matters little, my intent was to provoke, whichever way it went.

CHAMONIX:
OVER THE TOP OR

PARAGLIDER
IN FRONT OF
THE DRU LES
PRAZ DE
CHAMONIX,
FRANCE

UNDER THE GROUND

The sign reads "World Capital of Skiing and Alpinism." I call it the "Death Sport Capital of the World."

In Chamonix men achieve great things, and the Nietzschean ethic of surpassing one's previous best efforts plays out every day. As with all geographic sites of power, young people make the pilgrimage to measure themselves against the place and its people. Some commune with the mountain god and find their true selves among the ice and the stone. Others get slapped down and end up in the ground.

The cemeteries in Chamonix and Argentiere are beautiful. Rough-hewn monuments thrust through the earth like the mountains looming hungrily above them. They aren't homogeneous or polished like American tombstones or, for that matter, American lives. The carved stone speaks of great history. The SS used Chamonix for R&R during World War II. Monuments and tombs commemorate their victims. In fact, Axis powers battled the French high in the Vallée Blanche for several days after the armistice was signed. Neither side, it seems, believed the news.

In many visits to deceased friends I never realized how young most of the people lying beneath those stones were. Many of the interred were buried well before the end of their third decade. I met a grieving Swede whose daughter had been killed by an avalanche while skiing for Chamonix's other god, the camera. "In Sweden," he said, "you rarely see a headstone for someone under 40. What kind of sick place is this?"

Distracted by the power of the mountains and the hold Chamonix had on me, I wrote off his question to grief and anger. Today, I remember friends who've died up there and the ages on those monuments mock me because I was the guy who everyone said wouldn't live past 25. Dave Kahn taught me to climb; he died when he was 26. Fred Vimal was 26, Eric Mariaud was 24, Philippe Mohr was 28. I count 35 names on my list today—how many more by this time next year? I am sick of discovering what people mean to me by surviving them. I know the attitude that my friends and I share, not Chamonix, is to blame. Still, I fall into the trap of hating the place itself.

The finest skiers, alpine climbers, and paraglider pilots migrate to Chamonix to test and consolidate their power. It is a laboratory where the most difficult experiments are undertaken and the results are exported to mountain ranges throughout the world. The sheer number of participants combined with the typically cavalier French attitude toward death makes for fierce competition. New sports evolve with frightening speed. While athletes from other regions are content to progress soberly, Chamonix's climbers and skiers redefine human limitations almost daily. For example, in 1987 at the first annual Reunion of Ice Climbers held at the Cirque de Gavarnie in the Pyrenees the waterfall-climbing standard in France was pathetic compared to North America. In 1988 the world's first Grade VII waterfall was climbed in the Canadian Rockies. It took the French four years to catch up. By 1996 more Grade 7 waterfalls had been climbed in France than in the rest of the world combined. Many of the world's future Grade 8 and 9 routes would be climbed by an expatriate Brit living in Chamonix. How is this possible?

The topography and social structure of Chamonix virtually ensure that any visiting skier or climber comes away with greater skills. Being surrounded by great talent inspires you to surpass yourself. Socially, Chamonix is a meritocracy. No one cares which discipline you practice as long as you're good at it. Mercenaries all, if they can learn or gain by association with you, doors will open. Intent on becoming the best, the French share information, power, inspiration, even their women, if they think the overall standard will improve because of it.

We Americans, on the other hand, jealously guard what knowledge and power we have. We won't share or communicate because it may deny us the 15 minutes of fame we're "entitled" to. This selfishness prevents rapid progress and development. It blinds us to the fact that evolution as a process never stops. An open-ended supply of new participants brings fresh ideas and energy; thus, our isolationist attitude holds us back. Proof of this can be witnessed in two different disciplines.

By the mid-eighties, French alpinists were so good that the north faces of the Alps no longer offered much challenge by themselves, so they invented "enchainment": linking several faces into one nonstop marathon effort. When the ski areas, already radical by American standards, no longer presented significant challenge, the French invented "extreme skiing." I say "invented," although American skiers may disagree. Plenty of participants have died proving extreme skiing and snowboarding as practiced in the Alps is the real thing. What Americans consider extreme is, to the French, routine.

Keeping your shit together for a single leap from a 50-foot cliff is nothing. Compare that to the skill and discipline needed to ski a 3000-foot pitch of 55-to-

CEMETERY IN

ARGENTIERE,

FRANCE

65-degree snow interspersed with unskiable cliffs and certain death should you fall. No place in the Lower 48 features all the topographic threats an extreme skier deals with in the Alps: high altitude (most descents take place between 11,000 and 15,000 feet), weather, glaciation, remote terrain, sustained pitch. Adventure photographer Chris Noble worked with three of France's best: Jean-Marc Boivin, Pierre Tardivel, and Patrick Vallençant. He believes "extreme skiing in the Alps was a natural evolution of mountaineering, a sub-discipline to master. In the USA extreme skiing has nothing to do with mountaineering, because it evolved from skiing. American extreme skiers won't seek out the same terrain as the French, they aren't comfortable with it." Crested Butte is for spectators; Chamonix is for participants.

I originally went to Chamonix because of the attitude toward climbing I knew I would find there. I wouldn't have to justify my actions every day. It's a place that accepts and even venerates self-validation through dangerous practices. I'd progressed as far as an alpine climber could in the USA, so I sought the best in the world to teach me more. In Chamonix's meritocracy, my alleged success elsewhere was meaningless. I had to prove myself locally over and over again. To me, Chamonix was the center of the universe and climbing was all-important. I burned the torch brightly, alone or with partners, in my quest for power. In the beginning I believed the other players could do no wrong. Once the student became the master, however, I found fault everywhere.

Something was missing. Neither personal growth nor the grandeur of the mountains was enough. Although I was well accepted, had European sponsors, and even

SKIERS

DESCENDING

THE ARÊTE,

AIGUILLE

DU MIDI,

CHAMONIX,

FRANCE

starred in a French feature film, I could never actually settle in Chamonix. Ultimately, I did not fit in. I stayed in France for five years on a 90-day tourist visa. I expected to either leave or be put in the ground where I wouldn't need papers.

I found living a life where the obvious future was a six-foot dirt nap invigorating, but it wore me down nevertheless. With "no future" as my battle cry, I climbed as hard as I could and lived in the moment from one climb to the next. I didn't reserve myself a seat in the future because I wasn't in it. But it kept becoming the present, so I had to confront the fact that I might survive. I might have some kind of future—just not in Chamonix.

The last straw was the country's lack of cultural diversity. France is beautiful on postcards or for a vacation, but only the French can enjoy living there permanently. The same may be said of the USA. Ultimately, I wanted to own a big truck, exercise my Second Amendment rights, listen to hardcore music, and let my congressman know how poorly he represents me. None of this could occur in France.

When I said I hated the French and "things French," I really hated my own weakness for becoming one of them, for needing their "lab" to validate myself. My last two new routes and the attendant controversy surrounding them were my way of saying "fuck you" to Chamonix's incestuous thinking and lifestyle. They were hard routes—coveted by many locals—poached by two Americans who had finally sickened of France's claim to cultural and athletic superiority.

Once my infatuation wore thin, I realized that Chamonix, although an incredible place to live and train, is not, as residents believe, Mecca. It may supply the venue for some to fulfill their potential, but most people have never heard of the place. While useful as a tool, it's no basis for a religion. You can die ignominiously anywhere. They don't offer extra points for doing it in the shadow of Mont Blanc.

2000 AUTHOR'S NOTE

I wrote this three years after having left France for good. Neil Feineman at *Gravity* assigned the story, and it felt good to work out my perspective on paper. It was commissioned as a fluff piece, which I couldn't bear, so I added the dark overtones. Some sentences and concepts are clearly borrowed from my other writing. Rewriting it didn't affect me in the way that revisiting more specific periods of my life did, like that detailed in "Heaven Never Laughed."

VOICE of DISSENT —DR. DOOM

SPORTING THE LATEST IN FRENCH CLIMBING FASHION, CIRCA 1986, ON THE SERACS ON MOUNT RAINIER

DISSES
TRADITIONAL
VALUES

INTRODUCTION

This is the first of a series of "columns" the editors at *Climbing* asked me to write. I agreed on the basis that I am "allowed to rant as much as I like." I'll contribute two or three columns per year as long as the editors hold up their end of our verbal contract. I refused to sign a binding paper agreement because I want the freedom to pull the plug when my ideas and writing get stale. We've all seen how hard it is to come up with a relevant and interesting topic for every issue.

My column is called "Voice of Dissent" because I think you're all tightly sealed in Tupperware complacency, coasting along on the old ideals of the climbing-lifestyle dream. You need some heat. I am here to stir the pot. The climbing community used to be vibrant, genuinely alternative. Today, the original semi-anti-establishment climbers feed off the growing back of climbing's popularity, earning more money than they'd imagined possible. God forbid they should speak a disapproving word themselves or change a formula that is obviously working. The solution is to hire an independent thinker and contractor who's known to be critical, a punk the readers expect to speak and act radically.

My mentor John Bouchard once told me, "As soon as they invite you to sit on committees, judge mountain film festivals, or write columns, your climbing career is over." Until now I've avoided all of the above. I may, in fact, be done with climbing. I certainly don't do it in the "take no prisoners" style I once did in part because the current evolution of climbing, especially alpine climbing, disgusts me. Some days I don't like being associated with it, which brings me to this issue's diatribe.

DIATRIBE

In the Editor's Corner of #167 Michael Kennedy raised the curtain on the current fashionable controversy of summitless ascents. The guilty mentioned by name reacted badly to the finger pointing. Hearing this I laughed because I am guiltier than any of them, and I got off without a quip. However, I've never dressed failure up as anything else and admitted to it easily. Climbers competing for recognition, sponsorship, and the few remaining "firsts" are prone to stretching the truth. This tactic has always been part of the professional climber's repertoire—one of the "secrets of the pros." Kennedy calls it putting "the best possible spin on our outwardly fruitless struggles."

I love the phrase. It conjures the image of a climber thumbing his thesaurus for less negative-sounding synonyms to mask his failure. He draws his line on the photo of the face. Due to the foreshortened view from the base, he appears to have traversed off a few hundred feet below the top. On an aerial photo the line ends well below the summit. Naming his exploit is difficult. The magazines need a catchphrase, sponsors must write enthusiastic press releases. It has to be a "first" something. Perhaps it was a first one-day ascent? Although it took more than 24 hours, he decides to call it a "long" day. Why not call it "the first time I tell the truth about a route I've done?"

Kennedy states unequivocally that "summits are the yardstick of success in mountaineering." This traditionalist practice is carried over from the days when men were making first ascents of the actual peaks. The ethic is less important in an era when new routes are squeezed between existing "classic" lines. Using the summit as a measurement of success reflects the mortal injury done to climbing by our acquisitive society, which places great value on achievement itself and little on the process of achieving. I consider it a consumer mentality.

Due to the quest for new terrain and pure, gymnastic difficulty, traditional rock-climbing ethics changed radically during the last two decades. Once routes went to the top of the cliff. Today, the "top" of a climb is arbitrarily dictated by the midpoint of the rope. Should this evolution be exclusive to rock climbing?

The *American Heritage Dictionary* defines "route" as "road or way from one place to another," "customary line of travel," and finally "a means of reaching a goal." What is the goal of alpine climbing? Is it climbing and the psycho-physical experience of same? Or reaching the "most essential point," the goal traditionally perceived as the point of climbing mountains? Then ticking the summits off a list? If, as Scott Backes says, "The whole experience of climbing is important, not one specific point or moment," then why would anyone care about the topographic apogee when it is merely one component—essential or not—of the trip itself? For me, the point is not to climb the peak but to climb new ground both internally and externally. The judges and patron saints of mountaineering find this abstraction difficult to lay their hands on and categorize, so they condemn it. Happily, I am climbing for myself, not them. I can easily quantify my experiences and what they contribute to or subtract from me.

SAYING

HELLO AND

GOODBYE TO

FRANCE, AND

THE PRESS IN

GENERAL

I cite the new route Deprivation Scott and I climbed on Mount Hunter as an example: Our imperatives were first to survive; second, to go up and over in three days; and third, to go around difficulties rather than beating our heads against them. We lived. We walked into base camp exactly 72 hours after leaving our tent. We traversed 200 or 300 feet below the summit on our way to the west ridge descent. Scott and I wasted no time on the summit. We both believed we'd be going there for the traditional holy trinity of mountaineering judges: peers, media, and sponsors. Neither of us cares what the self-proclaimed guardians of tradition and ethics think one way or the other.

Scott climbs because "all climbing is anarchy," and he may do exactly as he pleases. Similarly, I climb because I can make my own rules for myself. Although I am free to do anything, my actions directly reflect my integrity. We both live by the words of the late Reinhard Karl, (I paraphrase): "No chalk? I'll smear their routes with jelly if I want to." We urge others to do exactly as they please because we certainly do. It matters little *what* you do, as long as you *say* what you do. You didn't go to the summit? You traversed to an easier route after the 10th pitch? You hooked your tool through the piton when no one was looking? Admit it. Believe in your actions enough that you don't care what others think. Attack traditional values. Right or wrong, we must constantly determine whether these values are defensible. Don't go along with what people say. You, the doer, empower them, not the other way around.

Every man must establish his own values and ask himself why he behaves as he does. "He" often assumes the values and traditions established by . . . whom, in fact? Religions are popular. The opinion leader for most climbers is the hierarchy of the climbing community. Suppose I deny those entities the authority to establish the rules I abide by and the right to judge me? Who, I demand, has the right to pass judgment on the actions of a climber? He who has the better route list? Who are they to set themselves up as the protectors of the current state of climbing? Why should you care what these judges say, unless of course you're climbing for the approval of others and not for yourself? Look in the mirror and think about it.

Do you intend to allow these so-called opinion leaders to determine how you behave, how you climb, which traditions to respect, and which new heathen practices to abhor? If you're the sheep I believe you to be, you'll gladly let others think for you.

I hear booing. Get off the high horse, you say. How is it that my shit doesn't stink? Here's the dirt you're after, you parasites. Log on to the nearest chat-room and discuss something that doesn't concern you. Steal some more of your employer's time and money.

1. Beyond Good and Evil, Aiguille des Pelerins, Chamonix, with Andy Parkin—the route ends at the Col des Pelerins, avoiding the final 300 feet to the true summit.
2. Richard Cranium Memorial, Les Droites, Chamonix, with Barry Blanchard—the route ends in a breche (steeper than a col) nowhere near the true summit.
3. Birthright, Grands Charmoz, Chamonix, with Scott Backes—the route ends 1400 feet up a 2000-foot-high wall on obvious terraces. We climbed ice and mixed terrain to the base of an overhanging rock wall, a type of climbing we prefer to leave to others.
4. There Goes the Neighborhood, Aiguille Sans Nom, Chamonix, with Scott Backes—the route ends where it joins the southwest ridge 200 to 300 feet below the true summit.
5. Deprivation, Mount Hunter, Alaska, with Scott Backes—we traversed south 200 to 300 feet beneath the summit to gain the west ridge and descent route.
6. Ghersen-Twight, Mont Maudit, Chamonix, with Alain Ghersen—we bypassed the summit after reaching the southwest ridge.
7. The Gift That Keeps on Giving, Mount Bradley, Alaska, with Steve House and Jonny Blitz—we stopped at a col approximately 400 feet below the summit.

I've missed the summit of every big new route I've ever done. I failed to climb Nuptse, Nanga Parbat, Everest, and countless others equally as meaningless. When

I climb several consecutive pitches of new terrain I call it a new route. I say it's a new way of reaching a particular goal, whether abstract or concrete. I don't care what the hierarchy says. I don't have to.

2000 AUTHOR'S NOTE

There's not much to add. This is one of the few opinion pieces I've ever written that did not generate huge quantities of negative mail. Readers must not have thought me too far wrong.

SMOKE GETS
IN YOUR EYES

I CLIMB
WHILE MARK
WILFORD
HOLDS
DIRECTOR
PAUL GIRAUD
STEADY.

A hundred feet up I drove my tool into a crevice. The ice answered with the whip-crack sound of a bullet going supersonic. Grinding aftershocks inside the ice vibrated through my tools. When I realized that I hadn't fallen, I climbed down.

Mark Wilford and I talked. We were still alive to do so. There's no instruction manual for climbing icebergs. We thought it might be better to solo wearing life jackets, but hitting water from a hundred feet would be like decking anywhere. Because we used the rope, we carried knives to cut tools and rope away, which might let us tread water more easily. Neither of us had dry suits so we wouldn't last long anyway. Under the 60th parallel the ocean is actually below 32 degrees, but the salt content keeps it from freezing. The ice itself is weird. Compressed on the continent for several thousand years, after it breaks off to become an iceberg, it tries to fall apart. Without support or geologic compression, gravity tugs from all angles while saltwater nibbles at integrity. Icebergs roll over without warning. People have seen them disintegrate for no reason.

Mark's unflappability renewed my courage. I chose a different line and climbed to the top. The iceberg measured 140 feet from the water to the summit. We fixed a rope and rappelled back to the Zodiac. Riding the chop toward the 200-foot Professor Khromov, I considered how to explain the situation to the film crew.

The "business" is autocratic, so I risked banishment from Hollywood by exercising my attitude problem. "What happened tonight proves that none of us know shit about climbing these things. If there's an accident, it won't be trivial—somebody will get killed." I stared at the Chief Rigger, Kevin Sweigert and said, "It's not safe and I don't think you can make it safe."

He tried finesse rather than force, countering with the familiar rationalization: "Nothing in this game is without risk, we won't be able to make it 100 percent safe. If that's what you want . . . " Having a guy who hasn't climbed on icebergs or done any difficult routes in the mountains tell me what is safe or unsafe for me did not sit well, but I sat still because I knew what was at stake.

The client, a cigarette company, invested 1.5 million dollars in the director, Paul Giraud, and allowed him three weeks on location to deliver dramatic footage. Antarctica is a brutish place where the weather is mostly foul. We'd filmed whales and icebergs, helicopters and occasional sunsets. Paul appeared anxious to film us climbing the following day.

I wasn't ready. "I want a day to climb on our own and check things out. No one here knows more than we do at this point, and we admit total ignorance."

Actually, Mark wasn't admitting anything. Privately, he showed some nervousness, but taking the film industry's money was important. Having climbed for Hollywood cameras before, he understood that the squeaky wheel usually gets greased, which is synonymous with axed.

Kevin suggested they begin rigging at 6 A.M. and be ready to shoot by 3 P.M., adding, "unless we run into problems making it safe."

The production team liked Kevin's attitude more than mine. I remained adamant, citing the poor integrity of the ice I'd hacked at that evening. My only ally was Amyr Klink. His solo 100-day crossing of the Atlantic in a rowboat qualified him as our Water Safety Officer. He thought the Hollywood folks were out of their minds to move so quickly. Should an accident happen, the film crew might be denied a finished product, but Mark and I might die. We compromised. Kevin would start rigging while Paul filmed Mark and I climbing easier ice elsewhere. At least we'd have something in the can.

As we filed out, Kevin signaled for a tête-a-tête. "Don't undermine me," he admonished, "we want the same thing. Getting it your way is antagonizing."

I waited.

"I may be telling them what they want to hear tonight, but I'll take as much time as I need tomorrow." He paused before adding in a soothing voice, "You'll get your extra day."

Just as I relaxed, he continued. "My wife said you'd stir the pot . . . I've been expecting this." I rolled my eyes. The Dr. Doom legend claimed another victim. I considered Kevin's assurances and said that if I disagreed with him, I'd do so silently until further notice.

Before I left he thanked me for fixing a rope to the top of the iceberg, acknowledging it would make his rigging job easier.

Back in my cabin, sipping a Quilmes Argentine beer, I thought about how I got to this place. After hearing Alex Lowe say, "The ice is the best in the world," I pulled out the stops on my audition tape. Because it was financially out of reach, I'd ride the television rocket to Antarctica or never see it.

Despite the cushy voyage, I remained ambivalent toward the film industry. I'd watched film crews trash locations and treat everyone from talent to indigens without respect. I saw directors and producers toss people over their shoulders after squeezing them dry. Compared to the anxiety the lower echelons of the film industry live with daily, the fear I feel while climbing is simple to deal with. At the moment of fear I have options, and an exit.

An exit is not necessarily available to the film crew, whose fears are insidious and quiet with no easy way out. Each day reminds them that they've handed control of their lives to someone else. Hundreds of other people are willing and able to do their job. One well-paid body is as warm as the next. Their futures don't necessarily depend on the quality of their output. Instead, they try to avoid getting caught doing something wrong. In Hollywood, whimsy carries as much weight as truth. When decisions had to be made, the crew vacillated until someone else took charge.

That someone ultimately was Paul Giraud. Because the bottom line rested on his neck, he was always right. He bore his responsibility gracefully. I admired his work ethic because he shot film at every opportunity and led by example. He was ruthless when someone let him down, which is always attractive.

Although I respected him, I remained suspicious. Hollywood hasn't made a good mountain climbing film or put authentic climbing action into films where it was called for. I was cynical about any crew's ability to capture the rare essence of hard climbing. On the other hand, the commercial was supposed to sell cigarettes—how good did it have to be?

We boarded the Professor Khromov (a Russian research vessel converted for tourism) in Ushüaia, at the southernmost tip of Argentina. Until we reached the Drake Passage, which separates South America from Antarctica, and were out of sight of land, the 200-foot boat felt huge.

As the swells increased, a general meeting was called below deck. Without a window to the horizon, I had no reference point. The Dramamine failed. Acupressure was futile. I turned green. I stood. I sat. I faced forward, then backward. Nothing made a difference. Choking the first convulsion back, I breathed deeply several times. Sweat stung my eyes. The second convulsion overwhelmed me. I sprinted toward my cabin with my hands cupped in front of my mouth. When I hit the stairs my mouth was full of puke. My tightly closed lips backed the next wave up into my sinus cavity—burning.

I erupted in the general direction of the toilet just as I crossed the threshold. I white-knuckled the toilet seat and dry heaved to exhaustion. I rinsed my mouth. During the next 24 hours I swallowed more than the recommended dose of motion sickness pills and studied my fellow man. Between the sick, all civility disappears. We are animals. The truth comes out when you start puking.

I eased awake to a calm sloshing. The ocean was flat, which meant the Antarctic

Peninsula sheltered us. I remained under the covers and hoped I hadn't set my expectations too high. I considered Antarctica a serious place, for serious adventurers. Here Mugs Stump climbed what he, with tongue firmly in cheek, said "may be the hardest route yet done by man." Messner had trouble crossing it. Ranulph Fiennes lost a quarter of his body weight here. Captain Scott lost his life. Men like Amundsen and Shackleton survived here "with the responsibility of proving that all the laws of chance were wrong." Failure meant you and your men died.

The first morning in Wilhelmina Bay shattered my preconceptions. On deck I was warm. The sky was hazy, without wind. The water was a soft black mirror, giant and slow like oil. The current had sculpted millions of fist-sized chunks of ice into long pathways a holy man could walk on. The sun hung low, its light burning through the big hole in the ozone. Everywhere I looked was more beautiful and inviting than any mountain range I had ever seen.

And there were whales. As they played and ate around the boat, they disguised their immense power and size by moving gracefully. The film crew took to the water in Zodiacs, giving the scene scale. Whales the size of submarines glided beneath the rubber boats. After they swam off, we continued south toward the Iceberg Graveyard, stopping to circle the occasional candidate. Paul filmed almost nonstop during the 17 hours of daylight.

We "interviewed" different icebergs and marked their locations with a GPS system. "Berg 6" (the sixth on our list) inspired more terror than any others. Of course, Paul decided to film the big action sequence there. Kevin and his crew rigged ropes for easy access, camera platforms, and a winch to hoist Paul and his camera into different positions.

The following day Mark and I waited for "Action" on a large shelf 30 feet above the water. Noticing a long horizontal fracture line through the ice, I placed my belay anchors above it and backed them up to a fixed rope. On command, Mark climbed toward the camera. The ice flinched under his tools, pops and cracks propagated through the iceberg. Paul shouted encouragement, assuring us the images were exactly what he wanted.

Once on top, we were lowered down the stark south face. It overhung the black water 12 or 14 feet in 140. The shaded wall was brittle and badly fractured, but the crew had drilled holes for our ice tool picks with a Bosch. We didn't excavate for good placements or drop ice on our belayers in the Zodiacs; we simply hooked our way up the 95-degree wall. It was the strangest climbing Mark and I had ever done.

We celebrated that night: the Hollywood folks because the hardest part was done, Mark and I because we survived.

The weather warmed to 45 degrees. Rain fell by morning. When the safety crew returned to remove the platforms, they discovered the shelf where we'd waited

IN THE
ICEBERG
CEMETERY
NEAR THE
LEMAIRE
CHANNEL,
ANTARCTIC
PENINSULA

floating in the lagoon. High winds and waves tore a house-size chunk away. Had it fallen the day before, 15 people from the film crew would have been crushed. Hearing this, I felt sick and righteous, my earlier ranting justified. The film crew barely reacted to the news. They had the action in the can, and despite my warnings, nothing bad had happened to them *while they were there.* Success can breed contempt and a casual attitude toward danger.

Heavy chop flipped one of the production crew out of a small Zodiac the next afternoon. The kill-switch cable wasn't attached to him, so the boat took off. It taunted him by circling further and further away. He tread water, thrashing because he'd left his life jacket aboard the Khromov. Eventually his cries were heard and he was rescued. It could have easily gone the other way.

Film crews often don't respect the power of nature because it's Disneyland to them. They act as if the gods grant them special privilege to document events in the often-savage arena without having paid their dues. When things go wrong, they rationalize that they responded correctly or their contingency plans worked.

The truth is that we were all very, very lucky.

While they did make mistakes, I have no right to judge them by my own standards. I can't expect them to know anything about my particular environment. I'm just as ignorant of theirs, and I'd make a fool of myself in Hollywood. I was prepared to hate them for trashing the location, but they sent a diver to recover a radio battery when it went overboard. When a storm nabbed two Zodiacs and blew them several miles from the Khromov, the crew could have written them off but recovered them instead.

While my prejudice insisted they couldn't film climbing properly, the 75-second commercial is an amazing tribute to Paul Giraud's vision and ability. When I saw it, I was so proud I cried. It will remain a monument long after I've forgotten my differences with Kevin and my fear of floating ice.

I laughed, though, when an actor took over the smoking moment. I may be a good climber, but to Hollywood I just didn't look cool inhaling.

1997 AUTHOR'S NOTE

There's a lot of antismoking propaganda in the news these days. The current PC view may criticize me for promoting tobacco products. But I say, "If you can't make a simple choice without being influenced by advertising, you deserve what you get." If you get addicted to something unhealthy and then don't have the sense or will to break free, ditto. And worse, if after all this you try to place the blame for your actions and your despair on someone else, you should be dragged behind a car. Although I have smoked at times, I'm a nonsmoker. I like the ritual, the smell of tobacco, and rolling my own cigarettes. I love the initial acrid whiff, first- or secondhand. But for my chosen lifestyle, wrecking my lungs is counterproductive. I made my choice *despite* the ads selling the great American dream: the dream in which smoking is cool and anyone can make it in Hollywood.

2000 AUTHOR'S NOTE

This commercial cured me of any heated desire to work with film or television people for a couple of years. I know my addictive personality would not fare well in Hollywood. Rather, it might fare too well, finding sources to satisfy all hungers. Best for me to stay at arm's length.

On the other hand, my good friend Kurt Johnstad works hard in Hollywood but has not disappeared into its maw. His company shoots climbing action occasionally, so he's brought me in to help a few times. Being paid well is so satisfying. And with these guys hip-waders aren't necessary. They tiptoe through bullshit wearing ankle socks, managing to eat healthily and stay fit despite hours on the set. There's always a gym nearby. If not, they bring one in the back of a semi. I love working their version of Hollywood.

For most climbers, though, the film business is a quick ticket to a negative power-to-weight ratio and weak lungs. The food is good, cigarettes aren't that bad, and the sport-fucking opportunities plentiful: "Oooh, you climb mountains?" And hanging around with folks whose values are evil does little for your own integrity, unless you're very hard indeed. Many of my friends own houses free and clear courtesy of film work, and some even continue climbing. Others have disappeared into the "business," replacing the mountains with piles of cash. I could take the same step, but I think it would kill me.

VOICE OF
DISSENT—
COMPETITION

WILL GADD

ON EUBANKS

CHIMNEY,

LONGS PEAK,

COLORADO

RUINS THE
FREE-FOR-ALL

The popularity of so-called extreme sports has both helped and hurt climbing. Climbing is coming of age. Like all sports at this stage, climbing and climbers are ripe for exploitation. Our sport is being redefined. Many crucial aspects are being decided by outsiders; government officials, big media, and by the public's demand for stronger vicarious sensations.

Sales of gear and instruction services, of magazines and stunts to feed the maw of advertising, are booming. Each time we sell risk, we trivialize it *and* the integrity of our sport and lifestyle. We downplay risk on camera and in print in feeble attempts at humility. Genuine accounts of high-risk climbs might scare new participants or paying advertisers. We've invented an aspect of the sport where risk is eliminated altogether, making it accessible to more people. Each time we take the freedom from regulation or the autonomy we enjoy for granted, we undermine our own foundations a little more. Freedom demands that one fight to maintain it, and here we are exploiting it for our own gain or ignoring it altogether. Risk and freedom are two factors that make climbing uniquely different from other sports.

These two things draw much attention to climbing. Hard consequences attract participants who fancy themselves "extreme," people who know no fear. This same risk compels the thoughtful person to give 100 percent all the time—something rarely demanded by other sports. The freedom invites not only outlaws who disagree with rules and structure but also people who don't fit in to ready-to-wear sports and lifestyles.

Compare the differences: there aren't "destination" basketball courts, and few people would travel halfway around the world simply to play at a particular place nor is there any serious consequence for missing a shot. In football you must earn your right to play against the best team through a laborious, structured elimination process. As a climber, if you want to try the hardest route in the world, you are free to do so. You may fail, but there are no restrictions against trying.

The more structure we bring to climbing—competitions specifically designed for public consumption do just this—and the more we bastardize the true nature of climbing in our quest to earn a living from it, the less freedom we have to express our love for it and the less accurately we communicate it. By inviting the big media machine to play with our sport, we encourage them to interpret it for us vis-à-vis the general public. Will Gadd doesn't believe that big media is influencing our sport, figuring that "all changes are being directed by the actual participants," which is true to some extent. But if the media's telephoto lenses weren't trained on climbing, if they weren't shouting its virtues far and wide, if advertisers weren't using it to sell everything from SUVs to hay fever medicine, the "gene pool" of climbers would look far different than it does. It used to take more effort to discover climbing and become a climber. I'm an elitist, but I also care about what happens to things I love.

It angers me that, to the public, climbing equals either "the Everest Tragedy" or Sport Climbing competitions (where runouts are exaggerated because huge falls have greater television appeal). Neither of these concepts has much to do with actual climbing. It angers me that the sport/lifestyle of climbing as I and my peers have pursued it is portrayed to the general public by hack ESPN2 commentators who compare "the adrenaline rush" of Modified Shovel Racing to the "thrill" of Ice Climbing. Why have ignorant outsiders become the spokespersons for climbing? Is it because the media machine is too big for our inexperienced ombudsmen to handle? Perhaps buyers and sellers and savvy middlemen rarely concern themselves with an outcome other than individual. I can't fight too hard against this because I believe everyone has the right to earn a living the way they choose. However, we must accept responsibility for how our choices affect the future of climbing, not just how they may fatten our wallets.

I played the sponsorship game in order to climb all of the time. I climbed for the camera to earn a dollar and promote my name. I became public personality and property. These acts killed the spirit of climbing inside of me. They demeaned the sacrifices and choices I made that had always led deeper into climbing. For a lousy buck . . . I am guilty. I atone in my own way.

What happened within me is happening to climbing itself. The presence of climbing in the public eye sparked a media feeding frenzy. Its popularity inspired organized competition tailored to an ignorant audience. Because watching climbing is incredibly boring, mainstream competition is as irrelevant to actual climbing as stock car racing is irrelevant to driving or sport shooting to combat.

Media were willing to pay for the right to televise contests long before climbers knew how to create an appropriate competition. Experts made valiant efforts to come up with a format similar to real climbing and develop criteria to compare competitors. Much of climbing is internal and personal safety is the sole discretion

of the climber. These concepts are unacceptable to spectators and organizers respectively so "races" were developed using the same tools used for real climbing, but the
events attempt to package climbing's most interesting moments in a 30-second video
bite. To purists, it's monotony contrived to crush the soul of climbing. To the young
competitor, it is competition plain and simple, a chance to win $6000 or more. Will
Gadd was truly enthusiastic when he shouted into the phone, "It's great. It's got nothing
to do with climbing; it's just a lot of fun!"

The obviously telegenic Speed Climbing event pits competitors against each other
and the clock. There's "little subjective interpretation" according to Gadd, "although
the medium does change over the course of the event."

The Difficulty category leaves much to be desired. At the 1997 X-Games the route
was barely Grade 5, so no one found it hard. Gadd figures the criteria in this event
"actually bear some resemblance to climbing." The racer is judged by the number
of times the tip of his tool touches the ice, "like climbing, the more efficiently you
swing your tools the less often you'll place them and the more height you'll gain
for a given amount of effort." As the ice is hacked by each racer, the playing field
tilts in favor of competing later. The ascent is clocked as well. Posting a faster time
subtracts a certain number of strokes from your ascent, which means more points
over all.

Anathema to myself, and the reason I declined my invitation to compete in the
X Games, is that these are judged events. I abdicate the right of judgment to no
man. Gadd's read is different: "The real problem for me is that no one actually wins
a judged event, no one delivers a crushing defeat to his opponent, but there's no
other way to decide an outcome in competitive ice climbing." There will never be
any world records to break either. And as long as this remains a judged event and
the medium changes over the course of the actual competition, ice climbing "races"
will always be defective and unsatisfying.

The upside is that competitions may raise the standard of climbing because
people train for them. Gadd's M9 test piece, Amphibian, in Vail was "a direct result
of my training for the X-Games. Best of all," he says, "competition places the psyche
under a microscope. Once an objective is clearly defined, each act can be defined
as either advantage or liability." Unlike casual climbing of any kind where excuses
are a dime a dozen, competition strips away the bullshit. And that's always a good
thing.

The idea of training to participate in a hollow imitation of climbing leaves me
equally empty.

I sound like a reactionary who's afraid of change. I am not afraid. Rather, I am
saddened by the way climbing is changing. My trad pal Mark Wilford feels the same.
"I used to get excited, bitching about rap bolting back when it was a new thing. No
one was bothered by it then and they aren't now. Climbing has been so bastardized

WILL GADD

ON THE

LOWER EAST

FACE OF

LONGS PEAK,

COLORADO

from my ideal that I don't really care about it enough to fight the direction it's heading. I just go climbing, and it's enough."

I used to participate in the development of the sport more stridently. These days I too prefer keeping my personal vision of climbing private. I nourish the spirit of climbing within me. I will pass it along, communicate it to those who can hear, but it isn't for sale. I suppose the soul of climbing never has been for sale. Only the fluff, the mechanics, can be sold. The soul of climbing has rarely been publicized by media in any form because it is personal, not universal. Climbing can be many things to many people. I know what it is to me. Alpine Style, light, fast, the biggest objective with the least amount of gear; obscure concepts to be sure, but I consider them evolution. Too bad they'll be denied public scrutiny in favor of 60-foot-high artificial ice walls and billboards featuring Nike climbing shoes.

However, climbing is beautiful because arguments and exploitation disappear while actually doing it. A sick runout above a fatal landing grinds all else into insignificance. I know if I go two days without food on a big alpine face and immerse myself in the uncertainty of survival, the last thing I'll be caring about is the supposed future of climbing.

2000 AUTHOR'S NOTE

This piece engendered some good mail. Readers accused me of bitching about competition because I was afraid my 15 minutes of fame might be stolen by the competitors. An employee of ESPN actually said the channel was providing great service to climbing by publicizing it and helping climbers to earn money doing what they love. Such self-sacrifice on his part.

Eventually I stopped being bothered by media and commercial exploitation and organized ice climbing competition. It thrives or dies whether I care or not.

In fact, there's a World Cup circuit now. It is so far from actual climbing that there are rules against competing with wrist leashes on the tools because "leashes make the routes too easy," said Gioachino Gobbi, director of the ice gear manufacturer Grivel. Will Gadd, who won the title during the 99/00 season, agreed that "the idea behind the leash change was originally stated to be 'safety,' as if tools flying through the air were safer. Eventually, they admitted the real reason was to make the climbing harder, especially for the stronger climbers. This basically fucked anyone who is an ice/mixed/alpinist type and gave the comp to strong Sport Climbers who can hang onto a round stick forever: people like two-time world Sport Climbing champion Francois Lombard and Daniel DuLac, French bouldering champion." This indicates greater separation between disciplines than I originally suspected.

All I can do is monitor what climbing means to me as I evolve personally and write about it when I'm able. I climb my own way on my own terms. Although I marvel at the steepness and difficulty of "sport mixed" routes put up by guys like Will, I have to ask if the ethical transgressions of bolts, rehearsal, and preplaced protection are worth this so-called progress.

THE GIFT THAT KEEPS ON GIVING

THE SOUTH
FACE OF
MOUNT
BRADLEY,
RUTH GORGE,
ALASKA

When you're looking at life through a strange new room
maybe drowning soon, is this the start of it all . . . ?
the lights look bright when you reach outside
time for one last ride
before the end of it all.

Ian Curtis, Joy Division

We arrived eight minutes late, which made us lame. Scott Backes and I had just climbed a new route up the south face of Pico del Norte in Bolivia. From our bivy at 17,000 feet we'd climbed the 2800-foot line in just over four hours. We did it naked; without ropes or packs. We carried water and GU in our pockets, stashed ice tools in the waistbelts of our harnesses when they weren't in our hands, and brought one collapsible ski pole each. Our light clothes kept us warm while moving but didn't allow us to stop on top for long. We hugged. I cried because this was our last alpine route together. Scott was retiring from the game. The route and the style testified to our closeness and the total trust of our partnership. After a few minutes on top, we downclimbed to the east. We'd passed the apogee of our climbing career together, and it was going to be a long, thoughtful road back.

In La Paz, after a day of psychedelic visions, celebration, and other Third World absurdities, the route named itself in our hotel room: "Fuck 'em, They're All Posers Anyway." Which is how we both felt about the alpine pretenders who were popping up on the scene—posers who wrote "Sea of Vapors, Grade 7" on their paper-thin resumés after they'd done it in Grade 5 conditions. Funny how so-called extreme events are becoming less and less remarkable.

Scott turned away from the hard and dangerous routes which had defined us to father a family. I watched, disappointed and jealous, angry and full of love. At first

I thought his absence wouldn't matter. But the more I considered sharing those routes with another person, the less they appealed to me. Who, for example, shared what Scott and I shared? Our tastes in music, art, trash, conversation, training, mountains, our transparent macho fronts and compassionate insides? Where were my peers? Some dead, some retired, most living elsewhere. Others were unknown. I was alone in a sea of human beings with whom I had nothing in common except breathing, eating, shitting, white skin, and trying to get by. Without the intimacy and trust of the partnership, climbing lost its attraction. My spirit for it withered, so I quit. I even stopped training for it and spent myself elsewhere. I felt a twinge of envy when I heard about guys getting up routes, or even failing marvelously. Not enough to draw me back. I kept my blinders off, stepped outside of the climbing scene, and took a good look around. I finally realized climbing is not the coolest thing in the world; some of the people I met outside it changed my life. I discovered nothing to change my elitist viewpoint, but the flavors were novel.

From out there, the state of climbing looks bleak. Its explosive popularity causes overcrowding and resource closures. Money-hungry manufacturers cut corners by addressing the new breed of casual user, leaving the hardcore hanging. Sponsorhungry FNGs spray half-truths and hype in hopes of attracting benefactors. I dig seeing another man's bravado, but only if such stands tall on the strong back of actual achievement. Instead, I saw fragile foundations and inarticulate sputtering. How could someone possibly be "redefining the sport of ice climbing" by doing routes in Vail and playing at meaningless competition? On the other hand, all the huffing and puffing apparently pleases someone. So who am I to criticize when I don't do it at all anymore?

John Bouchard came through town. Over breakfast he said it had taken him two years to become a climber again after a seven-year break. Realizing how soft I'd become, I started training after only a year off. The first few weeks hurt. Continuing took more self-discipline than I was used to. Small, sore muscles reminded me that alpine climbing is suffering and weakness, and maybe if I was lucky, fulfillment. When I climbed a lot, I had good days when the strength of the gods flowed through me, but I barely remember those. Instead, I see failure and ass-kickings stitched together by occasional success and slowly emerging self-confidence. Looking ahead, I knew exactly what I was in for when I started climbing again. There aren't any mountains worth climbing where I live, so I trained in the weight room, I punished myself on the Stairmaster, and occasionally ran up real hills. I love the weight pile and live for the ring of the steel plates. Newfound power bred ambition, so I returned some phone calls. After talking a bit, Steve House sent me a topo and pictures. We entertained ideas of going north in the spring, which was far enough off that I didn't have to start paying attention yet. It was just talk.

During my year off *Climbing* invited me to write a column of opinionated social commentary, "to help stir the pot" they said. I figured they wanted to forward the fiction of presenting both sides of the coin. Few subjects hit close enough to home to merit a good 1500-word rave. I was interested in writing words to provoke reaction and cause one or two readers to think for themselves. But the more I watched and read, talked and wrote, the more disgusted I became.

Man brought his emotional sloth and self-aggrandizing exaggeration into ice and mixed climbing when the disciplines were taken away from the risks imposed by the mountain environment. Mixed climbing is suddenly a "new" thing. Roadside hot flashes and grading arguments, overhangs, chipped holds, preprotected routes, exhibitions, competitions, and route rehearsal flourish. These same activities, which used to be called "training," have unexpectedly become a sport in and of themselves. Happily, few participants apply their newfound skills in the real mountains. Vail is an outhouse, keeping all the shit in one place. The hype pretends that M-graded routes of any kind had never been climbed until our scantily clad protagonists rap-bolted, rehearsed, climbed, and performed for photo shoots on an overhanging choss heap above the freeway. A new grading system developed, and the race is on to see who can claim the highest number. Sadly, tactics and attitudes are often polluted by the quest for pure difficulty. Petty personal battles rage between the most talented practitioners. They savage each other in pursuit of contracts, peer recognition, or the need to appear superior. The conflict crosses oceans and generations, allowing a look at the ugly underbelly of human nature.

The reality is that hard mixed climbing was going on in the mountains for a long, long time before the "M" grades were created. Most of this climbing was referred to on route topos as "hard mixed," an ambiguous description for an equally puzzling form of climbing on a medium that changes daily. For example: Jeff Lowe claimed in his book *Ice World* that a talented mixed climber could eliminate the aid from my route Beyond Good and Evil in the French Alps. Amusing commentary from a man who's never been there, but he was proven right. The aid *was* eliminated during the second and subsequent ascents. Not by talent but by ice plastered eight inches thick and six feet wide over a thin crack in a corner. Although conditions improved drastically over the three years between ascents, no one has repeated the last four pitches, which contradicts the numerous claimed ascents. This kind of misrepresentation makes me sick. But mere words cannot fight this disease. Talk – Action = Ø. A man must lead by example.

I'd been hearing about Steve House for a couple of years, knew he'd done the Fathers and Sons Wall and soloed a new route on the 6000-foot-high west face of the West Buttress, both on Denali. Barry Blanchard confirmed his talent. Bill Belcourt assured me that he "climbed like an old guy," meaning he put in gear like someone who had been, and wanted to be, around for a while. The ultimate recommendation came from Scott who christened him "the great white hope" of American alpinism. This I had to see.

Steve wanted to go to the Canadian Rockies, but I am persona non grata up there. My attitude problem is officially unwelcome. I suggested Valdez because I wanted to whip myself into shape and see if Steve and I could get along, but I quickly concluded that pissing energy away on roadside attractions was a waste of time, no matter the intent. I needed a big helping of alpine calories, an opportunity to bite off more than I could chew.

I'd heard the winter was mild in the Alaska Range, without much snowfall. I grilled my friend Daryl Miller at the Talkeetna Ranger Station for details. Russians were on the mountain attempting a "true winter ascent," something conceivable to my Western mind only in a mild year. I remembered the grin on Mugs' face when he talked about the Alaska Range in March. He admitted to dozens of lines frozen on absurdly steep faces, climbable if you had the vision, the skills, and were willing to take the temperatures. Alaska is a cheap date, where it doesn't cost much to get hammered by a world-class mountain range. Both Steve and I could afford it, and I'd already convinced Jonny Blitz to get off the couch. He hadn't been alpine climbing in nine years. Blitz and I had talked ourselves into failing on routes before and figured Steve was the perfect man to prevent us from doing so again. Besides, I wasn't willing to go north as a pair with a guy I'd be meeting for the first time at the airport. Three is safer, and there's less social stress. Then again, three dominant, willful personalities provide plenty of fireworks.

Steve Locher met us at the airport and mediated the initial territorial markings as he drove us toward Talkeetna. The road ran quickly beneath the wheels as we spoke. We talked about the savages we would become once the plane dropped us on the glacier, tried to adjust from the comfort of central heating and tap water to the instantaneous change predicted for the following day.

Everything froze. Olive oil, canned meat, cheese. Nothing escaped except the sweetened condensed milk and that's weird science I don't want to know any more about. The thermometer read below minus 30 degrees Fahrenheit until we broke it. Three days of normal Alaskan temperatures gave way to moderate conditions, so we decided to go climbing. Our recon ski tours hadn't yielded the endless supply of ice we expected. Most lines looked like powder snow over granite or were sunless 24 hours a day. One south-facing gully on Mount Bradley stood out. We packed three days of food and started up.

I backed off the first pitch, tools dragging through the thin coating of snow without even slowing down. Blitz traversed. Steve led through, hurrying. I pulled on a cam to avoid weighting a flake straight above the belay. Steve climbed up, then down, then up, and down again, all out of sight. When Blitz and I turned the corner, we found his pack hanging off two screws equalized in some snow/ice fluff. A steep wall leaned out above, holes gaping where his feet punched through. The chicken-scratching of tools that found no purchase were everywhere. Higher, Blitz ran out of rope and cracks at the same time, with no screws left he belayed off his tools. The gully split. The right branch was a dead end. But the ice in the left fork overwhelmed our collective psyche. We searched for a way to aid around it. We'd left the hooks behind. Compact rock shut us down. The weight in our packs shut us down. Our tactics shut us down. There were two hours of light left. We were failing. Steve took it harder than Blitz. No big deal for me though. I've failed a lot. It was just the Alaska Factor kicking in.

We skied and ate for two days. Paul Roderick flew in a pizza for us. We finally decided to try the route we knew the most about. At this level it's rare to on-sight a route. Failure in the name of research is the name of the game. Or maybe we're just too stupid to get it right the first time. We decided we'd settle for the redpoint just like the Sport Climbers do.

The first five pitches passed easily. I drew the fearsome ice pitch out of the dead end. Where the wall was steep, the medium was ice. As it laid back, ice turned to mush. With ice tool shafts half-buried, I pulled off a 90-degree wall onto a snow-covered, 75-degree slab. Twenty feet separated me from my last piece of gear. Facing a certain ledge-dive, I named the pitch: The Super Third Eye Opener. We were all sick of climbers naming the pitches of alpine routes after happy little experiences or to express their hippy-trippy love of the beautiful environment. Alpine climbing is hard. The fear up there is more intense than anything short of a drive-by down here. It's not beautiful. It's fucking war. The struggle is glorious in its own way, but beauty is for the ground, for postcards and for glowing prose written long after the fact.

Jon began by insulting Steve's next pitch, calling it "putzy" and telling him to hurry up. He changed the tune when Steve's crampons skated off, showering sparks. Steve continued into a broad snow gully. Another dead end. Three parallel runnels, no more than a foot wide, exited up the right-hand wall. Blitz took the lead. I belayed while Steve dug a bivy ledge. Following, I was certain that Blitz had soiled himself, I sniffed the air for evidence. A flaring offwidth coated with verglas rose 20 unprotected feet above a Stubbie in a patch of ice. I'd seen a good nut farther down, though. There were little nicks in the verglas.

Dusk was on us, but I wanted to wring one more pitch from the day. It all goes bad at once, never by degrees. Darkness fell. The ice thinned to veneer, then to no ice at all, and appropriately, no gear. I couldn't back down. The cam I might have used was in Jon's belay anchor. The size of my balls diminished. I squirmed unstylishly upward and finally, drove many, many pitons at the belay. I fixed the rope and we rapped to the bivouac. Over lukewarm soup, Jon christened his pitch The Super Butt Deodorizer. He'd needed one.

Jon jugged the single 8.5-millimeter for breakfast. Steve led through. His picks found rock beneath thin ice on every swing. The ice ended below an overlap. He detoured right. His belay wasn't big enough for three. I waited. Blitz followed. Steve continued on the sharp end, up The Hateful Wall, which offered ice to the leader, mixed to Blitz, drytooling out of a cave to the lucky third.

We belayed on the biggest snow mushroom I've ever seen. I backed off the next pitch, unwilling to take the risk it required. Steve grabbed the rack, fueled by desire, the resolve not to fail until stopped cold, and a bit of unspoken competition. He climbed into an alcove, placed some gear, and tentatively moved onto a free-hanging icicle. He made three moves before it snapped and he rode it down. The first piece ripped without activating the Screamer. He hit the snow slope at the same moment a cam took his weight. If I'd had any food in my stomach, I would have puked. It was a bad place to be falling off. Steve rested for a few minutes, but he didn't come down and said nothing. "Oh fuck, he's going to try it again," I thought, and put the viewfinder back up to my eye.

With another piece of gear in the cave he'd created, Steve pulled onto the remaining ice. He stemmed and hooked toward salvation. It wasn't there. Ice turned to snow; cracks disappeared behind it. He was 25 feet out before he could place more gear. The wall steepened. The anchors were below another mushroom and chockstone. After hearing two pins go in, I yelled up, "What do you think?" wondering if the chockstone was the end of the line. Steve answered, "I can't think yet . . ." More hammering yielded a five-piece, equalized anchor. He fixed the rope and rapped. "I'm sorry about that," he confessed uncomfortably, "that was too dangerous to be doing up here." I told him I respected his apology, that yes, the risk had not been solely his to take. We slept on it. By morning, the icicle had become justifiable. The runout above remained out of control, but the mind adapts. Success breeds ambition. Steve's certainly is strong. I'd like to see him survive it.

Our three days of fuel could be stretched to four, not more, so we punched for the top with no bivy gear, planning to go until stopped or we ran out of route. We wanted to move fast, but the pitch into the next system took awhile. Blitz aided off a cam, then his tools. He pulled on hooks, tied-off blades, and bad nuts. The back-cleaning ate the clock, but the Super Three-Hour Pitch ended on easier ground, and we started running. Higher, we stalled beneath another chockstone. Traversing around it inspired me to invent a new grading system (I want one of my own, too). The pitch is rated In Vail They'd Call It M7—But It's Not. "M" grades are more succinct, but mine communicates more information.

The next pitch had actual ice on it—briefly. Higher, Blitz shouted down from his lead, "What do we need one more of?" Steve and I simultaneously concluded another chockstone loomed above. "Is this ever going to end?" I asked. Steve answered, "The altimeter says we're close," as he put on his headlamp. Steep ice in The

STEVE HOUSE ARRIVES AT THE TOP OF THE FIFTEENTH PITCH, ON THE GIFT THAT KEEPS ON GIVING, MOUNT BRADLEY, ALASKA.

Glory Hole allowed us behind the chockstone. It was one of two pitches on the route where the ice was thick enough to take a 17-centimeter screw to the eye.

Loose rock gave way to hard névé, which welcomed us to the 8700-foot col where we agreed our route would end. Four hundred feet of easy snow—"easy" in this case meaning a guy would have a hard time falling off of it—disappeared toward the summit. I had a record to maintain and a lot of raps to my sleeping bag. It was 8 P.M. The black pyramid of Mount Huntington loomed nearby, and Denali, The Great One, made every other mountain look inadequate. We felt okay though.

We landed on the Super 'Shroom bivy at 1:30 A.M., but it was 2 A.M. before we freed the hung rappel. Sleep came easily. The Northern Lights shimmered across the few degrees of sky visible between the walls enclosing our route.

The next day flowed smoothly. Our rack disappeared for anchors, but we didn't mind because it meant less weight to carry on the ski back to base camp, which promised to be memorable.

There was a dark stain around the tents and I could see Steve circling somewhat aimlessly, unwilling to set his pack down. I brayed like a donkey when I realized that while we were climbing, God's cruel joke had been to visit the ravens upon us. No clean animals these, they went straight for the shit bags. "Pre-digested nuts, candy, grease, and meat . . . mmmm, good," I imagined them cawcawing amongst themselves. Apparently our feces gave them the runs, and in response they perched on our tents and let their diarrhea flow. The Alaska Factor kicking us again.

I faxed Scott the topo when I got home. I was proud of the climb and wanted to share it with him. It was the first hard alpine route I'd done without him in more than four years. I missed him. There's nothing as sacred as a partnership forged by shared risk and uncertainty, failure and success. We depended on each other for continued existence 24 hours a day. Our trust had taken years to build, and there was nothing like it on Mount Bradley. The three of us were simply men joined by a common goal, having fun, pushing the boat out, learning about each other, but something was missing. We weren't necessarily stronger as a team than alone. We feigned the closeness we lacked. We united ourselves into a team by poking fun at the outsiders. Anyone who wasn't where we were doing what we were doing was fair game. Although I've known Blitz longer than Scott, the intensity of what Scott and I have been through has scarred me deeper. The fax caught him off guard: "it was both amazing . . . and horrific, I'm proud of you Mark, but very sad I wasn't there."

Scott wrote me a letter before I went north, and I carried it with me. It finishes with these words:

"I grasp and gasp the knowledge of friendship
unimagined 'til now
the weight and light of it
my reflections pale against our toil together
my love, your love
hewn from rock and ice and bone
dovetails together
joined
flawlessly
finally."

The mountains won't ever feel the same without him. But his words remind me that the climbing wasn't foremost for us in the first place. Climbing mountains was just the start of it all . . .

2000 AUTHOR'S NOTE

I love the changes life offers up. Scott began climbing again. He jumped right back into the deep end with a new route on Howse Peak named "M-16," which Steve called "twice as hard as M8." Barry Blanchard rounded out the team. Now Scott has two children, and Steve and I have become quite close.

Some comments in this piece were directed at Will Gadd. Many readers got the idea I hated him, which is not the case at all. Will and I are friends. I respect his talent and drive enormously, but we agree to disagree, and he's a better man than I because he never stabbed my back in print. Our climbing goals are different, as are our ethics and tactics. Even though my ego demands I believe my way of doing things is superior, in calm moments I concede that it's all climbing, and people should do whatever they want. My ire rises when climbers misrepresent their actions. I don't care what you do, just say truthfully what it is that you do. Still, there are moments when I shout that alpinism properly occupies the top of the pyramid.

I'm not as pissed as I appear in this piece that Francois Damilano and Francois Marsigny had better conditions for the second ascent of Beyond Good and Evil either. For Damilano it was a personal vendetta; he'd been wanting to get back at me ever since I upstaged him at the Ice Festival in Gavarnie and a year later in the Canadian Rockies. Downgrading "Beyond" was his response to *Vertical* magazine heralding The Reality Bath as "the hardest route in the world" but neglecting to mention climbs he did in Canada during the same season. I'm told he threw a memorable temper-tantrum in the *Vertical* office over it too.

I was obviously angry with Jeff for speculating about how a more talented climber might free-climb "Beyond" in print. Not that it matters, or ever did. A little older and wiser, I managed to let go of it, but the same speculation is rampant among the younger generation. I heard of one young gun who, after failing on the north face of Jannu, said, "There's no way Tomo was soloing up there," as if the fact that he and his partners could not get off the ground precluded anyone else from doing so. We all pass judgment when we feel threatened. I suppose this is human nature and might never change. I try to recognize when I behave this way now. Recognition is the first step toward changing a bad habit, they say.

Climbing would not print the final words from Scott in their version of the article. The editors thought that theme detracted from the drama of the climb itself, but it was a big part of the motivation for doing the route in the first place. The piece was written as a tribute to him and to us. I speculated that *Climbing* worried about how one man describing his unconditional love for another might be received by the readership. I thought it tragic to cut away this depth.

JUSTIFICATION
FOR AN ELITIST
DEFINING

HOUR 27:
STEVE HOUSE
ON THE RAMP
AT 15,100
FEET. CZECH
DIRECT ROUTE,
DENALI,
ALASKA

ATTITUDE— CONSCIOUSNESS ON DENALI'S CZECH DIRECT

I spent my first trip of 2000 to Denali trying to put as much distance between my-self and my partner as possible. Mark Jenkins and I never climbed together before. I went because, at one point, it sounded like a good idea and I'd said I would. Our stated goal was to flash the Cassin. We were without a clever strategy though, and the West Buttress mentality seduced us upon arrival. There was nothing light, fast, or high about us.

Discord was immediate; he sang and whistled songs I detested. Mark isn't part of my crew, those few alpine climbers who are at the top of the game. Although he climbs because he loves it, and I do the same, there's an ocean separating how and why we each love climbing. Mark's technical ability and survival skills are unim-peachable. He's lived through some mind-blowing adventures, but I didn't trust his judgment, or care enough about him to make any concessions.

We hadn't shared enough to develop the belief in each other that dangerous climbs demand. And since I was only with him to train for a bigger route, I chose the West Buttress over the Cassin because it could whip me into shape as well as anything. The decision made little difference to me. Mark was disappointed and questioned why I didn't consider us a team. The climbing experience I'm after can't be had without the current of mutual love and respect electrifying the rope. When I climb with Scott or Steve or Barry the rope is a high-tension wire. The best part of the trip with Mark was untying from him at 10,000 feet. I turned up my Walkman, pointed 'em straight, and skied away.

When it was over and folks asked what we did, I answered that we barely got up the West Buttress. Denali by any route is a substantial undertaking and minus-40-degree temperatures level the field. Our toes were just as cold as the next guy's. But I couldn't truthfully say we "climbed" the mountain because there's no climbing on the West Buttress. Unless you call dragging a sled 11 miles, jugging fixed ropes up 500 feet of 35-degree ice, and hiking along a wide ridge-top "climbing." Folks call it whatever their egos need to hear.

A week after unroping from Mark I flew back to Kahiltna International with fellow cynics Steve House and Scott Backes. Each of us is intolerant of empty words and arrogant about action. The posturing among virgin Denali suitors sickened me more than it had in 1994. I guess the gray in my beard means I'm older, not wiser.

"Outside," in the Lower 48, it's not uncommon to hear a young buck claim he's going to do new routes on Hunter and Foraker, then blast the Cassin. I know. I was one of them once. Some men manage to posture all the way to 14,000 feet. During my trip with Mark I actually heard a guy say, "I'm doing the Seven Summits." When asked how many he'd climbed, he answered, "Well, um, Denali will be the first." Back at 7200 feet, more sober statements are exchanged: "Twenty-two days, not exactly what I envisioned," followed by pathetic rationalization about how no one else summited during that period either.

I'm an elitist prick and I think posers have polluted mountaineering. They replace skill and courage with cash and equipment. They make the summit, not the style, the yardstick of success. Only marginal minds or true individuals used to discover mountaineering. Lack of social support forced them to be autonomous, to turn climbing into a lifestyle, isolated from society. We had community back then. Now I'm embarrassed to call myself a climber, because close on the heels of the admission some dilettante will ask whether I've read *Into Thin Air* or done Everest.

Today's acceptance of climbing as sport, combined with technological and financial advances, allows casual participation. "How-to" books—including my own—offer recipes for success. Guidebooks for particular routes define the rules more specifically. I can't think of another mountain besides Denali for which such a rigid formula is prescribed: "Drag it all to 8K. Carry to 10K, sleep at 8K. Move to 11K, back-haul from 10K. Carry to 13K, sleep at 11K. Move to 14K, back-haul from 13K. Rest. Carry to 16K, sleep at 14K. Move to 17K with three days' food. If the weather's good, go for the top. If not, fetch enough supplies from 16K to wait out the storm." The indoctrination is so strong that some guys busy caching at 16K said, "You went to the summit from 14K? Wow. We didn't know you could do that."

Scott, Steve, and I skied to the base of Denali's south face. We spent two days trying to comprehend the massiveness of the wall and glassing features on the 9000-foot Czech Direct (CZD). The route was first climbed over 11 days in 1986 by a team of three Slovaks, who fixed 1000 feet of rope. Kevin Mahoney and Ben Gilmore repeated it at the end of May in a seven-day, Alpine-Style effort. Hearing they'd done it saddened us until we realized we didn't care whether we made the second, third, or eighth ascent. Only our chosen style mattered. In fact, a modern comparison would make our message that much clearer: We wanted to climb it in one push, without sleeping.

To go as fast as the dream demanded we had to acclimatize, so we pointed our skis up the West Buttress. Within 18 hours of arriving at 14K, Ranger Roger Robinson invited us to help rescue a 62-year-old climber with broken ribs and the onset of pneumonia from 17K. An armada of strong guys, including Joe Reichert and Pete Athans, made the rescue in eight hours round trip. Afterward I rhetorically asked Steve what my true motivation for helping was, and why I enjoyed being so skilled at it.

"Because it further justifies your elitist attitude," he replied, and it became our motto.

A *Nova* video crew pounced on us the next day. They acted as if we should be excited to answer questions about footwear. We gave the interview as a favor to our friend Colby Coombs, the camera crew's guide. Although I am happily orchestrating Steve's sell-out by introducing him to sponsors, encouraging media presence, and programming slideshows, I'm often galled by my own sleazy, subconscious attempts to claim any 15-minute period of fame within reach. Steve calls it The Poison Wanting and shames me for it. Two days later the shame spurred me to the summit in 5 hours and 39 minutes.

Back at the airstrip, bad weather stalled our return to the south face. Each day at 7K stole a bit of acclimatization. Each inch of fresh snow changed the route and its approach. Scott figured the gods made it harder because we had made ourselves stronger.

The Czech Direct posed many questions. As high pressure built, we raced up its first 1000 feet to determine how much they'd cost. Afterward we strategized. Proper timing was critical. So were hydration and nutrition. We'd stop every 12 hours to brew and eat; the first break during the afternoon's warmth would place the following one in the middle of the night. As a counter-measure each of us brought a two-pound Polarguard jacket and balaclava. We packed two MSR X-GKs, 22 ounces of fuel, and a titanium pot for each. Two stoves meant we could melt snow quickly enough to prevent an irreversible chill and loss of momentum while brewing. We split 55 pounds into two loads; 18 pounds were water. The leader would climb with a light summit pack or nothing at all.

We planned to ditch gear as it became superfluous: the rack, a rope, useless stoves. Armchair intellectuals will shout ethical opposition to this behavior, but until such critics confront the likelihood of death, they can't understand how easily ethics are traded for continued existence. Honor means winning, which requires surviving. This style of climbing isn't poetic. It's primitive battle with clubs and stones.

After dinner Steve read to us from Yukio Mishima's manifesto, *Sun and Steel* (1970): "Pain, I came to feel, might well prove to be the sole proof of the persistence of consciousness within the flesh, the sole physical expression of consciousness. As my body acquired muscle, and in turn strength, there was gradually born within me the tendency towards positive acceptance of pain, and my interest in physical suffering deepened." Mishima, who killed himself in 1970, had described our need to climb the CZD in a single push without knowing the context. We were on Denali to prove the existence of consciousness.

How far are we going to take this?
The question is not how far. The question is, do you possess the constitution, the depth of faith, to go as far as is needed?

The Boondock Saints

At 4 A.M., above the roar of the stoves, I listened to seracs disintegrating on the Ramp Route below the South Buttress. Mugs Stump died over there; buried by a collapsing crevasse lip a mile from our camp. I took these avalanches as his blessing. We knew he'd appreciate our plan because he had followed the European lead toward Single-Push climbing in the mid-1980s. Erhard Loretan, Jean Troillet, and Pierre-Alain Steiner climbed Dhauligiri in winter. Loretan and Troillet sped up Everest in 36 hours. Benoit Chamoux climbed K2 in 23 hours even though fixed ropes and camps threatened to trip him every step of the way. Cho Oyu, Shishpangma, G1, and G2 were also climbed without bivouacs. Europeans raised the bar a long time ago. Mugs took notice. He tested nonstop tactics on giant faces in Antarctica and refined them further during his 15-hour dash up the Cassin. Since his death in 1992, few have shown the courage to acknowledge his torch.

We crossed the bergschrund at 6 A.M., passed the Czech's second bivouac at 8 A.M., their third at 11 A.M. We reached their fourth bivy site on the first ice field at 2 P.M. and moved into a ledge chopped by Mahoney and Gilmore where we brewed, ate, and refilled our Dromedaries. We led in blocks of six pitches and simul-climbed or soloed what didn't merit a belay. I finally took the sharp end at 7 P.M. on the Czech's 32nd pitch. We were hauling ass and moved into another pre-chopped ledge at 1 A.M.

Scott led out at 3:30 A.M. Steve snored while I belayed. The topo showed ice steeper than 90 degrees. We joined Scott on his hastily chopped stance. He confessed that he was "glad to have gotten off that without getting hurt." Steve led through. His back-stepping and stemming told us everything we needed to know. From our belay it looked like Steve was connecting blobs of ice on El Cap.

As the sky lightened, Scott looked down.

"Do you see that?" he asked.

I looked over my shoulder and saw nothing unusual: Denali's shadow smothered Mount Hunter, the East Fork was almost a mile below us.

"What?" I asked.

"Look how far down the glacier is. We couldn't retreat if we wanted to."

Shit. The terrain would eat us. We pointed our faces upward.

Higher, Steve dropped a tool.

"I used that hammer on every route I've done since 1996," he said.

The list included his solo first ascent of Beauty Is a Rare Thing on Denali's Direct West Buttress, Mascioli's Pillar, King Peak, our new route on Mount Bradley, and M-16 on Howse Peak in the Canadian Rockies.

"At least it was KIA. I won't have to retire it when I don't trust it anymore and it never let me down," he said thoughtfully. We passed a silent moment in memory and honor. Most of the hard climbing was over, so it didn't matter.

An hour later we were lost. Mist lapped at the broken rocks and ice. Visibility was nil but we sensed Big Bertha, the serac dominating Denali's south face, pushing us west. That we were still conscious enough to be scared of falling ice comforted me. The topo was unclear and each apparently simple exit from the ice field proved more difficult than we could afford. I scouted toward the Cassin but saw no easy way out. Scott wondered out loud whether we were going to get off Denali at all as our collective confidence ebbed. We'd found the uncertainty Messner spoke so eloquently about 30 years ago but it wasn't as beautiful as he'd led us to believe. Our minds were fried. Making the decision to stop and brew up was a farce. Ticktock, tick-tock.

Thirty-four hours into it we scraped off a little perch at 15,900 feet. Calories and a break from the stress refreshed us. Scott traversed into a gully safely distant from the polished chutes and slabs beneath the serac. Sleep deprivation triggered our sluggish decline. No one could lead more than two pitches efficiently before indecisiveness and fear slowed his progress. Instead of adapting, we stupidly clung to the six-pitch block strategy that had worked so well 24 hours earlier. Scott placed four pieces of gear on a 30-degree ice pitch, he spent 20 minutes building an anchor. I'd never seen him that wrecked before. Steve and I were angry but said nothing because we knew fatigue worked its disease on us as well.

An ugly gale lashed spindrift against our goggles. We were too cold to climb further into its teeth and stopped in the lee of a massive boulder, hoping sun-up would calm the wind. Steve and I chopped hard for an hour. Scott watched with glazed-over eyes, too wasted to lend a hand. Things were falling apart. The stoves hissed away the last of their fuel at hour 48. Their silence sent my imagination down a deep, dark hole. We had eight lukewarm liters of water to get us to the top and down to our 11,000-foot cache but no idea how long it might take. Then Steve threw up, chucking 500 calories and a half-gallon of water into the snow. His stomach was troubled enough that he couldn't replace any of it. "Shit," I thought, "he's done." Out loud I asked if he was okay.

"Yeah," he said, wiping his chin, "I'm just defining my consciousness."

We couldn't retreat or escape sideways. I wasn't sure how much higher we'd get before Denali swallowed us forever. Cold numbed my toes and as the icy feeling crept up my legs I quietly accepted that we might have finally gone too light.

Survival instinct blinded us to the splendor of sunrise. Its beauty might materialize across years of memory, but seeing the sun right then just meant our jackets were finally warm enough. With the frigid Alaskan dusk another 18 hours away, Scott and Steve snatched a nap. Uncertainty about the remaining effort left me sleepless and vibrating. After 15 minutes I started packing, prepared to shut up, put up, and maybe die trying.

> It's one thing to hold a hammer in your hand, but do you have it in you, can you pound that nail? So many of you line up, but so few of you cross the line . . . Talk is talk. Kill is kill.
>
> **Henry Rollins, "On the Day"**

I climbed away from the ledge onto yet another amazing mixed pitch. Face to face with the upper edge of Big Bertha, I belayed from four tied-off pins. My partners followed quickly. The slope laid back so I ran on blunt frontpoints until I was out of rope, then shouted for them to move with me while I continued tugging.

"What about the anchor?"

"Leave it. We're done," I shouted back.

Before starting up I'd joked that the last 4000 feet would be my block, "since you guys won't be able to keep up anyway." We crested the Cassin at 17,400 feet, 56 hours above base camp. Two climbers shouted to us from above. They were high enough that we couldn't accidentally catch them and be compelled to break trail. They left nice tracks. The views behind us were heartrending, and the gods smiled.

I stomped one foot in front of the other, each step taking me higher. I used to love the sound of my crampons chewing up the ice and admire the brutal efficiency of my tools. Then, I felt invulnerable, as vanity overcame innocence. I've since crossed a pride-killing eternity. A 40-long list of dead friends and partners crushed conceit beneath the pressure of reality. I learned to respect my fear and sometimes dredge up the courage to face it. And despite understanding my humanity, I still feel superior within a narrowly defined discipline. Mostly because I've proven how far a disciplined mind can take the man that isn't particularly strong, or brave.

I couldn't believe Scott had emptied himself so completely but clawed enough from his reserves to keep going. If I stopped I fell asleep; when I slowed my pace it was the same. Previously unknown will moved my legs fast enough to keep me from falling off. We passed beyond any preconceptions of endurance, broke free of accepted limitations. Fatigue multiplied itself geometrically inside us: hour 56 was at least 12 hours harder than hour 48. Minutes were hours and hours meant nothing. We hovered across an unfamiliar landscape between the conscious and unconscious

SCOTT
BACKES AT
16,900 FEET,
FOLLOWING THE
FINAL HARD
PITCH ON THE
CZECH DIRECT,
DENALI, ALASKA

mind. We hurt, but we didn't feel it. We tired, but it did not matter. Concentration on the task was total. The "I" each of us revered so highly disappeared. We became each other and we became the mountain. Mishima was right: in our suffering we discovered the bright and ragged doors of perception, our exhausted minds were powerless to resist such pure, human experience.

Near the top Steve wanted to traverse west. I insisted we follow the tracks because it was so casual. Scott agreed. Fifteen minutes higher, Steve said he was going to traverse whether we came with him or not. I relented, and led the way for a bit. With self-preservation paramount, any action that made our push toward safety faster was fair.

Thin snow over rock required careful attention. Traversing made the big drop to our left more apparent and reminded us how careless of consequence we'd become. Halfway to salvation Steve apologized for his insistence and bad decision, admitting, "Staying in the tracks would have been easier." I accepted. Scott caught us and asked, "What the fuck are we doing over here?"

"I'm not sure," answered Steve, "I apologize though," and led through.

"This is scaring me," Scott admitted as we followed.

We pulled over a little cornice onto Pig Hill just below Kahiltna Horn, 60 hours after crossing the 'schrund. The summit was a hundred feet higher but light years away. As danger disappeared hard-won clarity faded with it. Dehydrated and hallucinating, we stumbled toward the trench thousands of thundering hoof-beats had pounded into the West Buttress.

During a break on the Football Field, I told Scott I hadn't had the will to resist Steve's desire to traverse, "and I couldn't let him take off alone. I can't think of a good reason for making that choice."

"I can think of 60."

"I don't understand."

Scott answered lucidly, "That you don't get it proves my point; 60 hours of climbing led to Steve's decision."

We drank the last of our water.

I test the power of a will according to the amount of resistance it can offer and the amount of pain and torture it can endure and know how to turn to its own advantage.

Friedrich Nietzsche, *Thus Spoke Zarathustra*, 1883-1892

We got to 14k at the 63-hour mark. Our brains were mushy, the offer of sandwiches and tea meant more than it would have any other time. We spent 24 hours being fed and nursed by friends in the Park Service Weather-Port, then hiked to our cache and skied from there to 7k. After a rest, we recovered the tents left behind in the East Fork. That same afternoon we flew the time warp between where we'd been and the rest of the world, between primordial and civilized man.

Steve left Talkeetna the following morning. Scott and I felt robbed. We wanted to hang out, to eat, drink, and talk it over. Instead we hugged one another and put Steve on the shuttle. Each of us knew without having the language to say it that the Czech Direct had been one of the most powerful experiences of our lives.

The pendulum arcs between chest-puffing egotism and the sense that success resulted from fantastic luck. It's a difficult route to live with. We were transformed during those hours and re-creating the "consciousness without exclusion" may be impossible. Visiting it in our memories is little consolation. I've tried to explain the crack we peeped through, but even close friends can't understand. What truth we learned is locked in our three hearts alone.

This is as simply as I can say it: we went north, we picked up Mugs' torch, and shined its bright light down the long corridor of potential. Who will take the next step?

2000 AUTHOR'S NOTE

This was a very difficult piece to write. I spent two months after the climb assimilating it, discussing it with Steve, Scott, and others before I came to the limited understanding described above. I don't think the bond forged between us can ever be broken; without filters or prejudice we saw each other's deepest strengths and weaknesses. Our love and respect allowed us to accept, without judgment, what we learned about each other and ourselves.

That said, our huge step into the future of alpinism left us little opportunity to draw parallels or find metaphors. I wanted to accurately communicate both physiologic and psychological aspects of climbing for 60 hours nonstop but found language wanting. I tried the military allegory; the guerrilla strike versus the huge, plodding formations of mechanized infantry. It fell flat. Finally, my partner on Mount Huntington in 1998, Bill Belcourt, exclaimed it was "like science fiction. You opened a crack in time and glimpsed the future." Less than a day later my friend Charlie Sassara, no stranger to the Alaska Range, wrote, "You guys just accomplished a Mars shot." It was that weird, a completely illogical compression of time.

Climbing the CZD in 60 hours was the culmination of all the lessons and attitude expressed in *Extreme Alpinism*. I walked my talk. I wrote to my nutritionist about how we had finally sighted perfection. None of us had actually seen it before but only posited its existence. To be sure, we made mistakes, but we were very, very close to climbing the route in exact accordance with its exigencies and our own stylistic demands. We could have shaved off 12 hours, I won't admit how just yet.

I tapped out a note to Steve on this subject as well:

"Perfection is something chased but never achieved. It is an evolution by small steps: progressing from the 7.5 or 8 (on a scale of 1 to 10) toward the 9, and the elusive 10. I think we are close, Steve. I see it receding over the horizon. A closer look will require more self-discipline, better science, and clearer strategy. We dissect such small details because we cannot ever expect better weather, better climbing, or better conditions. Or a route offering a better layout of terrain for both ascent and descent. The fact that the external was so accommodating forces our scrutiny inward, and we need a magnifying glass to see some of our mistakes. We've become such introspective nitpickers. Is this not the burden of the man who seeks personal evolution?"

This evolution has brought me to a position I never imagined I would occupy. I feel something swelling which is part ego but part duty and responsibility as well. In 1992, when my partner Randy Rackliff's girlfriend, Ruthann Brown, reached me in Chamonix to tell me Mugs had been killed, I wrote the following in the current notebook: "Mugs: dead, who's going to take over the spirit he worked so hard to develop? Who shall burn the torch?" I knew that I was not the one. I was too conflicted, too freaked out about my own life to give anything to anybody else. Besides, I'd never done any climbing I felt was worthy in comparison to his.

The CZD changed something for me. That, and the fact that *Extreme Alpinism* has altered the way people appreciate and/or deal with me, cause the sense that Mugs' mantle is passing to my shoulders. I am not the brilliant, visionary climber he was. I know that, but I am in a similar position to influence the way future generations climb mountains. Scott pointed it out before I recognized it. It's a strange thing to notice. At the risk of sounding egomaniacal I admitted my feelings to Steve. I said, "I recognize this, and I do not take it lightly. Being a duty, a debt I must repay to 'climbing,' it's not going to my head." I concluded by telling him, "You must know deep inside that this responsibility will pass to your shoulders some time." The future belongs to Steve's generation and those that follow.

As a role model I have tried to lead by example, but mine is not always a welcome one. Many climbers became such in an anti-establishment response to more fashionable, organized sport. Today particular climbing styles, attitudes, and ethical positions are so entrenched that they must be considered the current Establishment. As Morpheus said in *The Matrix*, "It is a system and it is our enemy." It's certainly mine. In keeping with the tenets of punk, I treat Alpine Style as rebellion; against an acquisitive climbing culture that is full of "collectors," against people in all disciplines who settle for less—especially those who know better. Alpine Style is rebellion but not revolution; I'm not talking about something new, I'm a conservative preaching a return to the most basic, minimalist approach to the mountains. I demand that practitioners place greater emphasis on their own power and skill rather than using technology as a crutch. No wonder my point of view is not enthusiastically adopted.

Steve Locher, who smoothed many transitions through Anchorage for me and always provided a sober sounding board for my ideas, suggested I not take it too seriously. He recognizes that a lone voice on the Stock Exchange floor is no match for the greed exhibited by people looking to improve their resumés. He wrote, "I believe in the long run that there will be a movement back to the roots of climbing, but right now, Caligula has taken power." Sadly, I believe his diagnosis is true, and without bright lights like Steve House, Rolando Garibotti, and Marko Prezelj, the future of alpinism and the mountains themselves would be dark indeed.

I'm concerned that some readers might take this article and this book as a message perpetuating the idea of "superstar climbers." It would be easy to read my words and say, "All that is well and good for Mark and his friends, but it means nothing to the rest of us." The superstar archetype causes a separation or distinction. It may also offer those who settle for less (in relation to their own potential, not in comparison to mine) a way out. It would disgust me to know that positioning myself and my message in a particular way provides built-in excuses for people who are too lazy to live up to their own promise. But it may be unavoidable.

I wrote in the main body of this piece that I've proven how far a disciplined mind can take the man that isn't particularly strong, or brave. Readers who are drunk on Dr. Doom Kool-Aid could easily miss the fact that I am less different from my fellow man than the media-generated hype pretends. Climbing is the means I have chosen to define and understand myself. I have given the mountains everything. I found the singular frequency at which my soul resonates and heeded its tone. My obedience taught me to be the man I am. My reward is freedom. As Brian wrote in the Foreword, it is "not the illusion of the freedom to choose, but the freedom to confidently follow the heart." This may be the only difference between us.

Hear and forget.
See and remember.
Do and understand.
Ancient martial arts dictum

WHAT'S IN A TITLE?

SOLO ON THE CHARMOZ
Named by Michael Kennedy at *Climbing*.

KISS OR KILL
Shouted by Exene Cervenka in a song titled "We're Desperate." It was my mantra, you either love what I say and do or hate it. I tried to live the all-or-nothing philosophy too. It didn't work out very well.

GLITTER AND DESPAIR
Struggling to live up to "Kiss or Kill," and falling short. It actually was poached from a song by The Stranglers titled "Paradise" in which the words "glimmer and despair" are sung.

THE REALITY BATH
A band from Austin, Texas, called Nice Strong Arm named their debut album "Reality Bath." I don't know what they meant, but the experience Randy and I shared on that particular route was exactly that.

RISE AND FALL OF THE AMERICAN ALPINIST
Coined by Michael Kennedy at *Climbing*. My working title is too embarrassing to even put down here.

I HURT, THEREFORE I AM
Obviously a play on Descartes' famous phrase. It was a rough, painful year and I discovered some of my true self by surviving it.

THE ABATTOIR
Literally, *slaughterhouse*. I heard the word in a song by And Also the Trees, looked it up, and thought it described the intensity of soloing difficult and dangerous routes.

HEAVEN NEVER LAUGHED
As with a lot of phrases I wrote or routes I named this came from having misunderstood the words to a song. Justin Sullivan of New Model Army actually sang "never-never land."

MY WAY: A SHORT TALK WITH TOMO CESEN
"My Way" was the title of Tomo's own article on the same subject.

PERESTROIKA CARPET RIDE

I fixated on having three words in the title. I wanted it to be funny and confusing. But I still can't recall where the phrase came from.

AGAINST THE GRAIN

The title of a Bad Religion song. Perfectly describes my attitude at the time.

HOUSE OF PAIN

It's where I lived while writing this article. I couldn't reconcile my own behavior or live up to my ideals. Scott Backes named my little studio the "house of pain" during his visit in May 1992. The name came from a song by Cyberaktif, a Skinny Puppy offshoot.

A LIFETIME BEFORE DEATH

I tried to find a phrase which spoke of how much a man can live in a short time.

DISTANT WARNING

Cevin Key shouts this in a Skinny Puppy song titled "Love in Vein." Since the routes described were a shot across the bow of French alpinism, I thought it appropriate.

THE REFERENCE POINT: INTERVIEW WITH JEAN-CHRISTOPHE LAFAILLE

Jean-Christophe pointed to his experience on Annapurna as that, a moment when his life changed forever.

NO TIME TO CRY

The title of a Sisters of Mercy song that I always wanted to use. It dovetails perfectly with Ian McCullough saying, "Do what must be done and don't say 'maybe'."

THIS IS WHAT YOU WANT, THIS IS WHAT YOU GET

John Lydon's masterful description of the experience of life.

TWITCHING WITH TWIGHT

Will Gadd named this in one of his finer hours. I was physically vibrating when I wrote it too.

CHAMONIX: OVER THE TOP OR UNDER THE GROUND

Typical Twight, just "Kiss or Kill" reworded.

VOICE OF DISSENT—DR. DOOM DISSES TRADITIONAL VALUES

Coined by Michael Kennedy at *Climbing*.

SMOKE GETS IN YOUR EYES

Neil Feineman at *Gravity* coined the title.

VOICE OF DISSENT—COMPETITION RUINS THE FREE-FOR-ALL

Climbing came up with the subtitle.

THE GIFT THAT KEEPS ON GIVING

The route on Mount Bradley kept "giving" us something more to overcome. Just when we thought we were done, the ravens visited base camp. I hate it when the route name is shortened to "The Gift" because a sport route at Red Rocks shares that name. It sounds like the climb was easy, a gift. Hardly.

JUSTIFICATION FOR AN ELITIST ATTITUDE

From a conversation Steve House and I had at 14,000 feet on Denali. I named the soundtrack CD I burned following the trip the same. The liner notes for the compilation also included the phrase, "We don't have to prove a point because we live it."

ACKNOWLEDGMENTS

Support: Scott Backes, without whom many of the routes herein would not have been done, I wouldn't have written so personally about them had I not felt his love and trust. Jonny Blitz reminded me I once used few words, then scolded me for writing too many as I aged. Barry Blanchard introduced me to Hemingway and unconditional love. Anne Smith put up with late nights and black thoughts. Anne-Sophie Charamel wouldn't let me have it my way, but compelled me to put the words to paper anyway. John Bouchard taught me the beauty of the concise phrase. Jon Krakauer didn't laugh at my early work because though badly written, it had heart. Alison Osius tried to teach me the technical bits she learned at University (I didn't listen). Lady Catherine spoke the truth. Michael Kennedy edited me well and loaned me his forum to express myself. Jim Martin taught me to write in an active voice and praised my "muscular" verbs. Lisa Boshard turned me into a "dog person," gave up her home so I had a place to write *Extreme Alpinism,* took care of me while I did it, and then married me.

Inspiration: Mad Dog (Kevin McClung, Cardinal of the Church of Tactical Truth) for marrying Lisa and I. Kurt Johnstad for working harder than anyone else I know. Bubba for still being alive. Steve House for burning the torch brightly. Carol Davidson for standing by me since the first reinvention. Andy Parkin who "maintained" despite an enormous setback. Alex Lowe who shamed me into exploiting my climbing talent instead of wasting it. Alison Hargreaves for her unbridled ambition. Will Gadd whose enthusiasm and self-discipline are infectious and who beat the Euros at their own game. Kristen Ulmer for "big air." Randy Rackliff for his art, which he should pay better attention to. Kevin Doyle who really was a better climber than anybody else. Brian Enos for illuminating the hidden doorways, and for teaching me to "be." Rolando Garibotti for his sense of humor and commitment to the ideal. Boston T. Party for reminding me that freedom is earned. Kitty Calhoun for making better fun of me than anyone else ever could. Thierry Donard for "Pushing the Limits." Gioachino and Betta Gobbi for showing me what marriage can be. Tad Linn for remaining my friend even when I disappeared. Francois Marsigny for originating the concept of the serial climber and admitting that he is one. Bryan Morgan for his contradictions and convictions. Bill Belcourt for his ruthless honesty. Blitz for "being." Jack Tackle for surviving to return the tool.

Bands: Sisters of Mercy, Trisomie 21, New Model Army, The Young Gods, The Clash, Echo and the Bunnymen, Poesie Noire, The Cure, Dead Can Dance, Marianne Faithfull, SNFU, The Sound, The Gun Club, Cassandra Complex, Frontline Assembly, DOA, The Sex Pistols, X, Skinny Puppy, Tool, The Damned, Treponem Pal, Joy Division, The Durutti Column, Killing Joke, The Wipers, Nirvana, Iggy Pop, The Nephilim, The Chameleons, Sixteen Horsepower, Social Distortion, Opposition,

Xymox, Ice T, Massive Attack, The Jam, The Dead Boys, One Minute Silence, Henry Rollins, and Arvo Part.

Writers: Isaac Babel, Yukio Mishima, Hemingway, Robert Stone, James Salter, Ayn Rand, and John Ross.

Finally, I honor my friends and climbing partners who are no longer alive to read this book. I told some I cared about them. Others, well, I hope they knew because I never said a word.

THUNDER KISS '65, by Ivan DePrume, Shauna Reynolds, Jay Yuenger & Robert Bartlett
©1992 WB Music Corp. and Psychohead Music
All Rights Administered by WB Music Corp.
All Rights Reserved   Used by Permission
WARNER BROS. PUBLICATIONS U.S. INC., Miami, FL 33014

PASSOVER, by Ian Curtis, Peter Hook, Stephan Morris, Bernard Sumner
©1980 Fractured Music, administered by Zomba Music Publishers Ltd. for the World
Sub-published by Zomba Enterprises Inc. for the US and Canada
All Rights Reserved   Used by Permission
WARNER BROS. PUBLICATIONS U.S. INC., Miami, FL 33014

ASSIMILATE, by D.R. Goettel, cEvin Key, and N. Ogre
©1985 Dig It Music (SOCAN) and Virgin Music Australia-APRA
All Rights Administered by Dig It Music.
All Rights Reserved   Used by Permission
DIG IT MUSIC (SOCAN), Chicago, IL 60612

ON THE DAY, by Henry Rollins
©UNI/Dreamworks
All Rights Reserved
UNI/DREAMWORKS, Santa Monica, CA 90404

Excerpts on pages 93 and 96 are from the book *North Wall* by Roger Hubank. New York: Viking Press, 1977. This book is now out of print.

Excerpts on pages 100 and 141 are from the book *The Gay Science,* by Frederick Nietzsche, translated by Walter Kaufmann. New York: Random House, 1974.

Exerpt on page 150 is from the book *See a Grown Man Cry, Now Watch Him Die,* by Henry Rollins. Los Angeles: 2 13 61 Publications, Inc., 1992.

Excerpt on page 198 is from the book *Thus Spoke Zarathustra, A Book for Everyone and No One,* by Frederick Nietzsche, translated by R.J. Hollingdale. Harmondsworth, Middlesex, UK: Penguin Books, Ltd., 1961.

Mark Twight is one of America's leading alpinists. His gripping accounts have been published around the world, translated into five languages. *Sports Illustrated, Outside Magazine, Rock & Ice* (and a host of European magazines) have profiled him. Twight was the first to solo the "Czech Route" on Peak Communism, and fastest to solo "Slipstream," a three thousand-foot-high waterfall in the Canadian Rockies (in two hours and four minutes; most parties take twelve hours). He made the first ascent of "Deprivation" on Alaska's Mount Hunter, climbed five extremely difficult new routes in the French Alps, and made a non-stop, sixty-hour ascent of Mount McKinley's "Czech Direct" (the previous fastest party took seven days). Twight works as a technical advisor for Patagonia and distributes Grivel ice climbing gear in North America. He develops cold-weather clothing systems for the Department of Defense and teaches climbing and crisis nutrition to U.S. Special Forces operatives. Home is wherever his wife, Lisa, and an 85-pound Akita named Zuma happen to be, which is in Utah for now.

Twight is the author, with Jim Martin, of the award-winning book *Extreme Alpinism: Climbing Light, Fast, and High.*

Foreword writer **Brian Enos** is a two-time NRA Action Shooting National Champion, a Masters International Pistol Champion, and a five-time Sportsmans Team Challenge National Championship team member. He has been a member of the United States IPSC Gold Team since 1983, and is a two-time Stock Gun World Speed Shooting National Champion. He is the author of *Practical Shooting, Beyond Fundamentals.* Visit his website at *www.brianenos.com.* Brian lives in Apache Junction, Arizona.

THE MOUNTAINEERS, founded in 1906, is a nonprofit outdoor activity and conservation club, whose mission is "to explore, study, preserve, and enjoy the natural beauty of the outdoors . . . . " Based in Seattle, Washington, the club is now the third-largest such organization in the United States, with seven branches throughout Washington State.

The Mountaineers sponsors both classes and year-round outdoor activities in the Pacific Northwest, which include hiking, mountain climbing, ski-touring, snowshoeing, bicycling, camping, kayaking and canoeing, nature study, sailing, and adventure travel. The club's conservation division supports environmental causes through educational activities, sponsoring legislation, and presenting informational programs. All club activities are led by skilled, experienced volunteers, who are dedicated to promoting safe and responsible enjoyment and preservation of the outdoors.

If you would like to participate in these organized outdoor activities or the club's programs, consider a membership in The Mountaineers. For information and an application, write or call The Mountaineers, Club Headquarters, 300 Third Avenue West, Seattle, WA 98119; 206-284-6310.

The Mountaineers Books, an active, nonprofit publishing program of the club, produces guidebooks, instructional texts, historical works, natural history guides, and works on environmental conservation. All books produced by The Mountaineers Books fulfill the club's mission.

Send or call for our catalog of more than 500 outdoor titles:

The Mountaineers Books
1001 SW Klickitat Way, Suite 201
Seattle, WA 98134
800-553-4453
mbooks@mountaineersbooks.org
www.mountaineersbooks.org

The Mountaineers Books is proud to be a corporate sponsor of Leave No Trace, whose mission is to promote and inspire responsible outdoor recreation through education, research, and partnerships. The Leave No Trace program is focused specifically on human-powered (non-motorized) recreation.
Leave No Trace strives to educate visitors about the nature of their recreational impacts, as well as offer techniques to prevent and minimize such impacts. Leave No Trace is best understood as an educational and ethical program, not as a set of rules and regulations. For more information, visit *www.LNT.org* or call 800-332-4100.